THE BLUELIGHT CORNER

THE BLUELIGHT CORNER

BLACK WOMEN WRITING ON PASSION,
SEX, AND ROMANTIC LOVE

Edited by
Rosemarie Robotham

A BALLIETT AND FITZGERALD BOOK

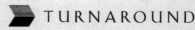 TURNAROUND

To Lascelles and Gloria, lovers through time—RR

UK Edition Published by Turnaround
Unit 3 Olympia Trading Estate, Coburg Road,
London N22 6TZ

Trade paperback original, published by THREE RIVERS PRESS, 1999

UK paperback edition published by Turnaround 1999

Printed in the United Kingdom by Caledonian International Book
Manufacturing Ltd, Glasgow

Interior Design by Susan Canavan

ISBN 1 873262 09 4
British Cataloguing-in-Publication data available

CONTENTS

. . . a good slow dance in a sacred place

where the lights stay dim all night

and the record is a longplay

and the bluelight corner

we have spidered ourselves into

is all night reserved . . .

—*The Turtle Ball*, Nikky Finney

THE BLUELIGHT CORNER

CHOOSING

Their stories multiplied. Papers overflowed my desk, books climbed in precarious towers beside my bed as the months rolled by and I gave myself over to the delicious pleasure of worlds so richly imagined. The difficulty was in choosing. So many stories insisted on being included, when only a handful could be. Indeed, I was often perplexed by having to choose what piece of writing by a single author I would use in one finite collection. In the end, geography, and the cultural legacies supported by a shared geography, became a defining principle—thus the decision to collect writings by women of African descent who live and work in North America. And the prism through which this anthology seeks to examine the lives of women of color at the dawn of a new century is *love*, the whole spacious ramble and reach of human experience converges here. There is, after all, no human experience untouched by love as an engendering influence, prevailing fact, or all too painful need.

Yet even as we defined the territory, the views were boundless. The talent and the range of experiences were boundless. And so, you see, the difficulty—the joyful, unsettling difficulty—was in choosing. So as you read these narratives, remember that behind these clear-sighted storytellers stand a multitude more Black women like them.

Many of the writers included here are not yet well known, while others are already cherished. All have given of themselves. All have crystallized experiences of mind, heart, and body to render Black women's lives in strong, evocative literature. Each of these stories also tells its own necessary truth about encounters with the erotic, for as the late Audre Lorde, visionary poet and muse, observed in her essay "Uses of the Erotic": "The very word *erotic* comes from the Greek word *eros*, the personification of love in all its aspects—born of Chaos, personifying creative power and harmony. When I speak of the erotic, then, I speak of it as an assertion of the life force of women; of that creative energy empowered, the knowledge and use of which we are now reclaiming in our language, our history, our dancing, our loving, our work, our lives."

The seeds sown by the pioneering Lorde and so many others have borne extravagant fruit. *The Bluelight Corner* bears witness to the ripening, for it recognizes Black women's erotic sensibility as something richer, far more inconvenient, and infinitely more tender than has been historically portrayed. Some might suggest that an anthology of this nature lends dangerous credence to the American mythology of Black women as overtly sexual archetypes. Such concerns among Black folks are understandable, born of a centuries-old need to protect against stereotypes that made Black women the object of tawdry fantasies, bringing rape and worse. In the face of this particular social danger, Black women learned to

suppress their sexual natures, learned to silence expressions of
love and longing that would reveal, and put at risk, the mul-
tiple dimensions of our lives.

But this, too, was a hollow projection of who we are, one
that deprived us of characters who could reflect the varied
truths of our experience. Mary Helen Washington, editor of
one of the earliest anthologies of Black women's fiction in
1975, appreciated this. "It is understandable that there is a
desire to protect and revere Black women's image," she wrote
in the introduction to *Black-Eyed Susans*. "But to write stories with one eye on upholding the sacredness of Black womanhood is to invite manipulation and distortion, when what
we need from Black writers is insight and honesty."

We have moved leagues since Washington wrote those
words. More than ever, the stories collected here show that
Black women's search for sexual gratification and need for
nurturing are far more complex than the mythology of skin
color. For while our experience of love is everywhere informed
by our racial reality, it is not defined solely by race. By collecting some of the very best work currently being produced by
women of African descent on the subject of passion, sex, and
romantic love, *The Bluelight Corner* seeks to explore the territory beyond the racial and sexual stereotypes, behind politi-
cally correct assertions.

And so you will find in these pages the quiet stories and the
ones that rage, playful narratives and surreal tales, explo-
rations both seductive and chaste. You will meet an abundance of characters: a single mother welcoming her lovers in
bougainvillea-scented darkness while her young son sleeps; a
teenage girl drawn again and again to the flickering images
inside the adult cinema in her south Georgia town; the Black
karate student who finds herself attracted to her white lesbian

friend; a man in his twilight years remembering lost love; pregnant urban teenagers attempting to make sense of their lives; a guitar-playing man with a secret past; a married couple in the aftermath of an affair; and the mysterious old woman who calls down the fates on a husband and wife.

You will read these stories and recall slow dances on hot, sticky Saturday nights; relive the heat of love on a bright winter morning; feel the vapor of a spirit lover more than a hundred years old. All these characters, all these expressions of the erotic are reflected here. And while many of these stories rejoice in our versatility and our resilience, others declare that even the most wounded among us will not be cast off. The abused child who grows to an unloving adult, the addict whose humanity cannot be extinguished, the HIV-positive artist reaching tentatively for affection—their truths, too, are examined, their pain rendered as they, like the rest of us, are reclaimed through Black women's creative honesty, fierce intelligence, and abiding love.

—*Rosemarie Robotham*

SECOND-HAND
MAN

Rita Dove

Virginia couldn't stand it when someone tried to shorten her name—like Ginny, for example. But James Evans didn't. He set his twelve-string guitar down real slow.

"Miss Virginia," he said, "you're a fine piece of woman."

Seemed he'd been asking around. Knew everything about her. Knew she was bold and proud and didn't cotton to no silly niggers. Vir-gin-ee-a he said, nice and slow. Almost Russian, the way he said it. Right then and there she knew this man was for her.

He courted her just inside a year, came by nearly every day. First she wouldn't see him for more than half an hour at a time. She'd send him away; he knew better than to try to force her. Another fellow did that once—kept coming by when she said she had other things to do. She told him he do it once more, she'd be waiting at the door with a pot of scalding water to teach him some manners. Did, too. Fool didn't believe her—she had the pot waiting on the stove and when he came up those stairs, she was standing in the door. He took one look at her face and turned and ran. He was lucky those steps were so steep. She only got a little piece of his pant leg.

No, James knew his stuff. He'd come on time and stay till she told him he needed to go.

She'd met him out at Summit Beach one day. In the Twenties, that was the place to go on hot summer days! Clean yellow sand all around the lake, and an amusement park that ran from morning to midnight.

She went there with a couple of girlfriends. They were younger than her and a little silly. But they were sweet. Virginia was nineteen then. "High time," everyone used to say to her, but she'd just lift her head and go on about her business. She weren't going to marry just any old Negro. He had to be perfect.

There was a man who was chasing her around about that time, too. Tall dark Negro—Sterling Williams was his name. Pretty as a panther. Married, he was. Least that's what everyone said. Left a wife in Washington, D.C. A little crazy, the wife—poor Sterling was trying to get a divorce.

Well, Sterling was at Summit Beach that day, too. He followed Virginia around, trying to buy her root beer. Everybody loved root beer that summer. Root beer and vanilla ice cream—the Boston Cooler. But she wouldn't pay him no mind. People said she was crazy—Sterling was the best catch in Akron, they said.

"Not for me," Virginia said. "I don't want no second-hand man."

But Sterling wouldn't give up. He kept buying root beers and having to drink them himself.

Then she saw James. He'd just come up from Tennessee, working his way up on the riverboats. Folks said his best friend had been lynched down there and he turned his back on the town and said he was never coming back. Well, when she saw this cute little man in a straw hat and a twelve-string guitar under his arm, she got a little flustered. Her girlfriends whispered around to find out who he was, but she acted like she didn't even see him.

He was the hit of Summit Beach. Played that twelve-string guitar like a devil. They'd take off their shoes and sit on the beach toward evening. All the girls loved James. "Oh, Jimmy," they'd squeal, "play us a *loooove* song!" He'd laugh and pick out a tune:

> *I'll give you a dollar if you'll come out tonight*
> *If you'll come out tonight,*
> *If you'll come out tonight.*
> *I'll give you a dollar if you'll come out tonight*
> *And dance by the light of the moon.*

Then the girls would giggle. "Jimmy," they screamed, "you oughta be 'shamed of yourself!" He'd sing the second verse then:

> *I danced with a girl with a hole in her stockin',*
> *And her heel kep'a-rockin',*
> *And her heel kep'a-rockin';*
> *I danced with a girl with a hole in her stockin',*
> *And we danced by the light of the moon.*

Then they'd all priss and preen their feathers and wonder which would be best—to be in fancy clothes and go on being courted by these dull factory fellows, or to have a hole in their stockings and dance with James.

Virginia never danced. She sat a bit off to one side and watched them make fools of themselves.

Then one night near season's end, they were all sitting down by the water, and everyone had on sweaters and was in a foul mood because the cold weather was coming and there wouldn't be no more parties. Someone said something about hating having the good times end, and James struck up a nice and easy tune, looking across the fire straight at Virginia:

> As I was lumb'ring down de street,
> Down de street, down de street,
> A han'some gal I chanced to meet,
> Oh, she was fair to view!
>
> I'd like to make dat gal my wife,
> Gal my wife, gal my wife.
> I'd be happy all my life
> If I had her by me.

She knew he was the man. She'd known it a long while, but she was just biding her time. He called on her the next day. She said she was busy canning peaches. He came back the day after. They sat on the porch and watched the people go by. He didn't talk much, except to say her name like that:

"Vir-gin-ee-a," he said, "you're a mighty fine woman."

She sent him home a little after that. He showed up again a week later. She was angry at him and told him she didn't have time for playing around. But he'd brought his twelve-string guitar, and he said he'd been practicing all week just to play a couple of songs for her. She let him in then and made him sit on the stool while she sat on the porch swing. He sang the first song. It was a floor thumper.

> There is a gal in our town,
> She wears a yellow striped gown,
> And when she walks the streets aroun',
> The hollow of her foot makes a hole in
> the ground.

> *Ol' folks, young folks, cl'ar the kitchen,*
> *Ol' folks, young folks, cl'ar the kitchen,*
> *Ol' Virginny never tire.*

She got a little mad then, but she knew he was baiting her. Seeing how much she would take. She knew he wasn't singing about her, and she'd already heard how he said her name. It was time to let the dog in out of the rain, even if he shook his wet all over the floor. So she leaned back and put her hands on her hips, real slow.

"I just *know* you ain't singing about me."

"Virginia," he replied, with a grin would've put Rudolph Valentino to shame, "I'd *never* sing about you that way."

He pulled a yellow scarf out of his trouser pocket. Like melted butter it was, with fringes.

"I saw it yesterday and thought how nice it would look against your skin," he said.

That was the first present she ever accepted from a man. Then he sang his other song:

> *I'm coming, I'm coming!*
> *Virginia, I'm coming to stay.*
> *Don't hold it agin' me*
> *For running away.*
>
> *And if I can win ya,*
> *I'll never more roam,*
> *I'm coming Virginia,*
> *My dixie land home.*

She was gone for him. Not like those girls on the beach: she had enough sense left to crack a joke or two. "You saying I look like the state of Virginia?" she asked, and he laughed. But she was gone.

She didn't let him know it, though, not for a long while. Even when he asked her to marry him, eight months later, he was trembling and thought she just might refuse out of some woman's whim. No, he courted her proper. Every day for a little while. They'd sit on the porch until it got too cold and then they'd sit in the parlor with two or three bright lamps on. Her mother and father were glad Virginia'd found a beau, but they weren't taking any chances. Everything had to be proper.

He got down, all trembly, on one knee and asked her to be his wife. She said yes. There's a point when all this dignity and stuff get in the way of Destiny. He kept on trembling; he didn't believe her.

"What?" he said.

"I said yes," Virginia answered. She was starting to get angry. Then he saw that she meant it, and he went into the other room to ask her father for her hand in marriage.

But people are too curious for their own good, and there's some things they never need to know, but they're going to find them out one way or the other. James had come all the way up from Tennessee and that should have been far enough, but he couldn't hide that snake any more. It just crawled out from under the rock when it was good and ready.

The snake was Jeremiah Morgan. Some fellows from Akron had gone off for work on the riverboats, and some of these fellows had heard about James. That twelve-string guitar and straw hat of his had made him pretty popular. So, story got to town that James had a baby somewhere. And joined up to this baby—but long dead and buried—was a wife.

Virginia had been married six months when she found out from sweet-talking, side-stepping Jeremiah Morgan who never liked her no-how after she'd laid his soul to rest one night when he'd taken her home from a dance. (She always carried a brick in her purse—no man could get the best of her!)

Jeremiah must have been the happiest man in Akron the day he found out. He found it out later than most people—things like that have a way of circulating first among those who know how to keep it from spreading to the wrong folks—then when the gossip's gotten to everyone else, it's handed over to the one who knows what to do with it.

"Ask that husband of your'n what else he left in Tennessee besides his best friend," was all Jeremiah said at first.

No no-good Negro like Jeremiah Morgan could make Virginia beg for information. She wouldn't bite.

"I ain't got no need for asking my husband nothing," she said, and walked away. She was going to choir practice.

He stood where he was, yelled after her like any old common person. "Mrs. Evans always talking about being number one! It looks like she's number two after all."

Her ears burned from the shame of it. She went on to choir practice and sang her prettiest, and straight when she was back home she asked:

"What's all this number two business?"

James broke down and told her the whole story—how he'd been married before, when he was seventeen, and his wife dying in childbirth and the child not quite right because of being blue when it was born. And how when his friend was strung up he saw no reason for staying. And how when he met Virginia, he found out pretty quick what she'd done to Sterling Williams and that she'd never have no second-hand man, and he had to have her, so he never said a word about his past.

She took off her coat and hung it in the front closet. She unpinned her hat and set it in its box on the shelf. She reached in the back of the closet and brought out his hunting rifle and the box of bullets. She didn't see no way out but to shoot him.

"Put that down!" he shouted. "I love you!"

"You were right not to tell me," she said, "because I sure as sin wouldn't have married you. I don't want you now."

"Virginia," he said. He was real scared. "How can you shoot me down like this?"

No, she couldn't shoot him when he stood there looking at her with those sweet brown eyes, telling her how much he loved her.

"You have to sleep sometime," she said, and sat down to wait.

He didn't sleep for three nights. He knew she meant business. She sat up in their best chair with the rifle across her lap, but he wouldn't sleep. He sat at the table and told her over and over that he loved her and he hadn't known what else to do at the time.

"When I get through killing you," she told him, "I'm going to write to Tennessee and have them send that baby up here. It won't do, farming a child out to any relative with an extra plate."

She held on to that rifle. Not that he would have taken it from her—not that that would've saved him. No, the only thing would've saved him was running away. But he wouldn't run either.

Sitting there, Virginia had lots of time to think. He was afraid of what she might do, but he wouldn't leave her, either. Some of what he was saying began to sink in. He had lied, but that was the only way to get her—she could see the reasoning behind that. And except for that, he was perfect. It was hardly like having a wife before at all. And the baby—anyone could see the marriage wasn't meant to be anyway.

On the third day about midnight, she laid down the rifle.

"You will join the choir and settle down instead of plucking on that guitar anytime anyone drop a hat," she said. "And we will write to your aunt in Tennessee and have that child sent up here." Then she put the rifle back in the closet.

The child never made it up to Ohio—it had died a month before Jeremiah ever opened his mouth. That hit James hard. He thought it was his fault and all, but Virginia made him see the child was sick and was probably better off with its Maker than it would be living out half a life.

James made a good tenor in the choir. The next spring, Virginia had her first baby and they decided to name her Belle. That's French for beautiful. And she was, too.

Born in 1952 in Akron, Rita Dove remembers the excitement she felt as a young girl when she first encountered literature that reflected her own life. Jean Toomer, Langston Hughes, and Richard Wright all helped inspire the woman who in 1995 became U.S. poet laureate, the first African-American and the youngest person ever to win that honor. Earlier, she had been awarded the 1987 Pulitzer Prize in poetry for her third collection, Thomas and Beulah, *a cycle of verses about her great-grandparents. Despite her years as an expatriate in Europe, studying at the Universität Tübingen in Germany, Dove crafts poetry and short stories that are rooted in the experience of her childhood home. "I could do nothing but describe the world I knew," she explained, "a world where there was both jazz and opera, gray suits and blue jeans, iambic pentameter and the dozens, Shakespeare and Baldwin." Dove is currently the Commonwealth Professor of English at the University of Virginia, and makes her home near Charlottesville.*

TRIPLE X

Shay Youngblood

T he summer I was sixteen years old, me and my aunt Sofine took the number thirteen bus downtown to the Triple X theater on North Main Street every Thursday afternoon. This idea came to Sofine one morning early in June. We both sat on the floor in my grandmother's kitchen in our bras and panties, sweating in front of a loud table fan set on high and a chipped white enamel bowl of melting ice. We dipped our hands in the bowl, flicking our cool, dripping-wet fingers at each other from time to time. Sofine laughed low down in her throat; her big breasts decorated with black lace trembled when she came across the small black-bordered ad in the movie section:

> First-run features. High-Quality Adult
> Movies. Air-conditioned. Thursday Ladies
> Free. Must be 18 years.

"Ladies free," she said.

"Air-conditioned," I repeated. I dipped my hands up to the wrists in the bowl of ice and water, then leaned forward, pressing my wet palms to Sofine's face like she'd taught me to do when I was a little girl and we'd spent hot summer days in my grandmother's house. She closed her eyes and smiled in my hands.

"This could be educational." Her long, thick fingers selected a small piece of ice and began sliding it back and forth across her bare, buttery shoulders.

My mother, when she left me at my grandmother's for the summer, insisted that I do something educational, that I think about what I wanted to do with my life. She and my father were not happy when I announced that I was thinking about dropping out of high school at the end of my junior year, just thinking about it. I was considering pursuing a career in acting, after knocking out the audience at Malcolm X High School with my original interpretation of Ophelia as a homegirl in a contemporary staging of *Hamlet*. Mama said I was just acting myself and didn't seem to think the reviews I got in the Afro-American weekly newspaper meant that I was Broadway stage material. Parker Henderson, the cultural critic, said I had promise, that my Ophelia was the most original he'd ever seen. My father, although he said he was proud of my performance, said he hoped I'd go to college before making my final decision to be a stage actress. I worked my behind off for that part. In Mr. Brandon's English class, the others were always laughing because I was a slow reader, but I fixed them. Mr. Brandon chose me to be Ophelia, and he helped me to create my role. He stayed after school with me for three weeks straight, helping me read Shakespeare. It might've been Greek, for all I understood in the beginning, but he took his time with me, and we cracked open the door to understanding.

"So you want to be an actress?" Sofine didn't act surprised or even laugh at me like my mama had when I told her.

"I *am* an actress. I was Ophelia . . ." Then I stood up in my grandmother's kitchen in front of the table fan in my underwear and gave Sofine and the kitchen cabinets all the drama of a mad Ophelia, heartbroken and abandoned. Sofine clapped politely.

"Mona Lisa, honey, get real; you can't afford to be playing Ophelia for the rest of your life. You a black woman living in America."

"Maybe I'll make movies," I said. "As a backup career."

"Well, there's an original idea." She took down my grandmother's coffee can filled with change from on top of the refrigerator and counted out bus fare for the both of us.

"Let's go do some research," she said, filling my hand with dimes.

The first time we went to the Triple X, the clerk, a bulky black man with a wild Afro and the mean gaze of a prison guard, asked us for ID. Sofine started to flirt with him, talking about how hot it was. He smiled, showing a gold tooth left of center, and winked at her.

"We get a lot of ladies come in, just want to be cool," he said, looking at her driver's license through the thick, dirty glass. She told him I'd lost my license at a baseball game two weeks ago. Her story was beginning to get long and I was losing my nerve, shifting my feet nervously, but the clerk wasn't interested and waved us in. The second time we came, he didn't bother to ask at all.

We lived in Atlanta then. My daddy delivered trailer homes cross-country. This particular summer he and my mama decided to use one of his long-distance deliveries to go on a second honeymoon. On their way out west they dropped me off in the small town in south Georgia where my mama grew up. I'll admit I was jealous of their adventure, had already begged on my knees at the dinner table to stay home alone so I could rehearse for my audition for Juliet in the Atlanta Festival of Stars Dinner Theatre production of *Romeo and Juliet* in the fall, but they just kept piling meat and potatoes on their forks and shoveling it into their mouths. Unlike most of my friends' parents, my mother and father were in love, and what I wanted didn't matter at all. The only saving grace to a hot summer in south Georgia was that my aunt Sofine was staying with my grandmother, and I knew she knew how to have a good time.

My grandmother was hard-of-hearing and spent her days piecing together quilts on the front porch when she wasn't watching afternoon soap operas and talking to the TV as if the villains inside could hear her harsh judgments of their sinful behavior.

Every Thursday all summer long, me and Sofine slept till ten o'clock, took a cool shower, and dressed in brightly colored tank tops and shorts and lace-up Roman sandals. We lotioned our bodies with cocoa butter, talcum-powdered between our legs and breasts, took three swipes of Mum deodorant under our arms, and picked our hair into big curly Afros that framed our faces.

I wasn't allowed to wear makeup at home, but Aunt Sofine put a thin line of black eyeliner on me, a little bit of blue eye shadow, and pink lip gloss that made my lips shine like glass. I began to feel glamorous. I had to look eighteen to get in the movies. Sofine let me wear her gold hoop earrings. I tried to give attitude like Lena Horne in *Stormy Weather*. I had to keep my glasses in Sofine's pocketbook until we got inside the theater. She said my glasses made me look like a square. It took Sofine longer to put on her face. The first layer was a liquid foundation that made her face look like a flat, dry pancake, then she painted on a thick line of black eyeliner, making points at the corner of her eyes to emphasize their slanted shape. My daddy said she looked Chinese, which she took as a compliment. Her lips she outlined in dark rose and filled in with Hawaiian Orchid, a kind of fuchsia color that matched her

stretchy tube top. Me and Sofine walked slowly to the bus
stop, so as not to encourage perspiration, and stood waiting
for the number thirteen to take us downtown. We could have
walked the eight or ten blocks, but it was hot, hotter than I
imagined hell could be on a summer day.

> *A hand rests on a swollen breast, thighs spread
> open like a Bible. A man bows his head in prayer
> before them, holy. Her head thrashes from side to
> side, eyes squeezed shut. Small whimpers. Pleasure
> out of sight.*

"You want some more popcorn?" Aunt Sofine whispers.
"No, I don't want no more." I cross my legs, shift in my
seat, and let out the air I've been holding in my lungs, but I
don't take my eyes off the screen. My mouth is dry, and
although the air conditioner is on full blast, my hands and
crotch are sweaty. I try to memorize the expression for desire.

> *A wide, red satin skirt lifted delicately above the
> knees. Thighs spread, lowered to the floor, hips
> dipping, picking up twenty-dollar bills. Smoke
> rings emanate from deep in her private parts.
> Perfect circles float in the air.*

At home I take off my panties, squat down, and try to pick
up a dollar bill, but my legs get a cramp and I lose my balance
and fall and scrape my elbow against the bathroom door. I'm
not allowed to smoke, so I can't try the smoke rings. Miss
Kitty makes it look so easy to be a movie star.

> *A pool stick aimed at the eight ball aimed at the*

*center of a womanly body spread open on a field
of green felt.*

My uncle High Five won't let me in the pool hall. He says
I can't play pool and besides, "This ain't no place for skirts."
He and his friends laugh and keep playing for quarters stacked
on the edge of the pool cue rack.

"I ain't no skirt," I say. "And anyway, blind Miss Lily could
beat you shooting pool." I knew I could beat him, too. All I
had to do was use my imagination. When I see High Five leave
the pool hall, I sneak in and rub my hands across the green
felt, hold the smooth, cool white cue ball in my hand, feeling
the weight of it, wondering if my aim would be sure. Practice
. . . rehearse . . . make believe . . . make it look easy . . . make
it look real. . . . Eight ball in the corner pocket.

*The frame is filled with moist flesh, steam heat, a
white washcloth makes a trail in the water of her
bath. The sound track is bland, nothing you could
dance to, but my body is rocking on the beat.*

At home I turn the volume on the radio up loud and sit in my
grandmother's room in the dark, rocking in her rocking chair
with my legs pressed together, a cool washcloth wadded into a
ball stuffed in my panties. I rock through the top ten soul hits
before my aunt Sofine bursts into the room and throws a comic
book at me and tells me it's time for bed. My bed is a narrow single cot next to the bed she sleeps in with her one-year-old baby
boy we call Honey because that's the color of his skin.

*A man and a woman, both naked, gallop through
a meadow on a white horse. Cut to interior bed-*

*room. Day. The man lies still on his back. The
woman sits on his lap and rides as if he is the white
horse.*

My aunt is munching loudly on the tub of popcorn balanced on her knees. She slurps her orange soda and watches
the screen as if it is a documentary on the secret life of a tree.
She watches as if she has seen it all before and is reduced to
looking at the background. Sometimes we see the movies
twice if the temperature is over ninety outside. We like it cool.
Sofine comments on almost every new scene: "I hope that
horse don't have fleas." Or "I would never sleep with a man
had a butt bigger than mine."

A hand on my shoulder, a whisper in my ear.

"You don't want to go for a ride with me, do you?" A voice
inviting, whispers in the darkness behind me. His breath
smells like licorice, his voice sounds like a little boy's, a boy
who is afraid the answer will be no.

"What you whispering in her ear?" Aunt Sofine turns
around to look him in the eye.

"I'll whisper in yours, too, if that's what you into." He
seems eager to please.

"We trying to watch the movie. Keep your comments to
yourself, soldier," she says without missing a beat. He gets up
and moves two rows behind us.

Sofine can tell a soldier from two hundred feet in the
dark. She should know. She's only nineteen years old, but
she's been married twice, both times to army men. Her first
husband married her when she was just one year older than
me. The problem with him was that he was already married

to a girl in New Mexico. Her second husband was a short, chunky brick-colored sergeant from Pittsburgh, who was twice her age and expected her to cook dinner and make up the beds every day. She left him after two weeks. She say she didn't have to work that hard at home. Honey's daddy was in the marines. Men liked Sofine and she loved men. She was sexy in a way that made them whistle, stop their cars in traffic, and made them want to give her things.

I want men to give me things—flowers on opening night and diamond rings for each of my fingers and toes. I want applause for a job well done.

The fourth Thursday in July, Sofine says she has a date with Honey's daddy. She gives me money to buy a loaf of bread, some sliced meat, and a carton of Coke at the grocery store. My grandmother is on a trip to the mall with a group of senior citizens. By eleven o'clock, heat rolls through the open windows of the house in thick waves. The fan just stirs up dust and blows dead flies onto the bed. I keep wondering what the movie this week will be. If I'll learn some new acting technique. I am itching to learn something new.

I am nervous and sweaty at the thought of going to the Triple X by myself. I take another cold shower and decide to put on my aunt Sofine's face and catch the bus downtown. One block from the theater, I put my glasses in the pocket of my shorts and the world becomes a blur. I manage to wave in the direction of the clerk behind the window who barely looks up from the comic book he is reading. I am a regular. I open the door and a blast of cool air freeze-dries the sweat rolling down the back of my neck. With the money Aunt Sofine gave me, I buy a tub of buttered popcorn and an Orange Crush. I sit in our usual spot three rows from the screen on the aisle. There are less than a dozen other people in the theater, scattered mostly in the back rows. The movie has already started, so I can't see their faces.

> *Underwater. Bodies in slow motion. Graceful as*
> *dancers. Slow-motion sex. Wet sex. Sunlight dances*
> *on their bodies. Two women kiss on the mouth. A*
> *man watches from a distance.*

I wonder if they could drown underwater, staying so long. Sofine would certainly comment on the man's hairy back or the woman's big feet. I squeeze my legs together, take a sip of Orange Crush, and hardly blink at the images on the screen. I want to be kissed underwater like that. I want the man to lift me onto his lap. There is a sudden movement next to me. I don't look directly, but out of the corner of my eye a body, a large male body, eases into the seat beside me. I sneak a look sideways. Muhammad Ali handsome. My guess, air force. His elbow takes over the armrest between us. His breathing is labored as if he is out of breath. He leans in my direction, close but not quite touching me. He smells freshly showered and shaved. His breath is minty.

"I could do that to you," the mouth next to me whispers, cool in my ear.

> *A girl and a boy are sitting on a sofa, watching TV.*
> *The boy tries to kiss the girl. The girl says no, but*
> *she is smiling. The boy tries to touch the girl*
> *underneath her dress. The girl says no, but she is*
> *smiling. The boy is frustrated. He pushes the girl*
> *against the sofa and pins her down with his body.*
> *The boy rips open the girl's blouse. The girl says*
> *no, she is breathing hard, putting up a fight, but*
> *she is still smiling. The boy is so overcome with*

passion at the sight of the girl's naked breasts that
he tears off the girl's skirt and panties. The girl
resists, but the boy is stronger. The girl struggles
for a while, but eventually she gives in.

My head thrashes from side to side, eyes squeezed shut. I am the girl in the movies who takes pleasure out of life. I am the girl who rehearses to become the woman who will win Academy Awards for her performances, the one who loves the sound of applause. I am the girl who takes the hand offered in the darkness. Small whimpers. Pleasure out of sight.

In her haunting coming-of-age novel, Soul Kiss, *Shay Young-blood writes of the search for familial love. Like her protago-nist, the author grew up with strong-minded relatives and neighbors in Columbus, Georgia. "This whole community of people, most of them much older than me and only a few of them bound by blood, took it upon themselves to raise me," Youngblood recalls. "I wanted to give them a voice." She reproduced their voices in* The Big Mama Stories, *and again in her plays* Shakin' the Mess out of Misery *and* Talking Bones. *Her other plays include* Black Power Barbie *and* Square Blue, *the Edward Albee Honoree for the twenty-first Century Play-wrights Festival. Born in 1960, Youngblood holds an M.F.A. from Brown University. She has served as a Peace Corps vol-unteer in the West Indies; as an au pair, artist's model, and poet's helper in Paris; and as a media specialist for the Black Women's Health Project in the United States. Youngblood teaches creative writing at the New School for Social Research in New York City.*

NIGHT WOMEN

Edwidge Danticat

I cringe from the heat of the night on my face. I feel as bare as open flesh. Tonight I am much older than the twenty-five years that I have lived. The night is the time I dread most in my life. Yet if I am to live, I must depend on it.

Shadows shrink and spread over the lace curtain as my son slips into bed. I watch as he stretches from a little boy into the broom-size of a man, his height mounting the innocent fabric that splits our one-room house into two spaces, two mats, two worlds.

For a brief second, I almost mistake him for the ghost of his father, an old lover who disappeared with the night's shadows a long time ago. My son's bed stays nestled against the corner, far from the peeking jalousies. I watch as he digs furrows in the pillow with his head. He shifts his small body carefully so as not to crease his Sunday clothes. He wraps my long blood-red scarf around his neck, the one I wear myself during the day to tempt my suitors. I let him have it at night, so that he always has something of mine when my face is out of sight.

I watch his shadow resting still on the curtain. My eyes are drawn to him, like the stars peeking through the small holes in the roof that none of my suitors will fix for me because they like to watch a scrap of the sky while lying on their naked backs on my mat.

A firefly buzzes around the room, finding him and not me. Perhaps it is a mosquito that has learned the gift of lighting itself. He always slaps the mosquitoes dead on his face without even waking. In the morning, he will have tiny blood spots on his forehead, as though he had spent the whole night kissing a woman with wide-open flesh wounds on her face.

In his sleep he squirms and groans as though he's already discovered that there is pleasure in touching himself. We have never talked about love. What would he need to know? Love is one of those lessons that you grow to learn, the way you learn that one shoe is made to fit a certain foot, lest it cause discomfort.

There are two kinds of women: day women and night women. I am stuck between the day and night in a golden amber bronze. My eyes are the color of dirt, almost copper if I am standing in the sun. I want to wear my matted tresses in braids as soon as I learn to do my whole head without numbing my arms.

Most nights, I hear a slight whisper. My body freezes as I wonder how long it would take for him to cross the curtain and find me.

He says, "Mommy."

I say, *"Darling."*

Somehow in the night, he always calls me in whispers. I hear the buzz of his transistor radio. It is shaped like a can of cola. One of my suitors gave it to him to plug into his ears so he can stay asleep while Mommy *works*.

There is a place in Ville Rose where ghost women ride the crests of waves while brushing the stars out of their hair. There they woo strollers and leave the stars on the path for them. There are nights that I believe that those ghost women are with

me. As much as I know that there are women who sit up
through the night and undo patches of cloth that they have
spent the whole day weaving. These women, they destroy their
toil so that they will always have more to do. And as long as
there's work, they will not have to lie next to the lifeless soul of
a man whose scent still lingers in another woman's bed.

The way my son reacts to my lips stroking his cheeks decides
for me if he's asleep. He is like a butterfly fluttering on a rock that
stands out naked in the middle of a stream. Sometimes I see in the
folds of his eyes a longing for something that's bigger than
myself. We are like faraway lovers, lying to one another under
different moons.

When my smallest finger caresses the narrow cleft beneath
his nose, sometimes his tongue slips out of his mouth and he
licks my fingernail. He moans and turns away, perhaps thinking that this too is a part of the dream.

I whisper my mountain stories in his ear, stories of the
ghost women and the stars in their hair. I tell him of the
deadly snakes lying at one end of a rainbow and the hat full
of gold lying at the other end. I tell him that if I cross a stream
of glass-clear hibiscus, I can make myself a goddess. I blow on
his long eyelashes to see if he's truly asleep. My fingers coil
themselves into visions of birds on his nose. I want him to forget that we live in a place where nothing lasts.

I know that sometimes he wonders why I take such
painstaking care. Why do I draw half-moons on my sweaty
forehead and spread crimson powders on the rise of my
cheeks? We put on his ruffled Sunday suit and I tell him that
we are expecting a sweet angel and where angels tread, the
hosts must be as beautiful as floating hibiscus.

In his sleep, his fingers tug his shirt ruffles loose. He licks his
lips from the last piece of sugar candy stolen from my purse.

No more, no more, or your teeth will turn black. I have forgotten to make him brush the mint leaves against his teeth. He does not know that one day a woman like his mother may judge him by the whiteness of his teeth.

It doesn't take long before he is snoring softly. I listen for the shy laughter of his most pleasant dreams. Dreams of angels skipping over his head and occasionally resting their pink heels on his nose.

I hear him humming a song. One of the madrigals they still teach children on very hot afternoons in public schools. *Kompè Jako, domé vou?* Brother Jacques, are you asleep?

The hibiscus rustle in the night outside. I sing along to help him sink deeper into his sleep. I apply another layer of the Egyptian rouge to my cheeks. There are some sparkles in the powder, which make it easier for my visitor to find me in the dark.

Emmanuel will come tonight. He is a doctor who likes big buttocks on women, but my small ones will do. He comes on Tuesdays and Saturdays. He arrives bearing flowers as though he's come to court me. Tonight he brings me bougainvillea. It is always a surprise.

"How is your wife?" I ask.

"Not as beautiful as you."

On Mondays and Thursdays, it is an accordion player named Alexandre. He likes to make the sound of the accordion with his mouth in my ear. The rest of the night, he spends with his breadfruit head rocking on my belly button.

Should my son wake up, I have prepared my fabrication. One day, he will grow too old to be told that a wandering man is a mirage and that naked flesh is a dream. I will tell him that his father has come, that an angel brought him back from Heaven for a while.

The stars slowly slip away from the hole in the roof as the doctor sinks deeper and deeper beneath my body. He throbs and pants. I cover his mouth to keep him from screaming. I see his wife's face in the beads of sweat marching down his chin. He leaves with his body soaking from the dew of our flesh. He calls me an avalanche, a waterfall, when he is satisfied.

After he leaves at dawn, I sit outside and smoke a dry tobacco leaf. I watch the piece-worker women march one another to the open market half a day's walk from where they live. I thank the stars that at least I have the days to myself.

When I walk back into the house, I hear the rise and fall of my son's breath. Quickly, I lean my face against his lips to feel the calming heat from his mouth.

"Mommy, have I missed the angels again?" he whispers softly while reaching for my neck.

I slip into the bed next to him and rock him back to sleep.

"Darling, the angels have themselves a lifetime to come to us."

Growing up in Haiti, Edwidge Danticat learned from the disappearances of novelists, poets, and journalists that writing could be a dangerous activity. "Perhaps it was the danger that attracted me," she admits, "the feeling of doing a high-wire act between stretching the limits of silence and telling the whole truth." In 1981, at the age of twelve, Danticat joined her parents in Brooklyn. It took her a few more years to master English, but after that, there was no stopping her words. A graduate of New York City's Barnard College, she finished her first novel, Breath, Eyes, Memory, *while an M.F.A. student at Brown University in 1993. She won a Pushcart Short Story Prize in 1995, and has earned numerous other fiction awards. Her second novel,* The Farming of Bones, *was published in 1998. "Night Women" is from her short-story collection* Krik? Krak!, *a 1995 National Book Award finalist.*

THE KICK
INSIDE

Martha Southgate

hen Rebecca kicked me in the stomach, it wasn't anything like what I was used to. I'd been kicked before, but this was different.

Before I started training, all I knew about karate came from Bruce Lee movies and from Wesley, this fool I lived with who had some nunchakus, those rubber things with a chain that you can throw at people. He thought he was real macho with those. After we'd been together for a while, he started talking about using them on me. That was when I threw his ass out of my life. I don't put up with that kind of treatment anymore. Not since I left home.

The good thing about it, though, was that I started thinking about taking karate myself. That plus I have this friend, Ruth, who used to take classes at this all-women dojo where I now train. She's real into women—she's the first black woman I ever met who calls herself a feminist—and she's got me almost convinced. Her life is so together. If hanging around a lot of women is a way to get to where she's at, I'll try it. I'm willing to try anything at this point.

Anyway, Ruth was always telling me how important it is to be around a lot of female energy, and she invited me to come and watch a karate class one day. I'd never seen anything like it.

Here were all these women, all different, sparring with each other and laughing, doing these beautiful forms called kata, looking so strong and sure of themselves. I was a little skeptical when I first walked in because almost all of the women were white and a lot of them were kind of butch-looking—lots of hairy legs—but by the time the class ended, I couldn't deny the power in that room. I told Ruth that day that I wanted to start training. She just smiled and said, "I thought you would."

Karla, my therapist, was all for me starting, too. She thought it would be a good way for me to "let go of some hostility in a physical way." I have to admit that I like all the yelling we do in class. I feel as if I've left my skinny-legged body behind, as if I'm all roaring voice and dark-eyed rage. And whenever we kick at the heavy bags or at the air, my father's face floats in front of me like one of those balloons on a string.

When Rebecca kicked me, I was sparring with her. I had just tried to throw a couple of punches, and before I knew it, she had flashed out this round kick and hit me dead in the stomach. My first impulse was to do what I had always done with my dad—get away first and plot my revenge later. I backed away fast, keeping my guard up. I looked at her small pale face and thought about how I would hit her if she kicked me again. I must have looked angry or hurt, because she stopped right away and asked if I was all right. She looked really worried.

I rubbed my eyes and took a deep breath, trying to stop the buzzing in my head. "Yeah, yeah, I'm fine. You just caught me by surprise."

"Still, I'm really sorry, Pam. You've only been training what, a year? I should have been more careful." Then she touched me on the shoulder and smiled. "You're sure you're okay?"

That touch was so different from what I'd expected. I was used to one kick following another, and then another after that. But Rebecca was really concerned that she'd hurt me. I rubbed my stomach for a second. "Yeah, I'm fine. Just let me catch my breath."

Afterward in the dressing room, she apologized again. Then she looked at me for a minute longer and asked, "Are you doing anything after class? Do you want to go get some lunch somewhere?"

I was surprised. Nobody at the school had ever asked me to do anything with them. Karla said that might have been because I was afraid to give them a chance to get to know me. I just figured I had nothing in common with these white girls.

"You really don't have to take me to lunch because you kicked me, you know," I said.

"That's not why I want to take you to lunch."

All right then, I thought, let's just see what she does want. "Okay."

We walked to this little coffee shop near the dojo. It's in this mostly white yuppie neighborhood. There were all these happy-looking couples out on the street, with babies in those blue backpacks and in expensive-looking strollers. I felt the same way I feel at work, as if I wasn't really a part of things, as if some kind of invisible shield had cut me off from the rest of the world.

Rebecca had her head bent, and I kept sneaking little looks at her. She's got short dark brown hair and blue eyes. Really perfect skin, that Irish skin that doesn't have any pores. Like a model's.

After we sat down, it was a little easier to talk. I could still feel the tender place where she'd kicked me. I didn't touch it, but I could feel it just above my belt buckle. It felt like it was going to bruise. She asked why I'd started taking karate.

"I never really thought about it a lot before. I guess I wanted to feel like I could beat up anybody who messed with me. I never thought I'd end up staying this long."

"I'm glad you like it," she said. She hesitated for a minute. "Sometimes I think it's harder for black women to stay at the school because there are so few of them in the classes. I think it's great that you've stayed."

"Did you want to have lunch with me to congratulate me for being black?"

She turned red and looked as if she didn't know what to say. "I . . . didn't want to sound stupid or patronizing. I . . ."

I let her stew for a minute. Sometimes you just need to pull these white girls up short. I've met so many well-intentioned ones—lots of times, they're the worst. But I wasn't really angry with her. And as I looked at her face, I realized I'd been messing with her for no good reason. Maybe this was what Karla meant when she said I pushed people away.

So I smiled and said, "Don't worry. I'm just giving you a hard time. I'm glad that you at least think about this stuff. A lot of people don't."

She smiled back and said, "Don't compliment me when I don't deserve it. I didn't mean to put you on the spot. Why don't we just start this conversation over?"

So we did. She told me how she'd started doing karate when she saw some women from the school at a rally. She works for a book publisher as an assistant. She actually likes her job. I can't imagine what that would be like. I do word processing. I hate it, but I don't know what else to do right now. I got my GED last year—I did really well on it, too—and I've taken a couple of classes at Brooklyn College, but it's going slow. Ruth's my only friend in the city, but since she got married and had a little boy, I don't see her as much as I used to.

It turned out to be nice, talking to Rebecca. She was really easy to talk to. Funny and smart. She started telling me this story about a trip she took out west, and then she said, "My old girlfriend and I always wanted to do it again sometime, but then we broke up, so we weren't able to. Maybe I'll get to go out west another time, though. With somebody else."

When she said that, it was like all the other noise in the restaurant stopped. I couldn't even hear the babies crying anymore. Her old girlfriend? Oh, man.

She kept talking, but her voice sounded real far away. A white girl and a lesbian. I'd never had a long conversation like this with a lesbian before. I'd been on my own for ten years, since I was seventeen, so I'd met a few, and I knew that a lot of the women at the school were gay. But I hadn't tried to talk to any of them. I had kind of steered clear of them because all the lesbians I'd ever known were pretty sad cases. Always fighting with their girlfriends.

Rebecca was different. She seemed real regular. She just talked to me like another person, not like a cultural experience. And she seemed honestly interested in what I had to say about things. But a lesbian. Wow. I always thought that didn't bother me that much, but now . . . I did feel a little funny. I hoped she couldn't tell.

We finished and paid. When we were outside, she looked at me that same direct way again and said, "I had a really good time. We should do this again sometime."

I was thinking that she wasn't like anyone else I knew. But all I said was "I'd really like that."

I was restless all that evening. I rented a movie but couldn't pay attention. I kept thinking about Rebecca. Knowing she was gay made me feel weird, but not bad. I never thought it was such a big goddamn deal. The worst thing you could call somebody back in Detroit was a dyke. I used to laugh along—I was afraid not to—but in my head I never hated lesbians. At least they had someone to love.

I thought about how unafraid Rebecca seemed. There weren't any secret messages hidden in the way she talked. She didn't seem to want to take anything away from me. She was just there, solid, not apologizing, not angry. I wanted to find that kind of confidence in myself, to take it in from her. I used to think that I didn't want anyone around me, that I could do everything by myself. Life was safer that way. But after I met Ruth and I started going to see Karla, things began to change. I don't know. It's scary, feeling things again. But I couldn't stop thinking about the way Rebecca had been so concerned about hurting me, and about the way her hands moved when she talked, like small white birds.

The next morning when I got up, I knew I had dreamed about her. Sometimes you wake up and you can't remember what the dream was, you just know who was in it and it's like they've touched you. Like you know them better somehow. I felt as if I'd had my hands in her hair all night.

When I was in tenth grade and my father was beating me up almost every day, I had this friend Sandra. I have one picture of us. We're both looking at the camera with our teeth showing in imitation smiles, our eyes flat and shiny with rage. Sandra was short and dark-skinned and fat and she wore thick glasses. People called us Fatty and Skinny after that kids' movie they used to show on Saturday afternoons. I think we got to be friends because we both loved to read but we didn't like school. We just wanted to read what we felt like. I remember she especially liked James Baldwin and that guy who wrote *The Postman Always Rings Twice,* James Cain. She turned me on to both of them. Her mother was drunk all the time, so Sandra was pretty much free to do what she wanted when she wanted.

We would sit behind the school, smoking cigarettes and plotting how we were going to get the hell out of Detroit and never look back. One time when we were hiding out there after an especially bad night with my father, I started crying real hard. I couldn't help it; I didn't know how much more I could take.

Sandra held me while I cried. Then without either of us knowing how it happened, she started kissing me all over my face, brushing the tears away. When we broke apart, our whole friendship was ruined. Sandra and I couldn't even look at each other. We stopped talking without even planning it. I met Kenny within a month and slept with him within a month after that.

I hadn't thought about Sandra in eight years. But ever since I talked to Rebecca all these kinds of things kept coming back to me. Stuff I thought I'd put behind me, stuff I hadn't even told Karla or Ruth. It was like something inside me got kicked loose that day. Everything began to rattle after that.

Weeks went by when I couldn't concentrate at work. I typed and didn't even know what I was typing. I went to class, I talked to the same few people I always did at work, asking what they had done over the weekend, and what about those Mets? I ate lunch outside at one of those little office plazas by myself, like I always did, but I kept thinking about Rebecca. I wished I could have lunch with her again. I saw her in class and we talked a little bit, but we didn't go out again. Because it was summer my therapist was on vacation, so she couldn't pick this thing apart. I didn't really want her to, anyway. Sometimes I hate telling her things. Ruth was on vacation with her husband and their son, so I couldn't talk to her either—not that I would have told her. What was to tell, anyway?

One Saturday about a month after I had lunch with Rebecca, I had a really hard time figuring out what to wear to karate class. I tried on three different T-shirts and wore my favorite shorts. I felt a little ridiculous but I couldn't stop myself. I knew that it had something to do with Rebecca, but I didn't know what.

The dressing room was crowded, as it always is. People were yelling back and forth, as they always are. Rebecca wasn't there, though. And she still wasn't there when we got called onto the floor.

It was really hot that day, so almost everybody was training in just a T-shirt or a tank top, not their *gi*. We were doing the warm-up exercises when Rebecca came in.

You know how you can see someone and everything is different all of a sudden? There's nothing gradual about it. You're just going along, minding your own business, and then, *pow,* there's this person that you have to be with and you didn't even know it? That's how I felt when Rebecca came onto the floor in a tank top.

At the sight of her arms, I thought I was going to start crying. I'd never seen anything so beautiful. I could no longer ignore what I was feeling. I didn't want to. In karate they're always telling us to follow our own path. And I felt that the sight of her arms, her face, the soft brown of her hair, that dream I had, were all lying in front of me like a dark road I had to travel, even though I didn't know where it would take me.

I went through the rest of class in a blur. After class, I went right up to her.

"Hi, Rebecca. How are you?"

"I'm good, Pam. How are you?"

"Good." I stopped for a minute. I thought of when I was little and things were still okay at home, the way my mother used to touch me on the back before I had to do anything I was afraid of. She said it would bring me luck.

"Listen," I said, "I hope you don't think this is weird but . . . are you free tonight? I'd like to have dinner with you or something."

"I'd love that," she said. "Where do you want to go?"

We went to this nice place in Fort Greene for dinner. It's

near where I live, and it's not too expensive. They'll let you sit
as long as you want. All afternoon, ever since I'd asked her, I'd
felt this quiet hum in the back of my head, like an organ note
in an empty church. It made it hard to hear what she was saying, made each feature separate and distinct. Eyes so blue you
could fall into them. Hair thick, dark brown, shiny. Strong-
looking hands that she kept gesturing with. I could only imagine them touching me, taking her fingers in my mouth. What
was she saying? She told me how she'd grown up in Kansas,
how she had moved to New York five years ago when she was
twenty-one. How her parents were upset when she told them
she was gay but then they came around after a few years.

She asked me how long I'd been in New York. Seven years,
I told her, since I was twenty. She looked at me the same way
she did when we had lunch, like she was really seeing me, like
I mattered. I felt like laying my head right down on the table
in front of her. I could barely breathe. But I could feel the
image of that bruise on my stomach. So I had to tell her.

I told her about my father, how he used to beat me up.
After my mother died when I was eight, something happened
to him. It started slow, just an occasional slap. I would almost
think it was a regular spanking. But then it got worse and
worse. He'd hit me in the face, on my back, call me all kinds
of horrible names. I never knew what would set him off. I put
up with it, hid the bruises once I got old enough. It was never
so bad that my teachers noticed. He seemed to know that if he
hit my face too hard he'd risk being caught. I managed to survive until I was sixteen and could leave school. But I learned
how to hide things. I learned how to hide everything.

I never fought back against my father until one night when
I was seventeen. I came home from my job at a 7-Eleven one
night and found him going after my sister. I didn't even think.
Everything went black, then red, in front of my eyes. He was

hitting her and hitting her, and somehow—I don't remember how—I got to the kitchen drawer. Got it open. Pulled a knife out. Screamed at him, "Get your fucking hands off her. Get them off her now!" She was only eleven, and she hung on to my leg so tight I could feel a pulse there; I don't know if it was hers or mine. I remember the way he looked at me, like I was something he'd found on the bottom of his shoe, his eyes all red. And then he just turned and walked out.

My sister and I left Detroit that same night. I spent all the money I had earned from my 7-Eleven job to buy our bus tickets. My sister lives with my aunt, my mother's sister, in Atlanta now. I can only afford to go down to see her a couple of times a year. She's doing pretty well. I worked there for a while, but then I followed this guy Wesley to New York. He turned out to be a user, not a savior. I would have left New York, but I met Ruth and she helped me get into this sliding fee counseling service. I'm trying to make my life into something I want. But it's hard.

My heart pounded the whole time I told Rebecca this. But I never thought about stopping. I wanted her to know everything.

Rebecca just looked at me when I stopped talking. Her eyes were very bright. "Your life then must have been awful."

I brushed at my eyes with the back of my hand. "Yeah."

She looked at her plate for a minute. Then she looked up and spoke abruptly. "Pam. I know you're . . . well, you've never been with a woman before, but I've got to tell you. You are so beautiful. I don't want to scare you, but I had to say it. I'm . . . well, you know . . . I want you very much."

She looked scared while she was saying all this, but she never turned her eyes away. It was like she was kissing me. I wanted to touch her so bad that I felt my heart contract under my ribs.

"Let's get out of here," I said.

We walked back to my apartment, our arms almost touching. There was nothing to say. We went inside and leaned up against the door, still not talking. Then my hands were in her hair and she was kissing me for real. It was like I'd never felt any pain in my life, only her hands on my back, her mouth on mine. I felt stunned, the same way I felt when she kicked me in the stomach. But this time it was a good surprise. Like the last Christmas my mother was alive. I remember running down the stairs, with that cold air on my bare feet, my mom and dad smiling at us. I felt that there were all these wonderful things ahead, that nothing bad would ever happen to any of us.

All of a sudden it was as if I'd stepped outside my body for a second. I saw myself in my doorway kissing another woman. And I froze. Just like that time with Sandra.

My eyes stung as Rebecca pulled away from me. "This isn't all right, is it?" she said softly.

My voice wouldn't come out right. "I don't know. I want to. I do. But I'm so scared."

She ran her hand gently across my face, my hair, and smiled a little. "Yeah. I know." She kissed me on the forehead. "I'm going to go now. But I gave you my number. Call me. Please."

I closed the door behind her and leaned against it for a minute or two. Then I slid down to the floor, bawling. I hadn't done that in years. I was so tired of being afraid. I was so tired of keeping it all in. I just couldn't do it anymore. After a while, I stopped crying and went to splash water on my face. I dried my hands and, without thinking, reached into my pocket. The little piece of paper Rebecca had written her number on was still there. I pulled it out and ran my fingers over the graceful writing, thinking about how much Sandra and I had loved each other and how we had thrown it away; what a stupid waste that was. Then I went and picked up the phone.

———◦—————

Martha Southgate's young adult novel Another Way to
Dance *explores the tensions faced by a young black dancer
as she tries to break into the overwhelmingly white world of
classical ballet. Published in 1996, the book received the
Coretta Scott King Genesis Award for best first novel and
was named an American Library Association Best Book of the
Year. Born in Cleveland in 1960, Southgate now lives with
her husband and two children in Brooklyn. She holds a B.A.
from Smith College and an M.F.A. in creative writing from
Goddard College. "The Kick Inside" was her first short story.
"People assume it's autobiographical, but it's not," Southgate
says. "I did study karate and I did share similar feelings
toward other women. But until I could step away and let the
characters become themselves, I couldn't complete the story."
Currently the books and articles editor of* Essence *magazine,
Southgate is at work on her second novel,* The Fall of Rome,
*as well as a contemporary young adult trilogy featuring an
African American girl.*

SECRET PLEASURES

AN EXCERPT FROM THE MEMOIR
Bone Black

bell hooks

I t may have been the pretend Tom Thumb wedding she had to participate in during first grade. It may have been that the tearing of her red crepe-paper bridesmaid dress convinced her she would fail at marriage just as she had failed at the pretend wedding. She knew that the pretend marriage had made her suspicious—nothing about it had been enjoyable. Whenever she thought of marriage she thought of it for someone else, someone who would make a beautiful bride, a good wife. From her perspective the problem with marriage was not the good wife, but the lack of the good husband. She is sixteen years old. Her mother is telling her again and again about the importance of learning to cook, clean, etc., in order to be a good wife. She stomps upstairs shouting, I will never be married! I will never marry! When she comes back downstairs she must explain why, she must find words—Seems like, she says, stammering, marriage is for men, that women get nothing out of it, men get everything. She did not want the mother to feel as if she was saying unkind things about her marriage. She did not want the mother to know that it was precisely her marriage that made it seem like a trap, a door closing in a room without air.

She could not tell her mother how she became a different person as soon as the husband left the house in the morning,

how she became energetic, noisy, silly, funny, fussy, strong,
capable, tender—everything that she was not when he was
around. When he was around she became silent. She reminded
her daughter of a dog sitting, standing obediently until the
master, the head of the house, gave her orders to move, to do
this, to do that, to cook his food just so, to make sure the
house was clean just so. Her bed was upstairs over their bedroom. She never heard them making fun sounds. She heard
the plaintive pleading voice of the woman—she could not hear
what she was asking for, begging for, but she knew that the
schoolbooks, the bit of pocket money, the new dresses, the
everything had to be paid for with more than money, with
more than sex.

Whatever joy there was in marriage was something the
women kept to themselves, a secret they did not share with
one another or their daughters. She never asked where the joy
was, when it appeared, why it had to be hidden. She was
afraid of the answer. They agreed with her when she said
marriage was not a part of her dreams. They said she was too
thin, lacking the hips, breasts, thighs that men were interested
in. But more importantly she was too smart, men did not like
smart women, men did not like a woman whose head was
always in a book. And even more importantly men did not
like a woman who talked back. She had been hit, whipped,
punished again and again for talking back. They had said
they were determined to break her—to silence her, to turn her
into one of them.

She answers her mother back one day in the father's presence. He slaps her hard enough to make her fall back, telling
her Don't you ever let me hear you talking to your mother like
that. She sees pride in the mother's face. She thinks about the
ways he speaks to her, ways that at this moment do not matter. He has taken a stand in her honor against the daughter.

She has accepted it. This, the daughter thinks, must be a kind
of marriage—and she hopes never to bear a daughter to sacri-
fice in the name of such love.

II

Masturbation is something she has never heard anyone talk
about girls doing. Like so many spaces of fun and privilege in
their world, it is reserved for the boy child—the one whose
growing passion for sexuality can be celebrated, talked about
with smiles of triumph and pleasure. A boy coming into awareness of his sexuality is on his way to manhood—it is an important moment. The stained sheets that show signs of his having
touched his body are flags of victory. They—the girls—have no
such moments. Sexuality is something that will be done to
them, something they have to fear. It can bring unwanted pregnancy. It can turn one into a whore. It is a curse. It will ruin a
young girl's life, pull her into pain again and again, into childbirth, into welfare, into all sorts of longings that will never be
satisfied. Again and again they tell their mother she does not
need to worry about them. They are not sexual. They will not
get pregnant, will not bring home babies for her to take care
of. They do not actually say We are not sexual, for the very use
of the word *sexual* might suggest knowledge—they make sexuality synonymous with pregnancy, with being a whore, a slut.

When she finds pleasure touching her body, she knows that
they will think it wrong; that it is something to keep hidden,
to do in secret. She is ashamed, ashamed that she comes home
from school wanting to lie in bed touching the wet dark hidden parts of her body, ashamed that she lies awake nights
touching herself, moving her hands, her fingers deeper and
deeper inside, inside the place of woman's pain and misery, the
place men want to enter, the place babies come through—
ashamed of the pleasure.

When she finally has a room all to herself she can go there when no one notices and enjoy her body. This pleasure is her secret and her shame. She denies to herself that she is being sexual. She refuses to think about it. Males are not the object of her lust. She does not touch herself thinking about their penises moving inside her, the wetness of their ejaculations. It is her own wetness that the fingers seek. It is the moment she thinks of, not as orgasm, for she does not know the word, but as the moment of climbing a tall place and reaching the top. This is what she longs for. There she finds a certain contentedness and bliss. It is this bliss the fingers guide her to. Like the caves she dreamed about in childhood it is a place of refuge, a sanctuary.

Like all secret pleasure she finds the hiding hard. She knows her sisters have begun to wonder about the moments alone in the dark cool room, the times in bed reading when they are outside. They watch her, waiting. They open the door fast. They pull the covers quickly before she can free her hands. They bear witness to her pleasure and her shame. Her pleasure in the body, her shame at being found out. They threaten to tell, they can't wait to tell. She prepares her denial. She goes over and over it in her head. Like a party ending because the lights are suddenly turned on she knows the secret moments are gone, the dark, the pleasure, the deep cool ecstasy.

III

No one ever talks to her about playing with herself, touching her body, about masturbation. She does not know if they told her mother. No one says anything. She is on guard, she is the watcher. She no longer touches herself. She does not like to mingle pleasure with fear. She does not like the smell of fear. She reads with passion and intensity. When she has read everything in sight she goes searching for something new, something undiscovered. Books, like hands in the dark place, are a source of pleasure. In her search for new reading she finds books kept in her father's private space, kept behind his bed. She has never heard the word *pornography*. To her they are just books with funny covers. The people on the covers do not look real. They are all white women, wearing heavy makeup, tight red dresses revealing body parts, they are naked. She does not know that these books are not to be read. She hides her reading of them solely because they can be punished for taking things from his private space.

In bed with her new reading she finds that the books are about kinds of sex, not the sex married, religious people have, but the dirty kind, the kind people have for pleasure. Excited by the reading, by the coming together of these two pleasures, books and sex, she learns that sex does not take place solely between men and women. Sex takes place between women and women, men and men, women and men in groups. Sex takes place with people watching—with people masturbating. Sometimes people like doing things with the sex she thinks are strange—whipping, eating, swimming. She finds that while reading these books her body is aroused, she feels the mounting wetness in her panties. She had thought the wetness came with the hand movement. This new discovery surprises her. It makes the touching more exciting, bringing images and fantasies to what was once just a good, warm wet feeling. Sex in these new books fascinates her. There are no babies to be had through the excitement these pages arouse, no pain, no male abuse, no abandonment. She never thinks much about the roles women and men play in the books. They have no relationship to real people. The men do not work, the women do not have children, clean house, go shopping. Sometimes the men make the women do sexual acts. She could never understand how the women did what they didn't want to do, yet felt pleasure in doing it. She never felt pleasure doing what she did not want to do.

It becomes harder and harder for her to take the books. She must wait until no one is watching. She must make sure she puts them back exactly as she finds them. She is caught creeping up the stairs with a book in hand. Her mother does not want to see the book, only for her to put it back where she found it, only for her to stop reading them. It is her favorite book, *Passion Pit*. It is the only book wherein she identifies with a woman in the one part where the man uses his tongue and fingers to sexually arouse his partner, then withdraws, telling her if she wants sex to ask for it, telling her to beg for it, to want it enough to beg. She can understand the intensity of the woman's longing, her willingness to ask, possibly even to beg. She knows this affirmation of the woman's sexual hunger is exactly what would be denied her in real life. Long after the books are all destroyed she recalls the image of the sexually hungry woman wanting it, wanting it enough to ask, even to beg.

IV

They are concerned because she has not shown the right interest in boys. They do not talk to her about what it is about boys that she finds boring, uninteresting. She cannot talk to them. She cannot tell them how much she hates anyone to lord it over her. She cannot tell them that this is what boys often want to do. She cannot explain that she does not like to be touched, grabbed at, without agreeing to such touching. She is disgusted by the grabbing, the pleading that she let them do this and do that. Even when she is aroused, the feeling goes away when boys behave as though there is only something in this moment for them, something they are seeking that she must give. She is not ashamed to say no. She does not care that the word gets around that she will say no. She cares that she is left alone. She has no date for the senior prom. Her would-be date, someone

she is talking to from out of town, someone who drives a sports
car, who has a job working for a newspaper, says he will come
when she asks him, then changes his mind without saying why.
They will not let her go with that theater crowd she hangs out
with, that group of rather wild white teenagers. They are concerned that she may be growing up funny. They watch her
behavior. They think about the way a certain funny grown-up
woman showed intense interest in her. They think that maybe
they were wrong to allow her to accept presents, a dress, a
watch with tiny diamonds. They are sure that she is not showing enough willingness to seek out boys and do what girls do.
They are watching.

Every now and then they agree that she can visit with a
girlfriend who lives across town, who is white, who drives
a convertible. They listen to their phone conversations to
hear what is being discussed, books, politics, boys. They
hear that she is mainly listening to the white girl talking
about the boys that interest her. They do not know that she
is interested in young men but does not talk about them
because they are not anybody the white girl knows. When
her friend drives her home from school they sit outside and
talk, sometimes for hours. They tell her this cannot happen,
that she must come inside and let that white girl go home.

She does not tell them when the white girl tries to kill herself. They are just glad that she no longer comes around. She
never tells anyone at home about the scars on her friend's
wrists. She never tells that she and her white friend share a
feeling of being outside, alone, that they comfort one another.
She knows that they will think it silly, downright crazy, to
want to die because some boy does not love you, does not
notice even that you are alive. She understands. She takes her
friend's hand. They embrace one another in the stillness of
the car. They share the promise that the friend will never

again act without talking about it first. They hold each other close, glad to be alive, glad to be friends.

When she enters the door her mother and father say nothing, even though they have been watching. Later in the night they keep her downstairs and want to know what is going on between her and the friend. She tells them they are friends, nothing is going on. Her daddy says, Don't lie to me. She looks at him with anger and contempt. She has no answers for them. They tell her that they will have none of this in their house, that she will have to go. She is not sure why they are so upset. She does not understand. Shaken by the fear of being told to leave, by threats of punishment, she agrees to stop seeing her friend. She does not understand why they want to take this friend from her. She does not know that they are worried that she may grow funny.

V

They are relieved that she is finally showing an interest in boys, but even that is something she does not do right. She likes a boy who is younger than herself—that is simply not done. They do not complain because they are so relieved. They laugh about it. They are glad at least that he is taller than she is, that he does not look younger. She likes him because he does not lord it over her, because he is always in a good mood. With him she is never afraid. It is not because he is younger, it is because of the way he is. He does not plead with her to give him some. They are content to touch each other, to explore. She likes to feel the wetness inside his pants. Now that she is interested in boys they are warning her not to become pregnant, not to bring any children into that house. She knows how to say no. She knows how to avoid getting to the place where no is hard to say. When she breaks up with him it is because he is someone she cannot talk to about the

things that really matter. He is only concerned with basketball. She likes basketball and watching basketball players. She
likes to see their bodies move. They remind her of deer, of tender fawns moving gracefully through the woods. She is interested in books and the grace of basketball, in ideas.

Another older basketball player interests her. He attracts
her eyes because he has skin that is a satin silklike black. Dark
enough to make the whites of his eyes look as if they are hiding, shielding themselves from the too much beauty he exudes.
She lusts after him. And she is not the only one. Daring in her
passion, she calls him to let him know. He is interested. She is
one of the good girls, the smart girls, one of the ones that will
go to college. He knows that she will not give him any. He
does not care. He knows where to go when he wants to get
sex. No one ever talks to him about ideas, life, and desire at
the same time. Her desire is curious and strong. Like homemade whiskey, it warms him quickly. Several times he tries to
move close to her. Yet he knows she is not for him. His own
mother has warned him. He has seen the stone-cold look on
her father's face.

He cannot believe she is not afraid. She slips into the backseat
of his car. He wants to show her that she should be afraid, that
she is not for him. She does not sit in front with him, choosing the
back. Her voice moves seductively in the night, caressing his ears
with the tenderness of her words. She feels safe with him without
knowing why. He stops the car out in the country on a deserted
road. She wants to know if this is where he brings girls on weekends after the basketball games. He does not answer. He moves
into the backseat as if he is entering a cage, a trap in which he and
not she will be imprisoned. He feels her innocence is too much.
She is beginning to feel afraid, afraid because she is innocent. He
has never let innocence stand in his way. It is her trust that

catches him. He is not to be trusted. Perhaps he, too, has heard the words A black nigger is a no-good nigger. He wants to be trusted. His cold hands around her neck do not make her afraid. He says no to her caresses and kisses. He says no, the night is fleeting—it is late—he must take her home.

———•—

Born Gloria Watkins in Hopkinsville, Kentucky, bell hooks took her great-grandmother's name in solidarity with generations of black women who have gone unheard. She lowercases her nom de plume to signify her skepticism of fame. Nevertheless, she is famous, the award-winning author of more than fifteen volumes of essays, poetry, and memoir, including such seminal works as Talking Back, Sisters of the Yam, *and 1981's groundbreaking feminist manifesto* Ain't I A Woman, *which Publisher's Weekly hailed as "one of the twenty most influential books by women in the last twenty years." hooks blends the rigors of academic writing with the art of storytelling in work that is at once intensely personal and searingly political. A Distinguished Professor of English at the City College of New York, hooks draws inspiration from her childhood in the segregated South, where she witnessed "the dignity and integrity of black womanhood in my church and in the domestic battles in my household."* Bone Black: Memories of Girlhood, *the literary memoir from which this excerpt is taken, is the author's unflinching examination of her own sexual and creative origins.*

TAMARIND
STEW

Gayle Gonsalves

Before I met Tony, I wrote stories. He wanted to hear them but couldn't find the time. There were so many things I wanted to tell Tony but never did. So he didn't know that I began to write when I was eight, or that when I first learned to read, I found the pictures more exciting than the words because the plots all sounded the same. There was always a princess being saved by a prince.

Tony was the first man I kissed. As I grew into womanhood, I watched him change from a gangly teen into a tall brown man with smooth skin and strong bones. His eyes were alert and captured everyone around him, but they shone when he was with me. There was a time when it seemed Tony couldn't do without me. When the sun rose, he'd make his way in the half-light to my house and lightly throw pebbles at my bedroom window. I'd sneak past my mother's room in my short, see-through nightgown to be with him. In the early morning, his lips held the freshness of dew.

Many mornings, as we sat at the seashore, we would imagine what lay beyond the sea. Our home was an island ten miles wide and ten miles long. But when I sat at the seashore with Tony's body pressed into mine, the horizon seemed endless.

—◆—

It was a hot afternoon when Tony and I first made tamarind stew. The sun was directly above when Tony arrived with a bag of tamarinds in his hand. Before we met, I'd pick tamarinds off the tree and eat them. Tamarinds have an over-powering sourness that is peppered by a faint sweetness, and I enjoyed bombarding my senses with their distinctive taste. Tony loved tamarind stew because he could disguise the sour-ness with brown sugar. I had never made tamarind stew until that hot afternoon when Tony taught me.

The first time we shelled tamarinds and poured them into a pot of boiling water, we nearly set the house on fire. As the pot simmered on the stove, Tony led me to the bedroom. The tamarinds melted in the water. They came together and bub-bled till the cover of the pot clinked from the steam, and soon the pot was on fire.

The burnt pot did not stop our desire, and a few days later we attempted to make tamarind stew again. While the pot simmered on the stove, I sat on the kitchen counter. Tony stood in front of me. With my arms wrapped around his shoulders, we both peered into the pot and saw the tamarinds dissolve and thicken. As he poured brown sugar into the stew, his lips tasted of steam. When it cooled, Tony dipped his hand into the pot. I licked the stew from his fin-gers. While we ate, a soft breeze blew through the window and caressed our skin.

I never heard fairy tales until I was six. My mother couldn't read, but she bought me books filled with pictures of power-ful lions and colorful birds. There were large castles with

princes and princesses. As I studied the enchanted animals and
fairy-tale people, I created stories. I imagined their world and
the lives they led. But my stories never had endings because I
didn't know how to finish them. I just kept inventing new
ways to live.

My first-grade teacher was the first person to read me a
fairy tale. Her voice droned the story in a flat monotone. As
she turned the pages of the book I had treasured, the animals
lost their magic. The castles were now hovels and the people
were no longer immortal. From the sound of her voice, I knew
my toys did not come to life at night.

When my period didn't come, Tony smiled and said it was
late. I wasn't sure. I drank some awful-tasting teas that tore
my insides apart. Tony didn't know. When the blood flowed,
I told him he was right. He believed me because we made
tamarind stew. He didn't know how my body ached as I stood
over the boiling pot. I didn't want to be a mother. The stories
I invented didn't have children. The world I lived in had too
many. The women dedicated their lives to them. They were
worn and tired by the end of the day and often forgot to
explain to their children that the stories they read at bedtime
were not real.

My mother didn't read me stories at bedtime. She didn't
know about enchanted castles and handsome princes until I
told her.

When I was eight, I read her a fairy tale.

She said, "That's not real life."

Then she told me the only story she knew. People were
chained and led across the ocean. They worked until they
died. They were buried in unmarked graves. I told her that
was a horrible story. She said it wasn't a story.

In the first tale I wrote, dragons conquered the world. Goliath survived in this story. When I read it in class, my teacher shook her head in disbelief. She told me it was blasphemous. I didn't understand what she meant. I thought it was a compliment because my story was different. All of the other girls' stories had the same plot. It went like this: "I went to the market with my mother to buy fish. The prince was passing by in a carriage. When he saw me, he thought I was the most beautiful woman in the land. He stopped his carriage and told me to hop in. As we rode around the land, we fell in love."

Tony and I graduated from high school at the same time. Though I was the more adept student, he got the better job. We worked different hours and saw less of each other. He said he was busy, but he was often just liming with his friends. I spent my time with my stories. Tony believed I was day-dreaming. I wanted Tony to listen to my stories, but he always had an excuse. Eventually we fought.

After my outburst, I walked to the shore and stared at the horizon. The sea lapped gently at my feet. It was warm and told me nothing. A ship sat on the horizon. It did not move. I walked back to town with no answers. The roads were narrow. People looked at me as I made my solitary way along the streets. My mother's image followed me as I walked. I thought of her life and I wasn't sure if I could walk alone as she had. That was why I never again asked Tony to listen to my stories.

One afternoon, when the breeze was still and the sweat dripped from our bodies and sticky tamarind stew simmered on the stove, Tony proposed. I cried. He saw the tears and told me he wished I had smiled instead. I don't know why I cried. Nor did I understand why I accepted. The love Tony and I shared was fading.

I asked my mother, "What do you think of Tony?"

She said, "He won't hit you."

"But he's no prince."

"Julie, there are no princes."

"But Tony doesn't know my soul or listen to me when I cry."

"No man has ever heard me, Julie."

On the morning of the wedding, large clouds covered the sun, allowing me to sleep. In my dream, a prince stood on the balcony of a castle. The people stood below him. His face was waxen as he waved to the crowd, which responded adoringly. I stood apart from the people. I felt that if the prince saw me, he would fall in love with me. My attire was shabby, and I believed that this was why he did not notice me. I rushed home and put on another gown, more elaborate than the one I had been wearing. I returned to the castle, but still he did not see me. Once more, I journeyed to my house and changed my clothes, to no avail. I kept changing my ensemble, but the prince never wavered from his mechanical role of waving to the masses. Finally, I put on a wedding gown, sure that this would get his attention. On my way back to the castle, I fell into a hole filled with water. Startled, I woke up. To my surprise, my bed was soaked and my body drenched in water. My mother stood next to the bed with an empty bucket.

"It's a chore, Julie."

I got up, wet and dazed from my sleep.

"What?" I asked.

"Love."

———•———

The sun did not shine much that day. Strange clouds hovered above. I was unsure of the hour. A spell left me numbed. My mother told me it was nerves.

Tony stood tall and strong as I walked down the aisle. His stance was majestic and his smile told me he believed I was a princess. His eyes glittered like the diamond upon my finger. At the reception, the guests congratulated us as the sun became a large red ball in the sky and started its descent to the horizon. In the semidarkness, I recalled all the fairy tales I had read. I stared at the orange sky with Tony by my side; his familiar body was pressed against mine. Nothing felt new even though everything I wore had never been worn before. I remembered how, earlier that day, I'd stood at the altar and sworn everlasting love to Tony. Even that vow was not new. Tony had heard me whisper those words many nights, but this was my first public declaration. Everyone in the room believed our story had begun. I alone knew it had ended.

Now I am married and Tony is never home. He tells me he is working, but I hear his voice at the rum shop. He never asks what I write. He does not concern himself with my needs. His wish is always the same: tamarind stew. One morning, as the cock crows, I realize that Tony has grown into a man who will never again throw pebbles at my window, so I decide to forget that sound.

My stories have no audience. I am tired of the echo that carries on the wind. I dream about the people who will respond to my words. The man who lies with me at night does not know this. His face will not be in the audience that applauds my work.

I think about all the things I've never told Tony. He has never heard me say, "My mother couldn't read and so she couldn't dream." He does not know that when I write, I touch my empty womb. I wonder if I'll read stories to my unborn children in the dull monotone of my first-grade teacher.

I learned to read so I'd be a different woman than my mother. She taught me to dismiss fairy tales but sent me to school to master reading them. She unleashed my stories but didn't tell me what to do with them. I have lived my whole life with each foot in an unmatched shoe. And I've walked with uneven footsteps. Now I shall discard those mismatched shoes and I will read my stories out loud.

It is late, well after midnight, and the moon is obscured by the clouds the night Tony hears my story. I have spent months writing this story and I want Tony to be the first person to hear it. The dampness in the air tells me that rain is on its way. Before it can fall, I do something I have never done: I go to the rum shop where Tony limes with his friends, and I stand outside and call him. Because he is in a drunken stupor, he comes to me. I tell him to listen and he does. I read him the story of an unknown god who defies the one named Tony. This god allows servants to become masters and love to defy tradition. I do not describe this god nor do I give it a gender. It is nameless, faceless.

When I am finished, Tony shrugs and says, "Nice. Now I know what you do with your spare time."

He walks back into the rum shop. He lifts a glass to his lips. I hear his voice chattering among his friends. He does not discuss my story.

The rain falls. It begins in little drops that become larger and larger. I walk in the downpour. It is hot and refreshing on my

skin. The darkness of the night does not frighten me. As I walk,
I shield the papers of my story from the water. My clothes cling
to my body and my hair looks like a mop. I take off my shoes
and sink my feet into the mud that rolls freely down the road.
When I get home, I climb into the bed that Tony and I share.
My muddied body leaves dirt marks on the sheets and on the
mattress. The rain sounds like a steel band playing music in the
yard. I fall asleep writing words to the melody.

———

*Born in 1963 in London, Gayle Gonsalves moved with her
West Indian–born family back to the island of Antigua as a
young child. In her twenties she migrated to Toronto, where
she now lives. But her characters still roam the sun-drenched
landscape of her island home. This excerpt from the author's
novel in progress, Tamarind Stew, examines the sweetness of
love and the bitterness of disillusion in a heartbreakingly
beautiful place, where the hypnotic voices of island people
create a seamless marriage of magic and realism.*

GOOD BROTHER BLUES

Pearl Cleage

I spend a lot of time talking to my sisters, and in between raising our children and earning our livings and struggling for our freedom and loving our women friends and building a new world, we *sometimes*—every now and then—talk about the brothers.

Invariably the discussion moves from vivid descriptions of the various ways in which the brothers stray far and wide from our definition of what constitutes "a good brother," to wistful expressions of disbelief at the unrelenting shortage in this area, to a resigned sigh and the unspoken question of why there seem to be so many more good sisters than there are good brothers.

Now I will admit that these are complex questions to consider, but how can we arrive at the correct position on the issues of the day without confronting them? Is Marion Barry, for example, "a good brother" with a few personal problems, under siege from the forces of racism and evil, or a physically abusive woman hater who regularly lied to his wife, manipulated his female employees and acquaintances, and backhanded his lover so hard he knocked her down before she had ever even met any FBI agents?

See what I mean about the complexity of the questions?

But I am optimistic. I believe we can work it out. I believe we have to and that time is getting very short . . .

So, as part of that move toward clarity, I offer the following Report from the Front Lines as part of our continuing examination of whatever it is that is going on between black men and black women.

Our latest research indicates that part of the problem is that most brothers don't have any clear idea of what we think a good brother is. This means that there is a strong possibility that it is their confusion, not their ill will, that makes the gulf so wide between us and them.

Perhaps the problem is that we haven't given them a current, updated, cross-referenced definition to work with. Maybe they are just sort of marking time, following their own black male instincts, until we reach consensus and begin to spread the good word.

And maybe, in this terrible vacuum of values and standards, they are simply following the lead of their white male counterparts, a thuggish group of violent, homophobic, woman-hating ne'er-do-wells, whose commitment to sexism is matched only by their absolute dedication to racism and their continuing quest to control as much of the world as they can get their greedy, warmongering hands on.

Assuming this is the case—and I know this comes under the category of giving the brothers the benefit of the doubt, but we have almost nothing left to lose and everything to gain— so *assuming* this is the case, I think it is time we put forward a working definition of who and what we are looking for.

We are looking for a good brother.

We are looking for a righteous brother. A *real* righteous brother. Not one of those singing white guys who made the loss of love sound so intensely intense that you had to fall in love every time the record came on.

We are looking for a real righteous brother. An all grown up, ain't scared of nuthin', and knows it's time to save the race righteous brother.

A good father/good husband/good lover/good worker/good warrior/serious revolutionary righteous brother.

A tuck the baby in at night and accept equal responsibility for child raising and household maintenance chores righteous brother.

A generate a regular paycheck *or* provide evidence of mutually agreed upon, full-time alternative service to the race or to the family, such as playing a saxophone or writing novels, or providing community defense, or taking primary responsibility for children's nurturing and education righteous brother.

A read a book and play a tune and dance your slow dance sweet and low down righteous brother.

A love black women, protect black children, and never hit a woman righteous brother.

A turn the TV off and let's talk instead righteous brother.

A turn the TV off and let's make love instead righteous brother.

A stay at home 'cause that's where you wanna be righteous brother.

A brother who can listen.

A brother who can teach.

A brother who can change. For the better.

A brother who can move. Toward the center of the earth.

A brother who is not intimidated or confused by the power and the magic of women.

We are looking for a righteous brother. What we used to call *a good brother*.

A brother who loves his people.

A brother who doesn't hit or holler at or shoot or stab or

grab or shove or kick or shake or slap or punch women or children.

A brother who doesn't call women hoes, bitches, skanks, pussies, dykes, sluts, cunts, etc., etc., etc.

A brother who knows there is no such thing as a rape joke.

A brother who uses condoms without being asked.

A brother who doesn't call sex screwing.

A brother who knows that time and tenderness are more important than size and speed and that reciprocity is everything.

A brother who knows that permission must be gained at every step before proceeding.

A brother who doesn't describe the details of an intimate heterosexual encounter by saying, "Man, I knocked the bottom out of it." Or: "I fucked her brains out." Or: "I drew blood from that bitch."

A brother who says: "I made her feel good. I showed her how much I love and cherish her."

A brother who says: "I rubbed warm oil on her."

A brother who says: "I kissed every part of her I could kiss."

A brother who says: "I made her feel so safe and happy and free that she fell asleep in my arms and her heartbeat sounded like the ocean after a storm . . ."

We are looking for a real good brother.

We are looking for a brother who will turn the ships around.

Now I know the whole boat question is a Serious Manhood Thing, and I know how dangerous it can be to offer an opinion about any topic that falls within their sacred circle, but I'll risk it for the sake of clarification. We can't afford to have any further confusion on these questions of what does and does not constitute manhood. Not from our side anyway.

In doing the necessary research to put forward our working definition of a good brother, it came to my attention that some brothers feel that we, their sisters, are giving mixed signals when it comes to the manhood thing. We want, they say, all the protection and safety offered by a strong man, but we are unwilling to accept the presence of the warrior's heart.

We, they say, are responsible for any confusion that exists on the manhood question; we are the ones, they say, that counsel caution instead of courage, diplomacy instead of defense.

They say that when the ships pulled up on the shores of Africa and the slavers came ashore to look for us, we were the ones who held them back, the ones who told them that it might be dangerous to go down to the water's edge.

We were the ones, they say, who encouraged them to stay at home, telling them how worried we would be if they went down there with the other warriors to turn the ships around, assuring them that if they just sat here by the fire with us, the white folks would probably change their minds and go away all by themselves. They say that's the reason why they didn't turn the ships around. Because they thought we didn't want them to.

Assuming this is a correct presentation of herstorical fact (and I am unconvinced), it is clearly one of the greatest examples of miscommunication in all of human herstory and one we should avoid repeating at all costs.

So let it be known that we are looking for a brother who will turn the ships around.

A brother who will go into the crack house and turn the ships around.

A brother who will go to the places where it is open season on our children and turn the ships around.

A brother who will hear the screams of sisters being beaten to death by the men who say they love them and turn the ships around.

A brother who will hear the whimper of our babies born with AIDS and turn the ships around.

A brother who will see the people sleeping on the street and turn the ships around.

A brother who will remember how freedom feels and turn the ships around.

A brother who will gather with the warriors and march down to the edge of the sea and turn the ships around/turn the ships around/turn the ships around/and this time, turn the ships around . . .

———

A leading African American playwright with such hits as Flyin' West (1992) and Bourbon at the Border (1997), Pearl Cleage is also a novelist (1997's What Looks Like Crazy on an Ordinary Day), essayist, activist, teacher (she is playwright in residence at Atlanta's Spelman College), mother, and wife, to name but a few incarnations. Born in 1949 in Detroit, Cleage recalls her preacher father encouraging her "to take writing seriously and then figure out what it could do for the people." What her writing could do, Cleage decided, was create a forum for debate, so in 1994 she published her book of essays Deals with the Devil and Other Reasons to Riot. "I wanted to see if I could talk about things in a form that invites political analysis and discussion rather than literary criticism," Cleage explained. One essay in that volume, "Good Brother Blues," generated so much discussion it was copied and recopied, often without proper attribution, on the Internet. Cleage, a columnist for the Atlanta Tribune, is a regular contributor to Essence and Ms. magazines.

THE TURTLE
BALL

Nikky Finney

for O K C Baker

This is not a saturday night
not a pumping pulsating dance floor
This is sunday
This is church
This is now
and as private as a first kiss

I have asked permission
from the Old Sisters on the front pew
and am already in good favor
with the deacon board
now if only you would say yes
to slowdancing
in church or some other
sacred and worshiping place
the ocean perhaps
then this private prom
could at last begin

This is not some ballroom
nor saturday
This is a tortoise dance
This
a snail prom
so if they want
let them say
I have been a slowpoke with you
cause   a good dance
a good slow dance in a sacred place
where the lights stay dim all night

and the record is a longplay
and the bluelight corner
we have spidered ourselves into
is all night reserved
and the record spinner himself
recently in love
is what I'm wanting

I have already said hello
and now am introducing myself
as the one who would sit out all the others
and wait for a slowdance with you

in gradual two-step time
and not all in the same sudden hello breath
but while all the other songs
go on and play
while I wait
for the right one

At first sight
there is always our hello hug
and you *don't know*
but I'm really practicing
how to lean into your arms
really   I'm noticing
where your hands might rest
that night at the ball
really   I'm chalking out
where our hips might ask each other to dance
I am imagining
how to ask for this dance of dances
from you

I am asking you
for a good   long   slow
deliberate turtle dance
and I am taking my time
snailing this one
all the way out
so everytime
my hands come near
don't know
they are
dropping some of myself
down inside your deepest pockets

don't know
of these places so far and down
that you can't check for lost coins
that you can't reach to warm your hands
it's too far and down
a place where even washermachine water
and dryer air   leave be
can't clean or dry
won't wet or heat
don't know
these deep and downy places
that have been put there

specifically
for things
for the saving
for the savoring
for slow notes

If I take my time
if I mosey and don't gallop
to the inside island landing of your arms
there is a chance
I'll get there
if I wait until the one slow song comes on
and skip all the fast ones in between
if I hoard my breath and bank my movements
I know the slow turtle anthem will play
the one
where your eyes are not given
but rather take
their brown tortoiseshell time
to see me
through and through

the one where you will size me up
with a Jamaican gauge
using increments of some secret family measure
where no hands are allowed
where no fingers can roam
the one where only legs may hold on
where one pelvis becomes an altar for the other
where arms have nothing at all to do
it might take some sweet time
but I want to get right there

A slow dance
cannot be hurried
and can never be asked
of just anyone
but I am asking   you

Come
to the center of the floor with me
and when the song is over
and my arms try talking
try telling me
that the dance is done
but my thighs refuse them attention

I will have waited
for the slowest one
for the turtle dirge
that always comes at the end
long after
all the others
the one that lasts
the last one
a longplay please Mister
the one everybody relaxes
and comes in close on
the one always remembered
always reminisced

the one
blouses run out of waists for
that one there
where shoes
kick themselves over to corners during
or at the first note of
the very one
where eyes have to be closed
or the music will stop
where hair of any crinkly crimpled kind

is left flat and damp and dewy
the one
that always comes on
just before those ruining lights do
the one I want to hear
right when I am
sweaty and tired and ready
to go home with you

Just so
we may never get
no place
too fast

———————

*"My first breath was drawn, my first words coaxed on a trian-
gular patch of sandy land," Nikky Finney writes in the introduction to* Rice, *her 1995 poetry collection in which "The Turtle Ball" appears. Born in 1957 in Conway, South Carolina, at
the foot of the Atlantic Ocean, the poet was raised in several
towns across the state. She has been writing for as long as she
has had memory. Choosing to remain in her beloved South-
land, she attended Tallageda College in Alabama, but later
moved to the West Coast. Her first book of poems,* On Wings
Made of Gauze, *was published in 1985. After eight years of
California life, she resettled in Lexington, Kentucky, where she
is a founding member of the Affrilachian Poets and an assistant
professor of creative writing at the University of Kentucky. Now
Finney is taking her love affair with words in a new direction:
She is at work on her first novel.*

ROSELILY

Alice Walker

early Beloved,

She dreams; dragging herself across the world. A small girl in her mother's white robe and veil, knee raised waist high through a bowl of quicksand soup. The man who stands beside her is against this standing on the front porch of her house, being married to the sound of cars whizzing by on Highway 61.

we are gathered here

Like cotton to be weighed. Her fingers at the last minute busily removing dry leaves and twigs. Aware it is a superficial sweep. She knows he blames Mississippi for the respectful way the men turn their heads up in the yard, the women stand waiting and knowledgeable, their children held from mischief by teachings from the wrong God. He glares beyond them to the occupants of the cars, white faces glued to promises beyond a country wedding, noses thrust forward like dogs on a track. For him they usurp the wedding.

in the sight of God

Yes, open house. That is what country black folks like. She dreams she does not already have three children. A squeeze around the flowers in her hands chokes off three and four and five years of breath. Instantly she is ashamed and frightened in her superstition. She looks for the first time at the preacher, forces humility into her eyes, as if she believes he is, in fact, a man of God. She can imagine God, a small black boy, timidly pulling the preacher's coattail.

to join this man and this woman

She thinks of ropes, chains, handcuffs, his religion. His place of worship. Where she will be required to sit apart with covered head. In Chicago, a word she hears when thinking of smoke, from his description of what a cinder was, which they never had in Panther Burn. She sees hovering over the heads of the clean neighbors in her front yard black specks falling, clinging, from the sky. But in Chicago. Respect, a chance to build. Her children at last from underneath the detrimental wheel. A chance to be on top. What a relief, she thinks. What a vision, a view, from up so high.

in holy matrimony.

Her fourth child she gave away to the child's father who had some money. Certainly a good job. Had gone to Harvard. Was a good man but weak because good language meant so much to him he could not live with Roselily. Could not abide TV in the living room, five beds in three rooms, no Bach except from four to six on Sunday afternoons. No chess at all. She does not forget to worry about her son among his father's people. She wonders if the New England climate will agree with him. If he will ever come down to Mississippi, as his father did, to try to right the country's wrongs. She wonders if he will be stronger than his father. His father cried off and on throughout her pregnancy. Went to skin and bones. Suffered nightmares, retching and falling out of bed. Tried to kill himself. Later told his wife he found the right baby through friends. Vouched for, the sterling qualities that would make up his character.

It is not her nature to blame. Still, she is not entirely thankful. She supposes New England, the North, to be quite different from what she knows. It seems right somehow to her that people who move there to live return home completely changed. She thinks of the air, the smoke, the cinders. Imagines cinders big as hailstones; heavy, weighing on the people. Wonders how this pressure finds its way into the veins, roping the springs of laughter.

If there's anybody here that knows a reason why

But of course they know no reason why beyond what they daily have come to know. She thinks of the man who will be her husband, feels shut away from him because of the stiff severity of his plain black suit. His religion. A lifetime of black and white. Of veils. Covered head. It is as if her children are already gone from her. Not dead, but exalted on a pedestal, a stalk that has no roots. She wonders how to make new roots. It is beyond her. She wonders what one does with memories in a brand-new life. This had seemed easy, until she thought of it. "The reasons why . . . the people who" . . . she thinks, and does not wonder where the thought is from.

these two should not be joined

She thinks of her mother, who is dead. Dead, but still her mother. Joined. This is confusing. Of her father. A gray old man who sold wild mink, rabbit, fox skins to Sears, Roebuck. He stands in the yard, like a man waiting for a train. Her young sisters stand behind her in smooth green dresses, with flowers in their hands and hair. They giggle, she feels, at the absurdity of the wedding. They are ready for something new. She thinks the man beside her should marry one of them. She feels old. Yoked. An arm seems to reach out from behind her and snatch her backward. She thinks of cemeteries and the long sleep of grandparents mingling in the dirt. She believes that she believes in ghosts. In the soil giving back what it takes.

together,

In the city. He sees her in a new way. This she knows, and is grateful. But is it new enough? She cannot always be a bride and virgin, wearing robes and veil. Even now her body itches to be free of satin and voile, organdy and lily of the valley. Memories crash against her. Memories of being bare to the sun. She wonders what it will be like. Not to have to go to a job. Not to work in a sewing plant. Not to worry about learning to sew straight seams in workingmen's overalls, jeans, and dress pants. Her place will be in the home, he has said, repeatedly, promising her rest she had prayed for. But now she wonders. When she is rested, what will she do? They will make babies—she thinks practically about her fine brown body, his strong black one. They will be inevitable. Her hands will be full. Full of what? Babies. She is not comforted.

let him speak

She wishes she had asked him to explain more of what he
meant. But she was impatient. Impatient to be done with
sewing. With doing everything for three children, alone.
Impatient to leave the girls she had known since childhood,
their children growing up, their husbands hanging around her,
already old, seedy. Nothing about them that she wanted or
needed. The fathers of her children driving by, waving not
waving; reminders of tunes she would just as soon forget.
Impatient to see the South Side, where they would live and
build and be respectable and respected and free. Her husband
would free her. A romantic hush. Proposal. Promises. A new
life! Respectable, reclaimed, renewed. Free! In robe and veil.

or forever hold

She does not even know if she loves him. She loves his sobriety.
His refusal to sing just because he knows the tune. She loves his
pride. His blackness and his gray car. She loves his understanding of her *condition*. She thinks she loves the effort he will make
to redo her into what he truly wants. His love of her makes her
completely conscious of how unloved she was before. This is
something; though it makes her unbearably sad. Melancholy.
She blinks her eyes. Remembers she is finally being married, like
other girls. Like other girls, women? Something strains upward
behind her eyes. She thinks of the something as a rat trapped,
cornered, scurrying to and fro in her head, peering through the
windows of her eyes. She wants to live for once. But doesn't
know quite what that means. Wonders if she has ever done it. If
she ever will. The preacher is odious to her. She wants to strike
him out of the way, out of her light, with the back of her hand.

It seems to her he has always been standing in front of her, barring her way.

his peace.

The rest she does not hear. She feels a kiss, passionate, rousing, within the general pandemonium. Cars drive up blowing their horns. Firecrackers go off. Dogs come from under the house and begin to yelp and bark. Her husband's hand is like the clasp of an iron gate. People congratulate. Her children press against her. They look with awe and distaste mixed with hope at their new father. He stands curiously apart, in spite of the people crowding about to grasp his free hand. He smiles at them all but his eyes are as if turned inward. He knows they cannot understand that he is not a Christian. He will not explain himself. He feels different, he looks it. The old women thought he was like one of their sons except that he had somehow got away from them. Still a son, not a son. Changed.

She thinks how it will be later in the night in the silvery gray car. How they will spin through the darkness of Mississippi and in the morning be in Chicago, Illinois. She thinks of Lincoln, the president. That is all she knows about the place. She feels ignorant, *wrong*, backward. She presses her worried fingers into his palm. He is standing in front of her. In the crush of well-wishing people, he does not look back.

———

With the publication of her epistolary novel The Color Purple, *which garnered both a Pulitzer Prize and an American Book Award in 1983, Alice Walker achieved worldwide recogni-*

tion as a writer of "womanist" literature. Born in Eatonton, Georgia, in 1944, the eighth and last child of sharecroppers, Walker attended Spelman College and earned her B.A. from Sarah Lawrence College in 1965. Her fiction, poetry, and essays explore the sexual and racial realities of black women in a world that seeks to stifle their power. Like much of Walker's work, her short story "Roselily," which appeared in the 1973 collection In Love & Trouble, attracted its share of controversy: It was briefly banned from the California school curriculum because it was thought to promote the idea that religion oppresses women. Walker, a gardener, world traveler, and spiritual seeker, admits to feeling singed by such criticism. In The Same River Twice: Honoring the Difficult (1995), she wrote: "I belong to a people so wounded by betrayal, so hurt by misplacing their trust, that to offer us a gift of love is often to risk one's life. . . ." Nevertheless, Walker, whose writing has received numerous honors and awards, continues to hone and offer her gift: She has just completed a new novel, By the Light of My Father's Smile. The mother of a daughter, Rebecca (herself a writer and activist), Walker currently lives in northern California.

THE CRY

Rosemarie Robotham

n Thursday, Cora woke up and knew she was in trouble. She knew it the minute she opened her eyes, knew that sometime in the night, while she slept, she had crossed the threshold into final despair. She'd been hovering on the brink of it for weeks, ever since losing her baby two months before. Since then, whispering veils of darkness had flapped about her like wings, first gently, then violently, threatening to wrap her completely and spirit her away.

Away to where she didn't know, but often in the last weeks, she'd wanted to stop fighting the veils, wanted instead to reach out the gossamer edges of grief, to pull its filmy fibers around her and sink into surrender. But everything she knew about living told her she must go on. She couldn't give in. That would invite the anxious, pitying scrutiny of people who cared: her husband Chris, her parents and relatives, well-meaning friends. Each one had echoed the same refrain. It's nature's way, they had told her, their voices stroking her pain.

That Thursday, Chris had already left the house when Cora awoke. He'd risen in the darkness and slipped out to work. Cora hadn't heard him leaving and, in the stillness of the house, she felt abandoned and alone. She didn't know what Chris felt about all this anymore; she couldn't pierce the silence he'd erected around himself like a wall. She imagined him safe within it, his sadness folded into its appropriate place so it couldn't keep tripping him as he maneuvered in the world.

Nights after work, they moved around each other carefully, fixing dinner and quietly setting the table. Then Chris would murmur that he wasn't hungry just yet, but he'd sit with her, keep her company while she ate. Cora noticed, sitting across from him, that little grooves had begun to etch themselves at the corners of his lips, and the crease between his brows had deepened. After they cleaned up, Cora would wander through the rooms of their apartment like sorrow's ghost, and Chris would sit perfectly still beside the living room window and track her with his eyes.

When it first happened, they couldn't have been closer, so that Cora had wondered if the little spirit that might have been their child hadn't given them a gift after all. Chris had been so composed the afternoon Cora had called him from the doctor's office to tell him there was something wrong with the baby. She was nineteen weeks pregnant, and a routine sonogram that afternoon showed that all the amniotic fluid had leaked away. The baby had ceased growing, its fragile skin collapsed on its bones like a wizened old man's. The doctors were advising termination. The word had sounded alien, and Cora couldn't comprehend that they were telling her to abort her child. She kept seeing the blurred image of her baby on the black-and-white screen: a skeletal little creature, heart pumping bravely in her dry womb. The doctors explained that the baby's lungs could not develop without fluid, that its limbs could not be exercised, the child could not survive once born. Its body would be twisted by horrible contractures; it would never draw breath. Cora's brother, a doctor, begged her to give up on this one and try again. Patiently, he explained that by delaying, Cora was risking an infection in her womb that would cause her never to bear children.

That night, Chris rocked her in his arms, buried his face in her hair and told her that there would be other children, but his concern right now was for Cora. Cora remembered feeling fortunate to be so loved. She thought about the life the child would have, if by some miracle it lived. She saw its crippled little body, tortured and accusatory, like the skeleton on the sonogram screen.

The next morning, at six-thirty, they drove to the hospital. Sunlight streamed through the ceiling-high windows of the hospital room to which they were taken. They might have been checking into a hotel, Cora thought as they explored the contents of the drawers and closets, noted the cleanliness of the bathroom. Cora remarked on the quality of light in the room, and the fact that they could see the river, with tiny sloops in the distance knitting the water.

Soon, a young resident arrived to take Cora's blood, set up her drip, and administer other tests. Cora had never stayed overnight in a hospital before, and she was feeling rather pampered. She congratulated herself on her sense of detachment. Chris being with her made the whole thing seem rather like an adventure, a new experience they were sharing.

At one o'clock, Cora's doctor arrived to administer the first suppository; she was to be given one every two hours until she delivered. The doctor had warned her that the pain would be excruciating, nothing short of "real" labor, with contractions and nausea and vomiting. "I've prescribed something for the pain," the doctor told her. "Don't hesitate to ask for it."

Chris stood to one side and looked away while the doctor put the prostaglandin tablet inside Cora.

"Well, the die is cast," the doctor declared, her voice falsely bright. A sudden chill rose through Cora. The sunlight dimmed a little; the adventure palled. She felt the first intimation of the dark veils that awaited her. She remembered something Chris had told her the evening before, when she'd wanted to wait, even though all the specialists had insisted that the baby had no chance of survival. Chris had whispered, "I hate to think of him suffering in there, gasping for breath, in pain." Those words more than anything had helped convince her of the path she should take. She clung to the words now, trying to remind herself that their decision was merciful.

At three, the contractions began. By seven that night, the waves were so close together they felt like one continual agony, and Cora wished she could drift into darkness rather than endure anymore. Chris was at her side the whole time, giving her water, holding the stainless-steel bowl as she threw up, wheeling the drip alongside her as she stumbled to the bathroom. Cora couldn't speak, couldn't cry even. She had to save all her wits for the pain. Her mind railed at God, at the bitterness of labor with no hope of a living child. And yet, in the midst of her desolation, she was overwhelmed by gratitude toward Chris, for his unflinching attention, his loving presence in the room with her.

At midnight the doctor came to check on her. She reached a plastic-gloved hand inside Cora's body and pulled out the dead fetus, placing its crumpled form in a clinical white bucket. She reached back in for the placenta, her fist inside Cora causing a pain more brutal than even the contractions had. Cora prayed fervently for the ordeal to be over, for the long night to end. But the placenta could not be reached. It was trapped somehow and Cora's body refused to deliver it. The doctor left with the nurse to find forceps, a better light, other surgical equipment. Cora breathed deeply, the pain momentarily gone.

Chris was standing over the bucket, which the nurse had

placed on the night table. Almost furtively, he nudged the cover aside and looked in. "It's a boy," he said. Chris had wanted a boy.

"What does he look like?" Cora whispered, afraid to know.

"Like a little rubber doll," Chris said, his voice also hushed. "Much bigger than I expected."

"How big?" Cora asked. Chris made a sphere with his hands; the circular air inside them was the baby's head.

"That big," Cora murmured and closed her eyes.

"Will seeing him give you nightmares?" she asked after a while.

"No," Chris said. "I'm glad I looked."

"Let me see, I want to see him, too."

"Are you sure? Cora?"

"Yes," Cora said weakly. "Very sure."

Chris brought the bucket to the side of the bed and held it low enough for Cora to look inside. Their baby boy, lying in profile in the bucket, looked perfectly formed. His head was smooth and incredibly round, his tiny ear exquisitely shaped. Two muscular little arms crossed his chest, five fingers curled inward, five delicate toes. He looked nothing like he had on the sonogram, a skeletal monster, more like a rodent, not human at all. In the bucket, in life, their baby looked flawlessly proportioned, impossibly human. A little rubber doll, Chris had said, serene-looking. Dead.

They took the placenta surgically the next morning, and at lunchtime Chris and Cora went home. Everyone called to offer condolences. The house brimmed with flowers and gifts. Cora thought how blessed she was to have so much support. But after a few days, she wished everyone would stop calling. Their voices over the phone were thick with pity, so that Cora felt obliged to act more damaged than she felt. Eventually, she stopped answering the phone. If Chris was home, she let him take the calls. "We just have to look ahead. We're young, we can start again," she heard her husband say over and over again. More and more often, she felt like weeping at the words. They might have other babies, she found herself thinking, but not that baby, not that little boy.

Her cousin, an apprentice healer, explained to Cora that on the other side, time is meaningless, a whisper, and that their baby's spirit would possibly come back to them in their next child. She speculated that the baby had come and gone so quickly to help Chris and Cora work out some mutual karma. With the loss of their child, she assured Cora, a mysterious debt from another life had quietly been paid.

Cora liked to imagine the possibility of other lives. She liked to think that souls came together after death, in a place where loved ones were reunited and all sorrow erased. If Cora could keep her mind running in this stream, she felt comforted, for she could contemplate the time that she would find her lost baby's soul. Her love would draw her to wherever he was.

After two weeks, Cora went back to work. In her head, she carried the perpetual image of her dead baby, small and serene on the floor of the bucket. Everyone had stopped calling by then, and now Cora, feeling unaccountably lost, began to call certain friends, hoping she might happen upon a definition of the melancholy that had begun to oppress her. But her friends were uneasy when she referred to her lost child.

"It was a fetus," her best friend told her firmly.

"Well, you still have Chris," another friend said.

Cora stopped reaching out. She looked up the word *miscarriage* in a thesaurus and found the words *failure, malfunction,* and *mismanagement*. She began to think she had sorely mismanaged her youth. She had smoked too much dope, had neglected opportunities for spiritual growth, and so was not worthy of the soul that would have been her child. She didn't know how to say these things to Chris. He would think her

melodramatic and would counsel her not to indulge in needless
recrimination. She must accept what had happened and simply
go on. That was the way Chris handled things. "You play the
hand you're dealt," he often said, as if life were as capricious
as a random tarot spread. Cora realized she had no heart anymore for the game. The cards were arrayed all around her,
their burlesque pattern mocking her imitation of sanity, divin-
ing her bottomless pain.

On that Thursday morning, she could feel the veils surrounding her more closely than they ever had. She knew there
was no question of going to work, so she sat in the dark
house, motionless as fractured stone. At nine o'clock, she
called in sick to her job. Then she lay down on her bed and
waited, waited numbly for the silken cloth to close over her,
for the rich veils of grief to smother her and deliver her over
to the other side.

But somewhere beyond the veils, sleep crept back in. Cora
fell through fiercely swirling silk into dreams of a little brown
child, breathless with life, with glossy black eyes like her husband's and brows that swept gently together over the bridge
of his nose. The child, a graceful, long-limbed boy, ran laughing among the veils, his wind-voice calling her name. Cora
stood transfixed, unable to move forward, still fearing the
heartbreak of hope. "Mama," the child called, and raised his
arms. The paralysis lifted. Trancelike, Cora began to move
toward the child, tentatively at first, then more swiftly, till her
feet were running behind him as he darted through the veils.

When she awoke, it was evening. Chris was bending over
her, his troubled eyes more familiar than they'd ever been, and
yet also more strange. Chris stroked her forehead, placed a
small kiss in the curve of her neck, then moved his lips to her
ear. It took another moment for Cora to rise out of the trance
of her dream, so she didn't hear what Chris whispered at first.

But as she furled herself against him, as his arms went around her, his words came through. "We'll find our baby," he whispered. In that moment the veils parted, and Cora knew it was true.

———◦•◦———

Born in 1957 in Kingston, Jamaica, Rosemarie Robotham grew up entranced by the lyricism of West Indian speech. Amid this music, she decided she wanted to write. At eighteen she moved to New York City to attend Barnard College and, later, Columbia University's Graduate School of Journalism. A reporter for Life *magazine for eight years, she is the author of the novel* Zachary's Wings *(1998), and coauthor of* Spirits of the Passage: The Transatlantic Slave Trade in the Seventeenth Century *(1996). Robotham was also anthologized in John Henrik Clarke's* Black American Short Stories: One Hundred Years of the Best. *In her short story "The Cry," she explores the resilience of women, the nurturing capacities of men, and the persistence of love. Currently an editor-at-large at* Essence *magazine, Robotham lives in New York City with her husband and two children.*

CHEESE GRITS
SWING

Pamela Johnson

The best meal I ever ate was at this spot over on Seventh Avenue, right here in Harlem. Don't even exist no more. But that morning they served me up some of the best cheese grits, fried chicken wings, and ham omelette I ever did eat. Course, I wasn't quite in my right mind. Me and Sweet T. had just danced all night at the Savoy; both our dogs was out of commission. We was just slung over that counter, our feet throbbing big time, waiting for something, anything, to be put under our noses.

Loved me some Sweet T. in those days. Sweet face, s'pose that's why they called her that; the T. was for Thelma. She was a little pretty thing. Dark girl when dark girls wasn't none too popular. But I never did run with the crowd on that one. For her height, 'bout five-feet-two, she had her some long legs. And she wore them cinch-waist dresses. Always laughing, too. Tell her a little joke, and that laugh start way down deep. And everything on her face full: lips, nose, cheeks, eyes like a doe. But what brought me and Sweet T. together at first was dancing.

She was with that old rascal Sonny when I first seen her. They was dusting it up halfway across the room. She didn't give him a second's delay. Put it in my file. As a young man, I was like that. Didn't necessarily have to act on something right away. Right away might not be the best time, you know, so I put it away. Then I watched her. Had my own girl then. Madlyn. Tall, brown-skin girl. Okay lookswise, but too clingy. Started every request with *Daddy*. I heard *Daddy*, I knew *gimme* was sure to follow. But Madlyn had a good nature. I didn't think we was no long-distance team, but she had a goodness about her.

Still, I kept my eye on Sweet T. Looked to see if any irregularity creeped up in her and Sonny steps. Kept track of them off ones. And when I notice them keep going out of whack, I start maneuvering me and Madlyn closer. Start doing my best moves, throwing a glance Sweet T. way now and again. Then one night, Count Basie and his orchestra was going at it in a frenzy, and I politely suggest me and Sonny switch partners. Couple months later, me and Madlyn done spun out and I see Sweet T. at the Savoy with other mens besides Sonny.

Always did feel I was a number one kind of man. When I danced with Sweet T., I glided her smooth. I worked hard, trying to make it easy on her. Wanted to show her what a real man could do, not like that process-head Sonny; wanted to burn his memory right out of her. And we go at it good, too. Do the jitterbug back. Keep my shoes shined and my suit pressed. This wasn't no dancing we was doing. I was making love to Sweet T. 'Fore I ever touched her, I was making love to her Friday and Saturday nights on the dance floor. I look into them doe eyes 'fore I turn her around, and I say everything better than I ever could put into words. When she fly between my legs and I swing her up and catch her, I was telling her how I would keep her safe. She knowed what I meant, too.

I wasn't the handsomest man, neither the most educated. But I kept myself nice. My thing was to be number one with Sweet T. I wanted that laugh to belong to me. Wanted her to depend on me. Might not know it 'cause she didn't act no particular way, but she had a college degree and was a professional teacher. She live by herself and didn't want nobody to forget that she could make her own way. Don't think she had nothing against me being a bricklayer. Besides the calluses on my hands, I probably had more problems with it than she did. Colored man in the forties, after the war, didn't get the respect neither the opportunities that white fellas got. They lay us off in a minute, keep the white fellas on steady. And just everyday indignity. Friday come, my body be in a knot. I soak in Epsom salts, and in a couple of hours I be new. Smelling good, clean pressed suit ready to swing.

T. say she think I'm special, but every time I bring up the subject of marriage, she ain't ready. She say she can't picture herself in no housedress. She say she love children, but she ain't certain she want to bring no more colored kids into this world. I figure she need more time. Eight years we dancing this lovemaking dance, and she ain't ready. Then she take ill. Breast cancer. She only thirty-four. They get to cutting on her. Cut her up pretty bad. Everytime I turn around, they ready to cut again. I think, T. losing her fight. Finally I can't take it no more. I say enough. I say, T., you coming home with me. I fix up the room for her nice, let her rest in peace. She sick as sick get, but time to time, I pull her out of that bed and hold her close. I do all the work so she can glide. I ain't much of a singer, but I sing soft to T. Her moaning go right through me, so I sing. I try to soak up her pain and bring it out in a little song. "Dream a Little Dream of Me," or "Someone to Watch over Me." One day I'm singing and T. just slip away. Nothing different in her face, but I know she gone.

Day after the funeral was the lowest of all my days. Up to the funeral, everybody so busy, hardly time to think. Her mama handle mostly all the details, but I make sure T. have on one of her cinch-waist dresses, red at that. Wasn't much of her left, though. Funeral director have to pin that dress in the back. Put on her dancing shoes. I sit right there at the end of that first pew the whole time. I let everybody else go up there and cry in the casket. In my heart, I know T. ain't at this affair.

Down the road apiece, I hook back up with Madlyn. She still out there throwing *Daddy* around like loose change. I see she weary. She need me. She come to depend on me. She a little reluctant since the Sweet T. thing, but deep down, I think she believe I mean to stay.

We married thirty-something years now. Each year, my sight get a little worse. Got arthritis bad, ain't danced in years. My next birthday, I'll make seventy-five. Madlyn do my running for me now. Mostly to the pharmacy. I can't be the man to her I once was. I used to could wear out a mattress in a week. Still she stay by me.

But every now and then, deep in the night, I stir. I'm back on that dance floor gliding with Sweet T. If I wake, my heart drop, but I get a comfort, too. In a way, T. be with me till my last day. But Madlyn's a good woman. She fuss over me and make my favorite dishes. I don't spoil it for her by telling her my taste almost gone, too. She do more for me than I ever done for her. But most of my best times is past. In fact, one of my choicest memories is that morning I was slung over that counter, dog tired and dizzy in love, and the Lord saw fit to slide me some cheese grits, chicken wings, and a ham omelette.

Now that was the best meal I ever did eat.

After sixteen years as a journalist working in television, newspapers, and magazines, Pamela Johnson is busy adding to her credits a trio of books—Santa and Pete: A Novel of Christmas Present and Past (1998), a novel in progress, and an anthology on the relationship between black women and their hair. A 1982 graduate of Stanford University, Johnson hails from the Los Angeles area but now lives in New York City, where she is a contributing writer to Essence *magazine. Of "Cheese Grits Swing" she says: "I had just finished eating at a restaurant and the waitress asked me how my meal was. I told her it was fine, but as she walked away I thought,* I should have told her that was the best meal I ever ate. *I think I must have wanted to say something extraordinary. Then I got to thinking,* What might make a person say that about a meal? *I realized it would have to be about more than the meal. The story started there."*

IN FRANCE

AN EXCERPT FROM THE NOVEL
Sarah Phillips

Andrea Lee

During the wet autumn of 1974 I heard a lot about another American girl who was living in Paris. Her name was Kate, and she was said to be from a rich family in Chicago—a word my French friends pronounced with relish, in a pidgin staccato. Kate was a photographer who specialized in making nudes look like vegetables; she lived on an immense allowance in an apartment near the Bois de Boulogne. She was an old friend of Henri, Alain, and Roger, the three young men with whom I lived, and in early October we tried several times to visit her, but each time a hostile male voice over the telephone told us she was busy, or out of town, or indisposed. Henri finally heard a rumor that she was being held prisoner in her apartment by her present lover and an ex-boyfriend, who were collecting her allowance and had bought a luxurious Fiat—the same model the Pope drove—with the profits.

The story was riveting enough when we discussed it over drinks at the Bill-Board, a nondescript café near the Rue de Rivoli, but none of my companions seemed especially concerned about Kate. Alain sighed and licked the ring of milk foam from his glass (he always ordered Ovomaltine); Roger thoughtfully rubbed his nose; and Henri, shaking his head at me in mock sorrow, said, "American girls!"

Kate came occasionally into my thoughts as I sat shivering
and watching television in the big vulgar living room of Henri's
uncle's apartment, where a penetrating chill rose from the marble floors. That fall I had only one pair of tights because my
supply of traveler's checks was dwindling and I didn't want
Henri to buy my clothes; over the tights, for warmth, I wore a
pair of white tennis socks I'd bought in Lausanne in the summer. The socks, which I seldom washed, were getting tatty,
brownish, and full of holes. I massaged my cold toes through
my socks and tights and thought idly about Kate the Lake
Forest debutante immured somewhere overlooking the rust-
colored chestnuts in the Bois. She seemed to be a kind of sister
or alter ego, although she was white and I was black, and back
in the States I'd undergone a rush of belated social fury at girls
like Kate, whose complacent faces had surrounded me in prep
school and college. Idly I sympathized with her, guessing that
she had a reason for investing in whatever thefts and embarrassments modern Paris could provide.

In October there was a French postal strike, which pleased
me: I had painstakingly cut off communication with my family in Philadelphia, and I liked the idea of channels closing
officially between America and France. The dollar was down
that year, and it was harder than ever to live on nothing in
Europe, but scores of Americans were still gamely struggling
to cast off kin and convention in a foreign tongue, and I was
among them. I had grown up in the hermetic world of the old-
fashioned black bourgeoisie—a group largely unknown to
other Americans, which has carried on with cautious pomp
for years in eastern cities and suburbs, using its considerable
funds to attempt poignant imitations of high society, acting
with genuine gallantry in the struggle for civil rights, and
finally producing a generation of children educated in newly
integrated schools and impatient to escape the outworn ritu-

als of their parents. The previous June I had graduated from Harvard, having just turned twenty-one. I was tall and lanky and light-skinned, quite pretty in a nervous sort of way; I came out of college equipped with an unfocused snobbery, vague literary aspirations, and a lively appetite for white boys. When before commencement my father died of a stroke, I found that my lifelong impulse to discard Philadelphia had turned into a loathing of everything that made up my past. And so, with a certain amazement at the ruthless ingenuity that replaced my grief, I left to study French literature in Lausanne, intending never to come back.

One weekend in Montreux I met Henri Durier, and at his suggestion quit school and Switzerland to come live in the Paris apartment he shared with his uncle and his uncle's array of male companions and his own two friends from childhood, Alain and Roger. There I entered a world where life was aimless and sometimes bizarre—a mixture that suited my desire for amnesia. Henri was nineteen, a big blond who looked more Frisian than French. Though he wasn't terribly intelligent, there was something better than intelligence and older than his age in the way he faced the world, something forceful and hypnotic in his gray eyes, which often held the veiled, mean gaze of one for whom life has been a continual grievance. He was, in fact, an illegitimate child, raised outside Paris by his mother and adopted only recently by his rich uncle. This uncle held a comfortable post at the Ministry of Finance, and Henri, who had an apprentice job in the advertising department of Air France, lived and traveled lavishly on a collection of credit cards. When I met him, he had just returned from touring Texas, where he had bought a jaunty Confederate cap. Throughout our short romance we remained incomprehensible to each other, each of us clutching a private exotic vision in the various beds where we made love. "*Reine*

d'Afrique, petite Indienne," Henri would whisper, winding
my hair into a long braid; he wanted me to wear red beaded
threads in my ears, like women he'd seen in Brazil.

Henri's ideas about the United States had a nuttiness that
outdid the spaghetti-western fantasies I'd found in other
Frenchmen; for instance, he thought Nixon was the greatest
president, Houston the most important city. I was annoyed
and bored by his enthusiasm for chicken-fried steak and
General Lee, and he was equally exasperated when I spoke of
Georges Brassens or the Comtesse de Noailles. He couldn't
begin to imagine the America I came from, nor did I know, or
even try to find out, what it was like to grow up in Lorraine,
in a provincial city, where at school the other boys gang up on
you, pull down your pants, and smear you with black shoe
polish because you have no father.

The apartment where we lived was in the Sixteenth
Arrondissement; it was a sprawling place, designed with fix-
tures and details in an exuberant bad taste that suggested a
motor inn in Tucson. A floor-to-ceiling wrought-iron grille
divided the living room from the dining room, and the
kitchen, hall toilet, and both bathrooms were papered in a
garish turquoise Greek-key design. Otherwise it was a wonderful Parisian apartment: tall double windows, luminous
wet skies, the melancholy soughing of traffic in the street
below. When I arrived, the place held handsome antique
wooden beds in each of the four bedrooms, and an assortment of boards and wooden boxes in the living room, dining
room, and kitchen. Henri's uncle, who spent little time there,
seemed indifferent to comfort, preferring to furnish his apartment with a changing assortment of male humanity. There
was Enzo, a muscular young mechanic, and Enzo's friends,
who were mainly Italian hoodlums; there was Carlos, a short
Spanish Gypsy, who lived in a trailer out by Orly; there was

a doddering Russian prince, and a wiry blue-eyed shadow in a leather jacket who Henri assured me was an IRA terrorist; there was an exquisitely dressed prefect of police, who sometimes lectured Henri, Alain, Roger, and me on *"la nécessité des rapports sains entre les sexes."* Manners within this motley company had assumed a peculiar formality: strangers nodded and spoke politely as they passed in the halls.

Alain and Roger both rented rooms in the Fifth Arrondissement, but they spent most nights with us, sleeping in whatever bed happened to be available. The two of them had grown up with Henri in the city of Nancy. Alain was twenty and slight bodied, with girlish white skin and beetling dark brows. He came from a large and happy petit bourgeois family, and although he tried hard to look as surly as Henri, he was generally amused rather than aggrieved, and a natural, naive joy of life gleamed out of his tiny, crooked blue eyes. He loved to improve my French by teaching me nasty children's rhymes, and his imaginative rendering of my name, Sarah Phillips, in an exaggerated foreign accent made it sound vaguely Arabic. Roger, a student who sprang from the pettiest of petty nobility, had flat brown hair and a sallow, snub-nosed face. He was sarcastic and untrustworthy; his jokes were all about bosoms and bottoms; and of the three boys I liked him the least.

The four of us generally got along well. I was Henri's girl, but a few times, in the spirit of *Brüderschaft,* I spent nights with Alain and Roger. At breakfast we had familial squabbles over our bowls of watery instant coffee and sterilized milk (one of the amenities Henri's uncle had neglected was the installation of a refrigerator); late at night, when we'd come back bored and dreamy from dinner or the movies and the rain on the windows was beginning to sound like a series of insistent questions, we played a game called Galatea, in which I stood naked on a wooden box and turned slowly to have my body appraised and criticized. The three boys were funny and horny and only occasionally tiresome; they told me I was beautiful and showed me off to their friends at cafés and discos and at the two Drugstores.

At that time, thank heavens, I hadn't seen or read *Jules and Jim,* so I could play the queen without self-consciousness, thinking—headily, guiltily, sentimentally—that I was doing something the world had never seen before. Two weeks after I had come to stay at the apartment, I returned from shopping to find the big rooms filled with furniture: fat velvet chairs and couches from Au Bon Marché, a glass-and-steel dining-room set, and four enormous copies of Oriental rugs, thrown down recklessly so that their edges overlapped to form one vast wrinkled sea of colors. "They're for you, naturally," Henri told me when I asked. "You were complaining about cold feet."

When Henri, Alain, and Roger weren't around, I loafed in the apartment or rambled through the Louvre; the painting I liked most was Poussin's "Paradis Terrestre," where a grand stasis seems to weigh down the sunlit masses of foliage, and the tiny figure of Eve, her face unscarred by recollection, looks delicate and indolent.

If I was idle, all France around me was vibrating to the latest invasion of Anglo-Saxon culture. The first McDonald's in Paris had opened on the Champs-Elysées. The best French commercials were those for Goldtea—artless takeoffs on *Gone with the Wind,* with Senegalese extras toiling in replicas of American cotton fields, flat-chested French belles in hoopskirts, and French male actors trying subtly to inject a bit of Wild West into the Confederate cavaliers they played. The hit song that fall was a piece by the madly popular cartoon canary TiTi, who had begun in the United States as Tweety; it was a lisping ditty in a high sexy voice, and it seemed to be ringing faintly at all hours through the streets of the city.

French girls were wearing rust-colored cavalier boots and skintight cigarette jeans that dug into their crotches in imitation of Jane Birkin, the English movie star. Birkin had the swayback and flat buttocks of a little girl, and she spoke a squeaky, half-hysterical, English-accented French. Henri, Alain, and Roger rolled on the floor in fits of insane laughter whenever I imitated Jane Birkin. I had a pair of cigarette jeans, too; they left a mesh of welts on my belly and thighs. Sometimes in the rainy afternoons when I walked in the Bois, I could hear TiTi's song playing somewhere deep in the dripping yellow leaves. Occasionally a wet leaf would come sailing out of the woods and affix itself squarely to my cheek or forehead like an airmail stamp, and I would think of all the letters I hadn't written home.

In October we went to England three times, on weekend excursions in Henri's plastic Jeep. We took the ferry to Dover, then drove up to London, where Roger thought it was fun to play slot machines late at night in a penny arcade in Piccadilly Circus. Each time, we put up at the Cadogan Hotel, charging a suite to Henri's uncle's credit card. The respectable English and Continental travelers eyed us surreptitiously, and we determined that if questioned we would say we were a rock-and-roll band. "Josephine Baker et les Trois Bananes," suggested Alain.

Some chemistry of air, soil, and civilization filled me with unwilling nostalgia, and I kept a sharp lookout in London for certain types of tourists: prosperous black Americans, a little overdressed and a bit uneasy in hotel lobbies, who could instantly identify where I came from, and who might know my family. During the day we would drive into the country and rent horses, prodding them into clattering gallops with Comanche yells. I was the official interpreter on these expeditions, and the times when I failed to understand a broad country accent, the three boys jeered at me. "What's the matter, don't you speak English?" they'd say.

Later that fall we tried to take the ferry from Normandy to the island of Jersey but were prevented from doing so by bad weather. We spent the night in Granville, in a tall, chill stone hotel where the shutters banged all night in a gale off the Channel. The next morning Alain got up, looking very skinny and white in a pair of sagging blue underpants, and ran shivering to the window. "We'll have to forget the island," he said, peering through the shutters. The waves were slate-colored, huge, with an oily roll to them and with shifting crests of yellowish foam.

Alain was in a bad mood because Henri and I had made love the night before in the twin bed next to his. "That was a charming thing to do," he said to Henri, who was pulling on his jeans. "To torture a poor adolescent. I couldn't get to sleep for hours!"

He tossed a pillow at Henri, who batted it away. Henri and I were in foul moods ourselves, mainly because the mutual fascination that had joined us suddenly and profoundly three months before had begun to break down into boredom and suspicion.

Still in his underpants, Alain jumped up onto one of the beds and began to yodel and beat his chest like Tarzan. "Aaah!" he yelled, rolling his eyes maniacally; then he leaped upon Henri, who had bent to tie his sneaker.

"Idiot! T'es dingue, toi!" shouted Henri, and the two of them began to wrestle, Henri easily gaining the upper hand over the bony Alain. Alain groaned in pretended anguish when Henri sat on his chest; it was clear that this attack and defeat were part of a ritual whose rules had been set in childhood. They were far closer to each other, I thought, than I would ever be to either of them.

When Roger appeared, he was in as bad a mood as the rest of us, his back aching because he had had to spend the night on a cot in a tiny *chambre de bonne* two floors above ours. "What a room!" he said, grabbing my comb and stroking his flat brown hair still flatter. "Good for a midget or a paraplegic!"

We gave up on the island of Jersey and drove inland toward Paris, past fields that were bright green beneath October mists, and through spare Norman villages, and then past brown copses and woodlands, all under a sky where a single white channel was opening between two dark fronts of autumn storm. Raindrops broke and ran upward on the windshield of the jeep, and I shivered in Henri's aviator jacket, which he had bought in Texas. To keep warm we sang, though the number of songs all four of us knew the words to was small: "Auprès de Ma Blonde," "Chevalier de la Table Ronde," "Dixie," "Home on the Range," and endlessly, endlessly, John Denver. "Country roads, take me home!" Henri, Alain, and Roger would warble, throwing their heads back with a gusto that was only partly satirical: they thought Denver's music was the greatest thing America had exported since blue jeans.

In between songs we talked about Roger's sister Sabine, who was engaged in a battle with her parents because she wanted to marry a Jew. "Sabine is a fool," said Henri. "The thing for her to do is to leave home and do exactly as she pleases."

There was silence for a minute, as in the backseat Alain glanced at Roger. All of us had heard how Henri had left his small family—his pretty, weak-chinned mother and his grandmother, a meddlesome farmer's widow from Berry. The story went that when Henri's rich uncle—whom the family discreetly described as *"misogyne"*—visited Nancy, he had taken a chaste interest in the fifteen-year-old Henri and had given

him twenty minutes to decide whether to leave the town forever and come to live in Paris. Henri claimed he had decided
in five minutes and had never looked back.

Alain looked out the plastic window of the jeep. "It's not
like that in my family," he said, his irregular face solemn for
once. "With us, attachments have an awful strength."

We stopped for lunch at the Cercle d'Or, a small inn near the
outskirts of Rouen. The place had a wood-burning oven, and we
ate lamb roasted over the coals, and goat cheese and Bosc pears,
and coupes napoléons, and then we drank coffee with Calvados.
By three-thirty in the afternoon, the semicircle of white-covered
tables near the fire was almost deserted and the restaurant
seemed hypnotically comfortable; padding waiters had begun to
set the places for supper. Outside, above a hill covered with
beeches, the rack of storm clouds had thinned into streaks of
blue, and a few rays of sun reached into the dining room.

A squabble had started between Alain and Henri when
Alain, for no reason at all, threw a mayonnaise-covered olive
into Henri's wine. The quarrel lasted through the coffee, when
Henri, to the amusement of the restaurant staff, ordered Alain
away from the table. Alain, swearing under his breath, shuffled obediently off to the courtyard and lay down in the back
of the jeep; through the window by our table we could see his
big sneakered feet protruding from under the rear flap in an
attitude of careless defiance.

When he had gone, Henri said, "Espèce de con!" and Roger,
who worshiped Henri and was always jealous of Alain, allowed
a faint smile to cross his face. After that Henri stubbed out his
cigarette on a crust of bread and began needling me about my
appearance; short skirts were out of fashion, he said, and mine
made me look like a prostitute. "And wherever," he added,
"did you get the idea that you could wear a green shirt with
blue denim?"

"Americans don't pay attention to little things like the color of their clothes," remarked Roger nastily, brushing a thread from the sleeve of his immaculate tweed jacket. "Or the style of their hair. Sarah, *ma vieille*, you're certainly pretty enough, but why don't you put your hair up properly? Or cut it off? You have the look of a savage!"

Henri giggled and grabbed my frizzy ponytail. "She is a savage!" he exclaimed, with the delighted air of a child making a discovery. "A savage from the shores of the Mississippi!" (He pronounced "Mississippi" with the accent on the last syllable.)

In the sunlight through the window, Henri looked very fair-haired and well fed. His round face, like that of a troublemaking cherub, was flushed with malicious energy; I could tell he was enormously pleased to be annoying me, and that he wouldn't let me off easily.

"I'm going to go see Alain," I said, and started to get up, but Henri held on to my hair and pulled me back.

"Don't go anywhere, darling," he said. "I want to tell Roger all about your elegant pedigree."

"Tell him about yours!" I said rashly, forgetting that Henri was illegitimate.

Roger gave a thin squawk of laughter, and Henri's face darkened. He picked up a spoon and began stirring the heaped butts in the ashtray. "Did you ever wonder, Roger, old boy," he said in a casual, intimate tone, "why our beautiful Sarah is such a mixture of races, why she has pale skin but hair that's as kinky as that of a Haitian? Well, I'll tell you. Her mother was an Irishwoman, and her father was a monkey."

Roger raised his hand to his mouth and made an indeterminate noise in his throat.

A small, wry smile hovered on Henri's lips. "Actually, it's a longer story. It's a very American tale. This *Irlandaise* was part redskin, and not only that but part Jew as well—some

Americans are part Jew, aren't they? And one day this *Irlandaise* was walking through the jungle near New Orleans, when she was raped by a jazz musician as big and black as King Kong, with sexual equipment to match. And from this agreeable encounter was born our little Sarah, *notre Négresse pasteurisée*. He reached over and pinched my chin. "It's a true story, isn't it, Sarah?" He pinched harder. "Isn't it?"

"Let me alone!" I said, pulling my head away.

"That's enough, Henri," said Roger.

There was a short silence, in which Henri's eyes were fixed cheerfully and expectantly on mine, as if he were waiting for a reward.

I said, "I think that is the stupidest thing I have ever heard. I didn't know you could be so stupid."

He waved his hand languidly at me, and I shoved back my chair and walked to the hall where the toilets were. All the staff had left the small dining room, which looked pretty and tranquil with the low fire and the tables freshly laid for dinner. The exception was the table where I had been sitting with Henri and Roger: the cloth, which hadn't been cleaned after the coffee, was extravagantly littered with ashes, wine stains, ends of bread, and fruit parings, as if filthy children had been playing there.

In the room labeled *Dames*, which was surprisingly modern— all red, with Florentine-gold faucets—I closed the toilet lid and sat down on it, bending double so that my cheek rested on my knees. It was a position to feel small in. I sat breathing soberly and carefully as I tried to control the blood pounding in my head.

I wasn't upset by the racism of what Henri had said. Nasty remarks about race and class were part of our special brand of humor, just as they had been in the wisecracking adolescent circles I had hung out with at school. On nights when we lay awake in bed, I often teased Henri into telling me nigger jokes, stories of the sexy, feckless little mulatto girl the French call Blanchette. His silly tall tale had done something far more drastic than wound me: it had somehow—perhaps in its unexpected extravagance—illuminated for me with blinding clarity the hopeless presumption of trying to discard my portion of America. The story of the mongrel Irishwoman and the gorilla jazzman had summed me up with weird accuracy, as an absurd political joke can sum up a regime, and I felt furious and betrayed by the intensity of nameless emotion it had called forth in me.

"Oh, dear," I said aloud in English, and, still bent double, I turned my head and gently bit myself on the knee. Then I stood up, brushed my hair, and left the bathroom, moving with caution.

In the vestibule I met the hostess, a stout woman with beautiful, deeply waved chestnut hair. She told me my friends were waiting in the courtyard, and paused to regard me with a shrewd, probing gaze. *"Excusez-moi, Mademoiselle, d'où êtes-vous?"*

"Je suis des États-Unis, mais jusqu'à présent, j'habite à Paris."

"Ah, bon, les États-Unis—j'aurais dit Martinique. Vous parlez très bien le Français."

"Merci. Je suis de Philadelphie, pas loin de New York."

"Ah oui, j'ai vu des photos. J'ai un neveu à Montclair, dans le New Jersey. Mais vous, vous avez de la chance, habiter à Paris."

"Oui, j'ai beaucoup de chance."

From an open doorway at the end of the corridor came the rich, dark smell of meat stocks and reductions; I could see into the kitchen, where a waiter in shirtsleeves was spooning up soup at a table. Beside him, a peasant in a blue smock and with a red, furrowed face had just set down a big basket of muddy potatoes.

When I walked out to the jeep in the courtyard, I found that the day had cleared into a bright, chilly autumn afternoon. The clouds had blown southward, skeins of brown

leaves rose in the wind and dissolved over the low wooded
hills and the highway, and the slanting sunlight on the small
gray village, with its thirteenth-century church, its lone
orange-roofed café and gas station, had the mysterious empty
quality one sees in some of Edward Hopper's paintings. It was
the kind of light that made me think of loss.

Henri surprised me by getting out of the jeep to apologize.
Apologies were hard for him, and he went about them badly,
using his blunt sexuality, his natural tendency to domineer,
and his adolescent harshness to turn "I'm sorry" into another
form of bullying. "Don't sulk," he said, drawing his forefinger gently along my hairline, and I gave a sudden giggle. I
could tell that he had been afraid not that he'd hurt me but
that I would hurt his pride by withdrawing before he had finished with me.

By the time we'd reached Chantilly, it had gotten dark, and
we were all feeling better. We had emptied a small flask of
Scotch, we'd planned a sumptuous new outfit for me—cavalier boots, lavender stockings by Dim, and a ruffled black velvet dress—and Alain taught me a song that went:

> Faire pipi
> sur le gazon
> pour embêter
> les papillons . . .

After that, as the lights of the Paris suburbs flashed by, we
sang more John Denver, yipping like coyotes at the end of
every line. In between songs, Alain sucked on a tube of sweet-
ened condensed milk, with a look of perfect infant bliss in his
crooked blue eyes. When Henri told him to stop, that it was
disgusting, Roger said, "It's no worse than your 'pasteurized
Negress'!" and I laughed until I choked; all of us did.

Back in Paris, we went to Le Drugstore Saint-Germain to have some of the fabulous hamburgers you eat with forks among all the chrome and the long-legged, shiny girls. Poor Roger tried to pick up two Dutch models in felt cloches (the film *Gatsby* had just opened on the Champs-Elysées), but the models raised their plucked eyebrows and made haughty retorts in Dutch, so that Roger was driven to flirt with a group of fourteen-year-olds two tables away, red-cheeked infant coquettes who pursed their lips and widened their kohl-rimmed eyes and then dissolved into fits of panicky laughter. In the record department of Le Drugstore, we ran into Alain's friend Anny. Anny was a tall, sexy blonde, a law student renowned for unbuttoning her blouse at the slightest opportunity at any social gathering to display her pretty breasts. She couldn't open her shirt in the record department, but she did take off her high-heeled black shoe to display a little corn she had developed on a red-nailed middle toe, at which Henri, Alain, and Roger stared with undisguised lust.

At eleven we went off to see *Il Était une Fois Dans l'Ouest*, and watching the shootouts in the gold and ocher mock-western landscape gave me a melancholy, confused feeling: it seemed sad that I had spent years dreaming of Paris when all Paris dreamed of cowboys. When we came out of the movie, the inevitable rain had started up, and red and green reflections from neon signs along the street lay wavering in puddles. Alain wanted to stop in at a disco, but Henri was sleepy, so we drove back to Neuilly, parked the jeep, and then dashed through the rain to the big icy apartment.

It was much later—after Alain and Roger had rolled themselves up in blankets to sleep on the couches, and Henri and I had gone off to bed to make love with the brisk inventiveness of two people who have never felt much kindness toward each other—that I awoke with a start from a horrid dream in which

I was conducting a monotonous struggle with an old woman with a dreadful spidery strength in her arms; her skin was dark and leathery, and she smelled like one of the old Philadelphia churchwomen who used to baby-sit with me. I pushed back the duvet and walked naked across the cold marble floor to the window. Through the crack between the shutters I could see a streetlight, and I could hear the noise of the rain, a rustling that seemed intimate and restless, like the sound of a sleeper turning over again and again under bedcovers.

Before that afternoon, how wonderfully simple it had seemed to be ruthless, to cut off ties with the griefs, embarrassments, and constraints of a country, a family; what an awful joke it was to find, as I had found, that nothing could be dissolved or thrown away. I had hoped to join the ranks of dreaming expatriates for whom Paris can become a self-sufficient universe, but my life there had been no more than a slight hysteria, filled with the experimental naughtiness of children reacting against their training. It was clear, much as I did not want to know it, that my days in France had a number, that for me the bright, frank, end-lessly beckoning horizon of the runaway had been, at some point, transformed into a complicated return.

I yawned and ran my hands up and down my body, pimpled with cold, feeling my usual absent-minded satisfaction in the length and suppleness of my limbs. Kate the photographer might make an interesting vegetable out of me, if I could only get to see her. Maybe tomorrow, I thought, I would go pound on her door; maybe her guardians would let me in. In a few min-utes I darted back to bed and settled carefully onto the big flat pillow where Henri had his face turned to the wall. Before I slept, I said to myself, "I can stay here longer, but I have to leave by spring." And that, in fact, is the way things turned out.

———

Like the title character in her 1984 collection, Sarah Phillips, Andrea Lee was born in Philadelphia in 1953, was the child of a Baptist minister, and attended Harvard University, from which she earned both a B.A. and an M.A. in literature. Her first book, Russian Journal (1981), was an autobiographical account of one year spent in Russia with her husband, a Ph.D. candidate in Russian history. The memoir was nominated for a National Book Award and received the 1984 Jean Stein Award from the American Academy and Institute of Arts and Letters. With the publication of Sarah Phillips, Lee was praised for her evocative, nuanced writing and complex characterizations. The story "In France" reveals a character grappling with issues of family and community and underscores the impossibility of ever fully escaping the bonds of culture, personal history, and race. A frequent contributor to The New Yorker magazine, in which many of the Sarah Phillips stories first appeared, Lee now lives in Italy with her husband.

LOVE

AN EXCERPT FROM THE NOVEL
The Hand I Fan With

T i n a   M c E l r o y   A n s a

Note: In this excerpt, Lena, the woman everyone turns to with their troubles, finds a sanctuary of her own in the form of Herman, a spirit she has conjured.

erman stood there before Lena in the middle of her Great Jonah Room a second, turning a bit, his hands hanging comfortably at his side, leaning back in his strong-looking legs, his head tilted to the side like an animal listening.

Lena thought for a second that he was waiting for a signal from the beyond. But he was waiting for the next selection to begin playing on the CD player.

"Good," he said as Duke Wellington and his band began playing "Mood Indigo." "It's a slow tune."

Then Herman turned to where she was sitting before the fire.

"Come on, Lena, baby." Herman extended his sturdy arm and asked gallantly, sweetly, earnestly, *"Dance wid me!"*

The gesture reminded Lena immediately of every teenaged black boy she had ever seen at a church social, prom, cotillion, sock hop, basement party or sweetshop coolly, serenely sliding across the dance floor headed for her, his next partner. Then, when he got there, not saying a word, not "Wanna dance?" not "Care to?" not "May I have this dance?" not anything. Instead, the young swain would throw his hand palm-up into her lap, look off into the distance as if he didn't care if she accepted or not, and wait for her to take his hand so he could lead her out onto the dance floor for a slow spin.

Lena hesitated a moment as she stared at Herman's hand. It was one thing to dance by herself over the floor of The Place when she thought no one was looking or to dance alone to Salt-N-Pepa naked in her bathroom mirror. Getting up and dancing with a new man—even if he was a ghost—was a different matter.

"Uh-uh, girl," he said with a serious chuckle. "I done waited a hundred years to dance again! And I get my first dance wid *you* and you sittin' up there sayin', 'No, thank you.' Uh-uh. Get up off your pretty butt and dance wi' me. Come on in my arms, Lena, and dance wid me."

He sounded almost as if he were singing to her, serenading her, cajoling her, just tolling her out on the floor. It was so seductive. Each time he said it—"Come on, Lena, baby. Dance wi' me"—it sounded more and more enticing.

Remembering her fiascoes on the dance floor ever since she was thirteen, she still hesitated. She just sat there rubbing her hands together in her lap.

"Aw, Lena, ain't no need to be shame or scared in front a' *me*," he said, his hand still hanging in the air in front of her. "Anything you do, any way you do it is fine wi' me."

Lena just wanted to grunt and say, "Ummm."

Instead, she rose from the soft leather couch and glided into Herman's open arms, the fire's light dancing in her eyes, placed one bare foot between his long strong legs, slipped her right hand into the space at the base of his neck under the bush of his hair, and lay the top of her head softly against the base of his throat where she could hear his heart beat. *Boom-boomp, boom-boomp, boom-boomp, boom-boomp, boom-boomp, boom-boomp, boom-boomp.*

Lena and Herman discovered immediately that they loved to slowdance together. Herman danced an old-fashioned two-

step, but he didn't move to the music like a country boy, studied
and rehearsed. Herman slowdanced like a block boy, like a
juker: slowly, sensuously, casually, unhurried. He curled her all
up in his arms and hunched his back over her frame just a little
bit so that it looked and felt as if she were inside his body, protected, loved, held. He wrapped his hand around her hand, then
tucked both hands in the cocoon between their dancing bodies.
He rolled his hips slowly and gently against the top of her pelvis
and guided her around the floor.

Lena was able to follow him right away. No awkward
movements, no bumping into each other, no stepping on toes,
no tripping over feet, no missing the beat.

And he moved unhurried, unhurried.

They danced all over her house, past still-burning, half-
burned and burned-out candles on plates and ashtrays and one-
of-a-kind glazed bowls, out onto the deck, by the foot of her
bed, past the pool, around the messy dining room table, back in
front of the fireplace in the Great Jonah Room, then back outside to dance under the stars.

"Look, Lena," he said in her ear, tipping her head back
with a gentle touch on her slender chin, "the sky is full a' stars
tonight. There's the Drankin' Gourd. There's the Serpent.
OOooo. Is that the Crab? There's the Virgin. You don't use-
shally see her this clear in April."

Lena had never enjoyed a dance so much. She felt lost in the
stars and lost track of the time. She felt they must have been
dancing for hours. They danced to Nat King Cole. They danced
to Otis Redding. They danced to Marvin Gaye. They danced
to Prince. They danced to Smokey Robinson. They danced to
Earth Wind & Fire. They danced to Jon Lucien. They danced
to Boyz II Men. So it had to have been a good long time. But
Herman danced as if he had all the time in the world.

Humph, I guess he does, Lena thought as she snuggled her cheek into the cave under Herman's jawbone and sighed as she settled into the slow, natural, easy rhythm of his slow drag. She didn't *think* of looking at her watch or her maternal grand-mother Lena Marie's pendulum clock.

Lena wanted to whisper into Herman's ear the way she had heard Protestant sisters prompt the preacher straining during an especially moving sermon, "Take your time, now!"

"I thought you wanted me to 'Quit,' " Herman said with a low sexy laugh in Lena's ear, and she joined him in sweet happy harmony. The sound of their laughter together raised such emotions in her that before she knew it, she was weep-ing, too. Try as she did, she could not remember the last time she had embraced a man and laughed at the same time.

And Herman just continued holding her. Lena could feel his penis growing harder and larger inside his pants and poking against her belly. His erection felt like life to her. And she did not try to avoid its touch when Herman sometimes dipped his pelvis down to catch Lena in the right spot. Then he'd straighten up and fly right for a while.

Even dancing to Al Green's "Love and Happiness," Herman remained unhurried, rocking Lena back and forth in his arms to the backbeat. They played it over and over. It was becoming *his song*. Herman would turn Lena loose, step back and do a little country-boy clogging step in his big black boots in time with the music as he sang along.

Now she could *see* the outline of Herman's hard dick straining against the front of his black work pants.

Lena, smiling and blushing and licking her dry crimson lips with the tip of her tongue, stood in front of the fireplace, bare-foot and still dressed in her red business suit, and tapped her foot and bopped her shoulders and head to the beat until he danced back over to her to place his left hand firmly on the small of her back and his right one lightly at the base of her neck. He drew her to him while he played with the small shiny hairs that grew down from the nape of her neck.

"Look a here at her kitchen. My baby, she still got baby hair," he said softly in wonder and amusement, twirling her short hairs around his index finger and humming along with Al on "For the Good Times."

Lena took that opportunity to bury her face deep in his throat and take a deep breath. Herman smelled like topsoil. Not like he had been working in it. Or lying six feet under it. But he smelled to Lena as if he were the dark rich crumbly earth itself outside her door. He smelled like the dirt she ate as a child when her mother wasn't looking. He smelled like the dirt she and her friend Sarah used to make mud pies. He smelled like the dirt in which Mr. Renfroe had just planted the new crepe myrtle trees.

She kept taking deep gulps of his scent and smiling as she was reminded of The Place the day before.

But the air surrounding this smooth, loving apparition was nothing compared to the air that moved in and out of his lungs. It was hypnotic. Each time she felt him breathing on her—her neck, her face, her hair—she fell more deeply and more deeply under his spell.

Their dancing slowed down a bit, and Lena leaned her head back, looking up into Herman's face. His lips were barely an inch away from hers. And she could feel his breath stirring the tiny hairs over her top lip. The hairs from his bushy mustache brushed her face, but he didn't kiss her.

She had to admire his ghostly restraint. She could still feel his erect penis against her stomach.

"I wouldn't push you fo' nothin' in the world, Lena," he said. "This time I'll wait for *you*."

Herman didn't have to wait long. Lena was ready for him.

She reached up, parting her lips slightly and sucking in, pulled Herman's head down to hers, pressed his mouth to hers, and kissed him. She wanted to watch this beautiful man kissing her back, but she couldn't keep her eyes open.

His mouth was barely moist and tenderly soft on hers. His lips, not quite as full as Lena's, seemed to fit inside the shape of her mouth perfectly. His bushy mustache tickled her own reddish fuzz. She felt his smile on her lips. The heat from his kiss radiated through her body, leaving her flesh hot and sensitive to his touch. When the tips of their tongues touched, Lena felt them both shiver. Her nipples were growing hard and large against the satin of her bra. She could feel his penis tug at his pants. Her vagina seemed to be tugging at her panties, too.

As they rubbed their bodies against each other, Lena felt her clitoris quiver. And she let out a little soft "uhh" from the pit of her soul.

Lena didn't know where they were standing, but she trusted Herman when they both, concentrating on tracing the other's lips with tongues, fell to the big leather sofa in front of the fireplace. One of his strong callused hands reached for the gold buttons of her jacket and the other began traveling under her skirt, up her thigh to the top of her dark gartered stockings, snagging the nylon gently.

Lena was surprised that Herman's clothes—the green shirt, the black pants, the leather belt—were actually real, firm to her touch. When she unbuttoned Herman's shirt, she was half expecting it to just melt away like cotton candy in a hot summer shower, leaving him covered with sticky sugar.

His skin *was* sweet. She couldn't help but lick it when they got each other naked.

And he did look good naked. A life of moving and work-ing and walking, a childhood of growing up in the wilds of North Florida, a life in the last century, had left him with a body taut, toned and strapping. She felt a responsibility to every woman who had ever wanted to make love to such a beautiful black man to run her hands over every millimeter of Herman as she kissed him all over.

"Good God, Lena, I'm already hard enough to plow packed earth," Herman said as she caressed his back and shoulders.

Herman was right. When Lena took Herman's big purplish penis into her hand she felt that it was hard enough to cut through Middle Georgia farmland. It leapt one quick time when she touched it. His pubic hairs were tight and nappy, rolled up into what looked like BBs all over his crotch. Down there, he smelled like the swamps in South Georgia. Lena played with his hairs awhile before moving on.

He was sweet all over, especially his throat and his deep broad chest where a few short black hairs grew inches apart from each other. She kissed each one. And when she fin-ished, Herman kissed her all over—from the palms of her hands to the soles of her feet.

In the midst of their first orgasm together, a core-shaking exquisite orgasm, with Herman inside of her and around her and right beside her coming, too, and watching her at the same time, Lena knew she would remember every detail of this night forever.

All during their lovemaking—from the great room to her bedroom—she saw what was happening between the two of them. Unencumbered by pictures from the past or conversa-tions from the future, she was filled with an intense awareness.

God, it's been years since I had my leg over somebody's shoulder, she thought.

Herman talked all through his lovemaking. "Oh, Lena, you so beautiful. Um-huh, look at my baby's *stuff!!* OOooo, I like the way yo' titties stand out like that. Uh, can I kiss there? You taste good, baby. Oh, Lena, I can't get enough.

"You can't tell me that ain't it!! That gets the butter from the duck!!!"

And he encouraged her to talk back to him.

"Tell me, baby. Tell me how that feel," he exhorted her. "I want to hear ya talk to me, baby. Come on, Lena, baby. Tell it like it is."

But Lena could not seem to form words with Herman under her and above her and inside her and all up through her. Making noises was the best she could do. She could hear her moans and screams and mewls and sobs echoing in the pine rafters of her house along with the scent of oak wood-smoke and love. Lena never knew how much she liked to holler during sex.

"OOOoo, I like when you get up on top of me like that and th'ow yo' body back, Lena, so I can still see yo' honey pot," Herman told her in breathy whispers. "What you like fo' me to do t' you?"

Lena was coming, so all she could do was let out a scream. But she thought, You doing just fine.

And Herman smiled as if he had read her mind.

All through their lovemaking, when he touched her breasts for the first time, tickling, licking and nipping at her hard erect nipples until she came again, he had whispered, "Oohhh, I can't get enough of you."

Lena did not want to break the mood so she stifled the questions that bubbled at her lips: "What do you mean, can't get enough? Enough what? Enough touching me? Enough fucking? Enough times?"

Herman smiled in her face, slipped his dick inside of her and said, "Enough of you, period."

Lena, who had never been able to get to the point of release with her other would-be lovers, came and came and came in Herman's arms.

As soon as Lena had unbuttoned the flap on his antique pants and freed his tight hard penis to bang against her chest, she thought briefly of trying to search up a condom somewhere in her house. She had not dealt with any other kind of birth control in years. Umm, now, I know I had some Trojans or something around here last time, she had thought, biting her bottom lip and narrowing her eyes in concentration. Now, just where was that? she asked herself. She tried to picture where she had been the last time she was naked and touching another human being. But Herman had slipped down her body and was just starting to kiss her all over with little puffs of breeze colored lime green and ocean blue, and she forgot everything except the fact that she was now making love to a ghost, a man dead a hundred years. And the idea of sexually transmitted diseases floated like a puff of smoke from her mind.

She sat naked astride him in the big suede easy chair the color of the Ocawatchee River when it wasn't Cleer Flo', her bare legs hanging off the arms of the big chair, her braids hanging down her back. In the light of the candles and the glow from the fireplace, Lena saw the sweat form on his beautiful broad brow. She smelled the chemistry of his come mingling with hers. She threw back her head and laughed when she saw that his thick curly eyelashes were sticking to the tops of his sweaty lids just the way hers did when she was a child playing out in the summer heat. Her mother sitting at her sewing machine would ask as Lena came inside, "Come here, baby, let Mama see how hot it is outside." Then she would check to see if the child's lashes were sticking to her lids and Nellie would call, "Yep, must be mighty hot outside."

It was plenty hot right where Lena and Herman were—on

the chair, on the floor, on the sofa, on the bed, on the deck—
making love.

There was no way she could forget for long that she was
making love to a spirit. One minute, he was as hard and real as
the granite of Stone Mountain. She could feel him inside her
hard, the veins in his dick throbbing against the walls of her
vagina. The next, he was mist, smoke, vapor barely grazing
down her breasts, stroking her between her legs, seesawing
between the folds of her vagina, easing up her back. Then he
would become a man again.

Lena sighed and shivered a bit at the feel of Herman and
the leather sofa on her bare back. She could feel the hairs
there sending out little signals of excitement to Herman
through the bare leg and shoulder he had resting on the back
of the sofa.

As she lay back on the leather cushions, cool against her
hot body, he spread her legs, one over the back of the sofa,
the other hanging to the floor, then reached down and
spread the lips of her vagina. Lena could feel his callused fingers scratch against the sensitive skin of her vulva.

"OOOooo," was all she could say as her body arched, then
went limp.

"Oh, 'cuse me, Lena," Herman said with a smile. But he
didn't mean it because he then brushed his callused fingers
across her tender vulva again. Slowly this time, leading to
her clitoris. And he moaned when Lena moaned.

Agile as a boy, he then jumped up on the fat padded arm
of the sofa, naked and muscular, and lowered his face into
her widespread vagina and traced the folds and flaps and
slits of skin and nerve endings with his tongue until she
screamed again, squeezing his head between her golden-
brown thighs.

Before she could recover, he slipped from the folds of her

vagina and crept into every little fold of her skin as a thick, dark gray, smoky mist.

She could feel him in the flap behind her ear. She could feel him in the folds under her full hanging breasts. She could feel him in the folds on the inside of her mouth. She could feel him in the folds of her eyelids. She could feel him in the folds of her knuckles. She could even feel him in the cursed new folds of her behind at the tops of her thighs and between the cheeks of her butt.

Then the smoke, the mist, the vapor that was Herman became a man again.

Herman turned his pretty pink tongue into a long thin soft red spiral that he coiled around the tip of her clitoris, played there awhile, then slowly pulled off as she screamed his name over and over.

"Oh, Herman! Herman! Herman!"

As he altered his consistency and shape to please Lena, he continued speaking his passion. Poking Lena with the tip of his penis, he said, "Baby, this one Georgia jumpin' root that's here to please." Then, he changed and modified not just his body shape but also the shape of his penis to accommodate, pleasure, tickle, tease and love his woman Lena. Looking down at Herman's dick, Lena was reminded of different vibrator selections in a small catalog of sexual toys Deborah had passed out at the office. As far as she could remember, Herman covered just about every one in the book.

And these strange metamorphoses of Herman's didn't frighten Lena a bit, no matter how bizarre and fantastic they might have seemed to someone standing out on the deck watching.

For one thing, Lena was on the receiving end of all the changes, and she wasn't about to pretend to complain. I wouldn't *think* of stopping him right 'long through here, she thought, sucking air through her teeth and moaning.

For another, no matter how many changes he went

through, he was still Herman to Lena. He was still the tall dark brown man who had been her love and guardian angel before she even knew it.

And Herman was a man of his word. He did nothing without first asking or moaning or groaning, "Okay, Lena?"

"Um-huh," she answered each and every time. Like I'mo say no, she thought as he continued touching her just the way she liked.

Herman went deeper and deeper inside her, touching spots and opening doors to room after room after room that Lena had never opened to anyone. Herman roused emotions she truly had not felt before. And she was grateful then for his sweet permission-asking, "Is that okay, Lena? Uhh, how 'bout that? And that? And that?"

They lay back opposite each other on the big soft couch to catch their breath. Lena did not have to ponder another second. She knew right then she would feel this way about this man the rest of her life.

When she was able to find her voice again, she said, "Herman?"

"Yeah, baby," he answered as he tucked one bare foot under her, threw the other over her and pulled her to him.

"You know, Herman, I think somewhere back there when we were dancing or eating or something, I decided."

"What you decide, baby?"

Lena loved how familiar he had gotten with her so quickly.

"Herman," she said, then paused and smiled. She loved to speak his name. "I decided I *am* your woman."

She had never said those words to a man before. Never. She liked the sound of them so much, she said them again.

"Herman, I *am* your woman. I'm so *glad* you came."

Lena could feel Herman smiling when he kissed her.

He lifted Lena and lay her nude body on top of his nude body—a pretty sight in the fire and candlelight—and held her close.

Slowly, Lena seemed to feel a change in her very blood chemistry. She had the sensation of barely falling—millimeter by millimeter, hardly falling. It felt to Lena as if she were sinking into the very center of the universe, a very warm and welcoming universe.

She began to perceive sparks of life all around her. The universe she was sinking into had a wide and complex life. She felt planets spinning by her in their orbits. She saw galaxies form next to her hips. Shooting stars and comets whizzed by from her vagina toward the top of her head, leaving tails of gold and red down her throat and stars in her eyes.

Herman had eased into her heart so smoothly that before she knew it, he had eased in and taken it over with old-time love.

As they lay in each other's arms all night long, stroking each other, licking, tickling, blowing, fingering, nuzzling, Herman turned to her again and again and declared over and over, "Lena, I am much in love wid you."

Lena—spent, sated, and content—dozed on and off throughout the night, smiling through little patches of dreams of floating on blue clouds. But she awoke each time she heard Herman's voice to reply, "Herman, I am much in love with you."

———

"In the South of the 1950s and 1960s, where I was raised, black folks talked all the time about spirits and hants, dreams and visions, feelings and ghost tales that were true," Tina McElroy Ansa says, to explain her fascination with the spirit world. In The

Hand I Fan With, *Ansa's best-selling third novel, the world of
things unseen achieves full embodiment in the character of Lena's
ghost lover, Herman. The book won the Georgia Authors Series
Award in 1996; Ansa's first novel,* Baby of the Family, *won the
same prize in 1989.* Baby of the Family *was also named Notable
Book of the Year by the New York Times and an American Library
Association Best Book for Young Adults in 1990. Ansa's second
novel,* Ugly Ways, *was published in 1993. Like her other books, it
examines our responsibility to family, community, and ultimately,
self. A native of Macon, Georgia, Ansa is a widely published journalist and essayist. She taught creative writing at Spelman College (her alma mater), Brunswick College, and Emory University
before moving with her husband, Jonèe, to the Georgia Sea
Islands. There, she tends her moonflowers, collard greens, and
black-eyed Susans in between lecture tours, taping segments of
CBS News Sunday Morning's "Postcard from Georgia" and writing her new novel,* You KNOW Better.

THE WIFE

Jennifer Jordan

onight his snoring was loud, irritating. It was strange how the sound affected her. When she was overcome by some nostalgic remembrance of how it used to be or when she received his love-making with both resentment and grateful relief after one of those long droughts, the steady drone was almost comforting. She would fall asleep, listening to the little ebbs and flows and holding on to the low rumble as if it were a lifeline that bound them together and kept their heads above water.

But tonight was not a good night. He had had too much to drink. He lay on his back as motionless as a dead man, his legs spread-eagled over most of the bed. If he hadn't been snoring, his stillness would have tempted her to reach out and feel for his heart. But the snore was very much alive. For long moments it sounded like the fitful grinding and whining of an old car refusing to start on a too cold morning. Or like her Hoover trying to eat the tassels on her Oriental rug. The sound made her stomach ache. She wanted to pinch him in some excruciatingly tender spot or snatch a single hair out of his well-trimmed mustache.

She pulled the light blanket, which covered her third of the king-size bed, up to her chin. It was July and very hot outside, but Jonathan liked to sleep in an ice-cold bedroom.

Even though the electric bill was a fortune each month and the chill kept her on the edge of awakening, she had long ago decided that it was easier to use a blanket than to argue about the setting of the thermostat.

Jonathan had always wanted his way, even as a young man. She met him when he was a student at Howard's law school. He lived in an efficiency apartment over an antique store on Mount Pleasant Street in that kind of grubby poverty that middle-class graduate students accepted as one of the penances suffered in the cause of higher education. Jonathan was at home there, negotiating his way through the winos, exchanging his few words of Spanish with the Hispanic neighbors, tolerating the cockroaches. It was his notion of the bohemian life.

Marta, as middle class as Jonathan but basically a South Carolina country girl, felt inept in that environment. She was always nervous running the gauntlet of drunks, who yelled out obscure phrases she suspected were obscene. She much preferred the quiet northeast neighborhood where she rented a basement apartment from the Cuthberts, a couple she had met at church. Mr. Cuthbert was one of those elderly men who like to pat young ladies on the fleshy part of their bare arms, a gesture that might have been either lecherous or paternal. At his age it was hard to tell. Mrs. Cuthbert claimed to be from a distinguished old Washington family, part of the colored gentry, and had the sour disposition of a woman who felt she had married down.

On their second date Marta had gone to pick up Jonathan at his apartment. His ten-year-old Triumph was in the shop again. Because his apartment building had no intercom system, she had blown her horn to let him know she was downstairs. The loud honk of her Chevrolet Malibu made her self-conscious, although the people hanging out in front of the

North Carolina Barbecue never missed a beat in the rhythm of
their busy posing. Instantly she felt uncertain about her clothes.
She looked like the schoolteacher—and the daughter of school-
teachers from Cheraw, South Carolina—that she was. High
heels; a short, straight skirt; a short, nonswinging version of
the Jackie Kennedy pageboy; and a string of pearls. Somehow
she knew the look was too careful, definitely not the kind of
thing a trendsetter would wear. But even at twenty-two she
knew she was no trendsetter.

Jonathan opened the locked door of the building. He was
dressed in a pink button-down shirt, beige jeans, and loafers.
Twenty years before it was the thing to do, he wore no socks.
Immediately Marta felt apologetic about her own meticulous
appearance. She didn't want to appear prissy.

"Go on up," he said as he urged her to climb ahead of him
the three flights to his tiny apartment.

"Watch out for the third step on the next landing. The carpet is torn. The last girl who went tripping up these steps in
high heels tumbled over me on her way back down." He
grinned. "She was a pretty healthy mama, too. I felt like I had
been hit by a Mack truck."

Even as she laughed, Marta wondered how many girls regularly climbed those steps. It occurred to her that he was probably
getting a good look at her legs and behind as she moved only
inches in front of him. The thought made her uptight. In his presence she always felt she was being judged and found wanting.

Jon obviously was unconcerned about impressing her.
His apartment was a mess. Dirty dishes sat in the sink. One
of those aggressive Washington roaches, with their usual
disrespect for company, made an appearance. Jon was
unembarrassed. He didn't even try to kill it. Marta, who had
come to D.C. thinking that only the disreputable and trifling
had roaches, stifled an urge to smash it.

"Do you like Greek food?" he asked.

"I don't know. I've never had any."

Marta could have added that in segregated South Carolina, most black people thought pizza was an exotic dish.

"Would you rather go someplace else? How about Chinese? Italian? This new Greek restaurant, Taverna's, has got great lamb and terrific baklava, but we don't have to go there."

Greek food was Greek to her and Italian was problematic. Despite the familiarity of spaghetti, Marta didn't think she could negotiate a plate of it without wearing some of it home on her blouse.

"Chinese might be nice," she ventured.

He looked disappointed, even slightly annoyed. It was obvious that he had his heart set on the Greek restaurant. Who was she to deny him?

"Of course, I'd love to try Greek food. I'm always game for something new."

A look of instant satisfaction came over his face. "Greek it is!"

He insisted on driving her car, although Marta considered herself quite a good driver. He gave her canary-yellow Malibu a quick once-over. His reaction was a bit scornful.

"American cars are okay. But they aren't built to last," he said. "Now the BMW's the car!"

Marta wasn't quite sure what a BMW was. Where she came from, people raved about Buicks and Cadillacs. But even as she lamented her own lack of taste in cars, it occurred to her that a Chevy that ran was preferable to a Triumph that didn't. What was that verse from Ecclesiastes? Something about a living dog being better than a dead lion. The irreverence was fleeting. She vowed that she would learn about foreign cars.

The dinner at Taverna's was a success. Marta began to believe that she was in love with this man who charmed Greek

waiters, knew exactly what to order, and calmed her fears by
his own intuitive understanding that he belonged anywhere he
wanted to go. He seemed a world traveler even though he had
grown up in a Washington as restricted and racist as South
Carolina. Mrs. Cuthbert had told Marta about the days when
black people couldn't go into Garfinckel's department store
unless they were carrying a mop, but Jonathan had none of
Marta's fear of whites. He felt the world owed him whatever
he could take.

Marta also lacked Jon's ambition. She had no desire for
fame or fortune. But she knew there was something more
than the quiet responsibilities and dulling restrictions of
Cheraw, South Carolina, or even northeast Washington. She
had a notion of a domestic future gleaned from *Father
Knows Best*, romance novels, and 1950s Pepsi commercials—a life where she could be honest and loving, a life
where she was comfortable in a house with appliances that
never broke down, a husband who adored her, and children
who never disgraced her. The bills would always be paid—
on time. At the same time she dreamed of trips to Paris and
weekends at romantic inns in Virginia hunt country. She
didn't decide at once that Jonathan would give her these
things, but she did believe that he was a man who understood the way to such a life. She wanted to be near him if
he would have her.

It was not that she thought of herself as worthless. She knew,
despite her inexperience, that she was an intelligent woman, not
beautiful but good-looking enough to evoke catcalls from the
brothers on the corner. She had, above all, the kind of loyalty
that is usually found only in small children and large dogs. She
hoped something in her reminded Jonathan of desire.

After dinner Marta climbed Jonathan's stairs and didn't come
down again until morning. Back in his apartment, a twin bed

that served as a sofa was the only thing that would accommodate the two of them. Apologizing for the lack of air-conditioning, Jonathan opened a window and turned on a small fan. Its hypnotic drone merged with the buzz of street noise and the distant sound of salsa from someone's apartment.

"Have a seat while I get us a glass of wine," Jonathan said. It was a command, not a request. Marta searched his face for a sign that a seduction was being staged. His cinnamon-colored eyes in his black face were startling. They were friendly but cool. She was vaguely disappointed by his seeming indifference.

He offered her in one of his two wineglasses a pink bubbly substance she could not identify.

"I didn't know if you would like a white or red wine. I settled on a bottle of Lancer's. I thought a sparkling rosé would be a nice compromise. A kind of poor man's champagne to celebrate a good evening."

Marta studied the contents of her glass. She wondered if he was trying to get her drunk. At all-black South Carolina State the guys drank mostly beer or rum-and-Coke. She had known only two women who drank regularly, a wild Geechee girl from Charleston and a New Yorker who suffered culture shock and went back North. Marta had usually nursed the obligatory one beer at the fraternity parties she and her girlfriend frequented. Wine in thimble-size glasses was what you drank on first Sunday at church. Or if you were an Omega or Kappa, you bragged about the destructive powers of Ripple and Thunderbird.

Marta took a sip and decided she liked it, but she was determined that this one glass would do for the evening. She wondered how long it would be before he tried to kiss her.

Jonathan had not sat down with her yet. He stood with his glass in his hand, his muscular body balanced calmly and solidly over her. When he moved, it was a slow, lazy amble.

Sort of like Leroy Jones from home returning to the huddle after he had steamrolled over half the opposing team on the football field. Jonathan paced back and forth in front of her as if delivering a summation to a jury.

He sat down on the bed next to her and took the hand without the wineglass. Marta put down her drink and steeled herself for the grab and the grope. Instead, he lifted her hand and lightly brushed her palm with his mustache and lips, a gesture that instantly penetrated the anxiety he made her feel. She was willing to allow all of his kisses and caresses and even his unhurried, expert removal of most of her clothes. But she had no intention of giving up so soon, even though she was technically not a virgin. During her junior year at State, she had succumbed to a star basketball player out of curiosity rather than passion. But Ronnie's idea of a conversation was a monologue about the highlights of his last game, so she never slept with him a second time.

She wasn't looking for a genius or a millionaire. Just a man who knew things she didn't know, who wasn't afraid. She was waiting for such a man. She wanted to *live* life, and she was too timid to do that alone.

That night on the narrow bed, Jonathan did things to her that made her want to say yes, but she thought about the other things that she wanted and her mother's warning that a man never married a girl who seemed easy. Until she knew he was the right one, the answer would be no.

She was expecting rage or at least a prolonged sulk in response to the refusal. Having long ago taken off most of his clothes, he simply gave her a couple of lingering kisses to test her resolve and promptly went to sleep. Marta, not quite knowing how to get up to leave and frightened at the prospect of braving the winos and would-be rapists on Mount Pleasant

Street, waited out the night. The fan's breeze was now unpleas-
antly cold, but she didn't think it was her place to cut it off. As
she listened to just a hint of a snore and contemplated his face
in the soft glow from the streetlights, she didn't have the heart
to wake him.

The next morning, with a stuffed-up head and a headache,
she put on her rumpled clothes and headed back to northeast
D.C. and to the astonished stare of Mrs. Cuthbert, who stuck
her head out the door to pick up *The Washington Post* just as
Marta hurried around to the side entrance.

The ritual of the interesting dinner, the good conversation,
and the attempted seduction continued through the month of
June. They went on walking tours of Georgetown and Alexan-
dria. They ate the cuisine of China, Thailand, Brazil, and Cuba.
They, or at least Jonathan, talked about John Kennedy and his
relationships with Khrushchev, with black people, and with
Jackie; about Martin Luther King and the efficacy of nonvio-
lence. Marta, the good listener and quick study, marveled at
his knowledge and accepted his judgments as gospel.

By July she was doing more than sleeping in his bed. She
had also been the donor of substantial supplements to his rent
money, which he evidently spent feeding her in all those quaint
little restaurants. By October of that year they had formed a
financial and sexual bond that made marriage seem inevitable.
Just as Mrs. Cuthbert had become explicit about her disregard
for young lady tenants who frequently stayed out all night,
Marta had announced that she and Jonathan were getting
married.

Now, as she contemplated the years and next month's electric bill, she studied his face with a cold appraisal usually
reserved for strangers. Asleep he had none of the pugnacity
that made him a successful lawyer and kept her afraid to chal-

lenge him. The dark brown face with its usually rock-hard jaw
was relaxed into almost toddlerlike roundness. Some nights,
watching him in the vulnerability of sleep, she had conflicting
urges to kick and kiss him. Tonight, for the first time in twenty-
eight years, she merely wanted to hurt him.

Marta tried to figure out what had destroyed the wonder
of it all. By the fifth year Jonathan's brilliance no longer
overwhelmed her. She discovered, after absorbing the things
he taught her and reading much more, that she had opinions of her own. At first when her ideas contradicted his,
she was contrite, then truly hurt by his resistance to her
ability to think for herself. He had finally reached the point
where any independent thought on her part brought petty
remarks and put-downs, often in front of other people. His
insecurity saddened her, not because she had grown egotis-
tical, but because it made him less a man in her eyes. It tar-
nished the beautiful image of him as a kind of black giant,
arrogant and unperturbed.

Despite the cracks in the armor, she admired the vitality
that was still there. He was considered one of the most com-
petent criminal lawyers in town, but he had developed a dull
ache in his gut as a result of constantly comparing himself
with the hundreds of men in D.C., black and white, who had
more prestige and power than he had. Most people would
have considered his income impressive, but over the years it
was Marta's salary as a teacher that paid the mortgage note
month after month. Jonathan kept the family in debt acquiring the BMWs, the trips to Haiti, the handmade shirts. Marta
shopped at seasonal sales, kept her old car, and nursed her
hurt feelings when he decried having married such a Bama.

She was the one who worried about food bills, the utilities,
their daughter's private-school bills. Kim, the product of the
dregs of their passion, thought Dad was "neat" and Mom was

"a pain." Daddy was the promise of a car for college; Mom would probably be the one who made sure that tuition and book bills were paid.

In the last year Marta had been suffering an almost constant headachy feeling reminiscent of PMS. She finally identified it as her growing resentment of Jonathan's charmed life made possible through her anguish. She was, however, unable to pinpoint the now distant moment when he had stopped even feigning interest in her.

He was rarely home. They had never really talked, but now he didn't even bother to deliver those erudite lectures that she had found so interesting in her more limited days. She understood too well that Jonathan needed an adoring, attentive audience. But no woman with an ounce of brains and integrity could maintain, after more than twenty-five years of marriage, that rapt look—eyes sparkling, instantly responsive to the touches of wit; lips parted in a breathy smile; body thrust forward as if to capture sooner the gems of wisdom.

She hadn't realized how vital such unalloyed devotion was to Jonathan until today, when she had walked into the American Café on Capitol Hill and seen him with the young woman, a youthful Diahann Carroll type, without the camouflaged hardness. She looked like a young lawyer dressed for success and conquest as she leaned across the table in her eagerness to hear and learn. That she had already slept with the prosperous, smug man who was the center of her gaze was clear in the confidential slant of his head and the absentminded way he toyed with the band of her Gucci watch. His touch had a proprietary air. Marta surprised herself and Jonathan by walking up to their table.

"Hello, Jonathan. Fancy meeting you here."

Jonathan would not be Jonathan if he had shown any sign of discomfort.

"Hello, baby. I don't usually hang out in the American Café, but Miss Lawrence suggested it as a nice place for a quick lunch. Marta, this is Saundra Lawrence, the counsel for the city council's zoning committee. Saundra, my wife, Marta. I'd invite you to join us, sweetheart, but we have to run to a meeting."

If Marta had any doubts about Jonathan's relationship with his companion, Ms. Lawrence's response dispelled them. She was nervous at meeting the great man's wife face-to-face, but not so nervous that she failed to give the competition a thorough inspection. She checked out the gray temples and the shape of the body, made observations about the taste in clothes, searched the eyes for any signs of recognition or hostility.

Good manners for people raised to be polite die hard. Marta smiled, assured them that she did not feel neglected.

"That's quite all right. I'm meeting Phyllis for lunch in a few minutes. I haven't seen her in months, and we have a lot of gossip to catch up on. It was nice meeting you, Ms. Lawrence."

At home Marta had cried bitter, urgent tears. She was surprised by the ferocity of her response. She had always felt that Jonathan availed himself of the opportunities that most men had in D.C., with its hordes of attractive, smart, unattached women—black, white, and Hispanic—who fought for jobs and men with a spunky, dog-eat-dog combativeness. But she had no notion of how to deal with the reality of unfaithfulness. Maybe she could put on that Nancy Wilson song "Guess Who I Saw Today, My Dear?" and then rush to pack her bags. But then what would she do about Kim, who would be sure to announce that she was staying with her beloved daddy? Maybe she could pretend she didn't know, but even her loathing for confrontation would not allow her to ignore a situation that was making her sick with grief.

Tonight as they sat in bed, he watching television, she reading a book, she blurted out her suspicions without introduction or evasion.

"Jonathan, are you having an affair with that woman you introduced me to today?" Marta said this without looking up from the book in her lap.

She could imagine that he furrowed his brow and that his brown eyes were hostile. The few times she had risked a battle he had been fierce in squashing the rebellion. When she finally looked over at him, he was still watching the eleven o'clock news. His body was almost too casual in its repose.

"Marta, be serious. I'm not going to dignify that remark with a response. You come into a restaurant, see me with a woman with whom I have a professional relationship, and jump to some wild conclusion that I'm screwing her. You've always been jealous and paranoid, but I'm not going to allow your insanity to make life miserable for me."

It was at this point that he usually marched into the bathroom and slammed the door. Ordinarily Marta would back off and try to control whatever anger or anxiety she felt. Tonight she was not interested in control. Something like bile rose in her throat, and just as he tried to get up from the bed, she snatched the end of the belt on his robe with such force that she tore off a loop.

"You are going to listen to me. Do you think I'm going to sit here while you parade some young thing all over D.C.? I suppose everybody knows about this but me. Phyllis was probably feeling sorry for me all through lunch. 'Poor Marta's getting old. Gray pubic hairs, dragging titties, and a stomach that will never be flat again. Poor thing ain't even in the running.' Well, Jonathan, I won't be pitied. I won't be pitied."

She was still convulsively clutching his belt. Jonathan was taking off his robe in his haste to get away.

"Woman, you are losing your grip. They say the change of

life makes you all crazy. When I come back to this room, you better have yourself together again. I'm going to get a glass of wine. Do you want red or white?"

Marta stared at the belt in her hand. When she didn't answer, he left the room, a furtive, almost fearful glance the only hint that tonight was any different from all the nights they had coexisted in civil indifference.

Later on, as she lay in bed shivering from the cold and from the violence of her suppressed rage and hurt, she tried to understand what all of this meant. She was pained not merely at the thought of him in bed with a younger, receptive woman. It was also that, in all the years that they had been married he had never given her credit for the things she contributed to their life. In fact, her growing competence was, to Jonathan, her biggest flaw. He was beginning to detest her because she was no longer that little South Carolina girl who thought he was hot stuff because he drove a British car and had been to every restaurant in town.

She turned her back to him and pulled the covers up to her ears. Jonathan rolled over to her side of the bed and threw one arm across her hip. She heard him call her name in a voice that seemed a plea for help. She realized that he was asleep only when the familiar droning of the snoring resumed. Over the years the occasional call in the night allowed her to fabricate a fiction to live by and served as a sign that he needed her. Those ambiguous night noises made the waking hours possible.

She knew she wasn't going anywhere. She didn't have the energy. Some days she even thought she loved him. Tomorrow she would get up and go off to work. Tomorrow night the two of them would sit up in bed. She would finish the last chapter of *The Color Purple*. He would watch the eleven o'clock news. Meanwhile, she would add this dose of bitter gall to her

store of slights, bad memories, and disappointments and pray
that, when the next blow came, she could remember one taste
of honey.

———◦————

*Jennifer Jordan was born in Fort Benning, Georgia, in 1946,
and grew up in Phenix City, Alabama. She received a B.A.
and an M.A. from Howard University and a Ph.D. from
Emory University in Atlanta. As an associate professor in
English at Howard University, she has published numerous
scholarly articles on African American literature and was the
recipient of a Ford Foundation postdoctoral fellowship, which
supported her study of contemporary black women novelists.
Her fiction has appeared in* Essence *magazine and was
anthologized in John Henrik Clarke's* A Century of the Best
Black American Short Stories: One Hundred Years of the Best
and Brooke Stephens's Men We Cherish: African-American
Women Praise the Men in their Lives. *Of her short story "The
Wife," she says: "I tried to capture that particularly torturous
moment in a marriage when you discover that a man is not
'The One,' but you can't find the courage to move on."*

INVENTING
THE FOOD

Akua Lezli Hope

for Shimmer

and this stretch across the oceans of our difference
and this straddling our continents of concern

a wild mashing of parts   a mingle of limbs
bee swarm   cicada songs and sweat
dripping silences   a purple burst
galaxies in paw   swimming milky way
braids on fire   flame sprouts

a delicate meshing of mutual endowments
conspiratorial giggles and royal jelly
sharing cheese and licking fingers

you dressed in the bright suit of morning
beckon through the wall of winter and want
saying sisterwoman teenager please
an mbira tinkles
stroked tines for the fork
that will imagine
the necessary food

"I write to record the urban, black, émigré, technopeasant mythos," says poet Akua Lezli Hope. *"I work to lengthen my reach, to better block, strike, pluck, or embrace."* A native New Yorker, Hope grew up in the South Bronx and Queens, studied psychology at Williams College in Williamstown, Massachusetts, then went on to earn graduate degrees in business and journalism at Columbia University in 1977 and 1978. The recipient of numerous creative writing fellowships and awards, Hope has been widely anthologized. Her most recent collection, Embrouchure (1995), *"uses the lens of jazz to explore the sensual and sexual."* An area representative for Amnesty International, USA, and a member of Amnesty's Cultural Diversity Resource Group, Hope lives in Corning, New York, where she sings, gardens, plays her saxophone, reshapes thread, and *"makes good dreams manifest."*

TOUCH

AN EXCERPT FROM THE NOVEL

Charlotte Watson

Sherman

January 13, 1994

I wish I believed in Circe's God. Wish I could fall down on my knees and pray, pull from that disintegrating well of Negro spirituals, get happy, throw up my arms and run through the streets of this city with my skirt hiked above my knees, crying out in this wilderness of isolation and death.

Wish I could look into the darkness of my future standing atop the bones of the believers, the seers, those who can heal with their hands, can make my flesh whole with their tears, the comforting holy water of their tears.

I wish I could stand in the center of the world surrounded by a gospel choir in golden robes, the resolve in their faces lifting me up in the arms of their belief, their voices rising like saviors to the heavens. I wish I could turn this sorrow into a blessing. I wish when I looked inside the hollow of my spirit, a starling of hope would rise inside me fluttering for the first time up through the bitterness of my soul breaking it down into something sweet like hope like forgiveness like salvation.

I wish I could feel anything other than the emptiness I feel when I think about my spirit and ask God, why me?

154

March 11, 1994

Last night I dreamed about Theodore. I was painting again. I was naked when he rang the buzzer. I didn't put any clothes on. I answered the door, just like that, naked. It was warm in the apartment. Warm like summer.

He wasn't surprised when I opened the door. He came and sat down on the floor where I was painting. I had yellow and green and purple streaks of paint on my thighs where I wiped my hands on my legs. My naked legs. I talked to him about the painting, what I was trying to do. The woman in the painting looked familiar, but I didn't know who she was trying to be.

Her eyes are smart, Theodore said. I looked at him. The large size of him. The strength of his hands and forearms.

God, how I liked this man. I put my bare foot on his crossed knee and pressed on it slightly. He ran his hand up my leg. He kept talking to me about the intelligence he saw in the woman's face. All the while stroking me. I kept painting. I didn't want him to stop. I opened my legs and he moved his hand over the terrain of my legs, the valley there. I was trembling by then. He kept talking. I focused on the painting while he stroked and talked, a gentle rhythm to it. He picked up one of my feet and kissed it, toes, sole, ankle. He was tickling me. I didn't laugh. I had to concentrate. Concentrate on the most beautiful man in the world. No, the painting. I had to focus on the woman's mouth. His kisses moved up my leg. I knew where this was going. And I was not afraid. He kissed my belly, below my breasts, circled my nipples. He stooped in front of me with my nipple filling his mouth. His large hands cupped my behind and squeezed. He pulled me to him. One long hug. I took the paint brush and dipped it in a pot of blue. I pulled the brush across his chest, his muscled stomach. I painted him. Drew lines on his gleaming skin. His nipples became cobalt blue, his navel, chartreuse. I painted red polka dots on his ass. He laughed when I took his penis in my hand and painted it purple, dark as the night without moon.

March 12, 1994

I told Theodore I was positive last night. On the Ferris wheel. At the top of the world. He was more afraid of the height than what I had to tell him.

His brother died of AIDS.

Sheila calls what Theodore has "survivor's guilt." Theodore has always felt guilty. His work with Mrs. Jenkins and her Dancing Unicorn House kids helps him with that. But I can't help wondering, How do you look into the eyes of a dying child and stay sane?

Theodore wants to keep seeing me.

When we got back to my apartment, I lit my candles and we sat on the area rug on the living room floor. Theodore took off his coat but left the rest of his clothes on. I had on my denim skirt and black tights. My sweater without a bra.

We don't have to be afraid of loving, he said. This is not the time to be without touch, he said. Now is when we need it more than ever. And I'm not talking about sex, I'm talking about touch, he said.

He took my hands in his and kissed them. I started to feel afraid for him. He placed my hands on his face and shook his head until I stopped being afraid. He laid me down on the rug. He slipped off my shoes, pulled down my tights. He brushed his lips gently across my toes, then kissed each one. He raised my leg and brushed his mustache across my ankle, over the soles of my feet. His breath was hot when he blew on my calf.

It tickled. He trailed his tongue along the inside of my thigh and I started to squirm.

You want me to stop? he asked.

What could I do but moan?

He ran his hands over my behind under my skirt, squeezing, kneading, caressing. He put his head under my skirt and planted kisses around the edges of my panties.

Wait, I said. Wait.

He stopped.

His lips had branded my skin. Don't stop, I said, remembering Sheila and Janice's encouraging words: I am alive and a sensual being. I am entitled to this pleasure.

I felt so alive beneath the warmth of his breath. His lips made me think about anything but death.

Theodore helped me remove my sweater. He traced circles around my navel, then slid his tongue to my nipples where he took one, then the other, between his teeth. He kissed my stomach before he blew his breath on my neck. My legs began to shake.

Just a minute, he said.

I was still, but my body was making a sound something like humming.

Theodore returned with the Kama Sutra massage oil. Chocolate Mint. He opened it and told me to lie on my stomach. His hands smoothed the oil on my body, into my hungry skin. He held my calves, thighs, buttocks in his hands and stroked them, massaged my back until not one knot of tension remained. Easily, he rubbed my neck, pushed his tongue into my ear, rolled me over and massaged the front of my body, my thighs, my stomach, my breasts, my shoulders, and then when I was nothing but honey beneath his hands, he laid his body on top of me and we lay like that until I started to rub myself against him, against the rough texture of the pants that covered his muscled thigh, then I pushed myself against his body until he lay beneath me and I was astride him and able to ride until I reached a land where there was no AIDS, no terror, no secrets, only this grinding pleasure, this wicked wetness between my legs.

And that's just a taste of what safer sex can be like, he said.

We lay on that rug for hours breathing together, licking, rubbing, holding, being still. It was as if the HIV had broken something open in our relationship; there was no room for lying or secrets. There was not even space for promises. Those, I told him, are forbidden. He made me promise to meet Mrs. Jenkins and her kids, though. So I will do it. For myself and for Theodore.

How could I say no to a man who can caress me with words like that?

————

Charlotte Watson Sherman is the author of Killing Color, *a collection of short stories;* One Dark Body, *a novel; and a children's book,* Eli and the Swamp. *Her second novel,* Touch, *published in 1995, deals with a woman's search for love and meaning after being diagnosed as HIV-positive. "I had heard stories about mothers not wanting to see their sons dying of AIDS and parishioners not wanting to sit next to fellow church members suspected of having AIDS, and I wondered how such behavior could be allowed to go unchallenged," Sherman recalls. "In* Touch, *I wanted to show what safer sex could be, that we did not have to lose touch with our ability to arouse and be aroused, that we could continue to express our erotic natures." Sherman lives in Seattle.*

ETTA MAE JOHNSON

AN EXCERPT FROM THE NOVEL
The Women of Brewster Place

Gloria Naylor

tta, Etta Mae!" Mattie banged on the bathroom door. "Come on out now. You making me late for the meeting."

"Just another second, Mattie. The church ain't gonna walk away."

"Lord," Mattie grumbled, "she ain't bigger than a minute, so it shouldn't take more than that to get ready."

Etta came out of the bathroom in an exaggerated rush. "My, my, you the most impatient Christian I know."

"Probably the only Christian you know." Mattie refused to be humored as she bent to gather up her sweater and purse. She turned and was stunned with a barrage of colors. A huge white straw hat reigned over layers of gold and pearl beads draped over too much bosom and too little dress. "You plan on dazzling the Lord, Etta?"

"Well, honey," Etta said, looking down the back of her stocking leg to double-check for runs, "last I heard, He wasn't available. You got more recent news?"

"Um, um, um." Mattie pressed her lips together and shook her head slowly to swallow down the laughter she felt crawling up her throat. Realizing she wasn't going to succeed, she quickly turned her face from Etta and headed toward the door. "Just bring your blasphemin' self on downstairs. I done already missed morning services waiting on you today."

Canaan Baptist Church, a brooding, ashen giant, sat in the middle of a block of rundown private homes. Its multi-colored, dome-shaped eyes glowered into the darkness. Fierce clapping and thunderous organ chords came barreling out of its mouth. Evening services had begun.

Canaan's congregation, the poor who lived in a thirty-block area around Brewster Place, still worshiped God loudly. They could not afford the refined, muted benediction of the more prosperous blacks who went to Sinai Baptist on the northern end of the city, and because each of their requests for comfort was so pressing, they took no chances that He did not hear them.

> When Israel was in Egypt's land
> Let my people go
> Oppressed so hard, they could not stand
> Let my people go

The words were as ancient as the origin of their misery, but the tempo had picked up threefold in its evolution from the cotton fields. They were now sung with the frantic determination of a people who realized that the world was swiftly changing, but for some mystic, complex reason their burden had not.

> God said to go down
> Go down
> Brother Moses
> Brother Moses
> To the shore of the great Nile River

The choir clapped and stomped each syllable into a devastating reality, and just as it did, the congregation reached up,

grabbed the phrase, and tried to clap and stomp it back into
oblivion.

> Go to Egypt
> Go to Egypt
> Tell Pharaoh
> Tell Pharaoh
> Let my people go

Etta entered the back of the church like a reluctant prodigal,
prepared at best to be amused. The alien pounding and the
heat and the dark glistening bodies dragged her back, back
past the cold ashes of her innocence to a time when pain could
be castrated on the sharp edges of iron-studded faith. The
blood rushed to her temples and began to throb in unison
with the musical pleas around her.

Etta glanced at Mattie, who was swaying and humming,
and she saw that the lines in her face had almost totally van-
ished. She had left Etta in just that moment for a place where
she was free. Sadly, Etta looked at her, at them all, and was
very envious. Unaccustomed to the irritating texture of doubt,
she felt tears as its abrasiveness grated over the fragile skin of
her life. Could there have been another way?

The song ended with a huge expulsion of air, and the congregation sat down as one body.

"Come on, let's get us a seat." Mattie tugged her by the arm.

The grizzled church deacon with his suit hanging loosely
off his stooped shoulders went up to the pulpit to read the
church business.

"That's one of the widowers I was telling you about,"
Mattie whispered, and poked Etta.

"Unmm." The pressure on her arm brought Etta back
onto the uncomfortable wooden pew. But she didn't want to

stay there, so she climbed back out the window, through the glass eyes of the seven-foot Good Shepherd, and started again the futile weaving of invisible ifs and slippery mights into an equally unattainable past.

The scenes of her life reeled out before her with the same aging script; but now hindsight sat as the omniscient director and had the young star of her epic recite different brilliant lines and make the sort of stunning decisions that propelled her into the cushioned front pews on the right of the minister's podium. There she sat with the deacons' wives, officers of the Ladies' Auxiliary, and head usherettes. And like them, she would wear on her back a hundred pairs of respectful eyes earned the hard way, and not the way she had earned the red sundress, which she now self-consciously tugged up in the front. Was it too late?

The official business completed, the treasurer pulled at his frayed lapels, cleared his throat, and announced the guest speaker for the night.

The man was magnificent.

He glided to the podium with the effortlessness of a well-oiled machine and stood still for an interminable long moment. He eyed the congregation confidently. He only needed their attention for that split second because once he got it, he was going to wrap his voice around their souls and squeeze until they screamed to be relieved. They knew it was coming and waited expectantly, breathing in unison as one body. First he played with them and threw out fine silken threads that stroked their heart muscles ever so gently. They trembled ecstatically at the touch and invited more. The threads multiplied and entwined themselves solidly around the one pulsating organ they had become and tightened slightly, testing them for a reaction.

The "Amen, brothers" and "Yes, Jesus" were his permission to take that short hop from the heart to the soul and lay all pretense of gentleness aside. Now he would have to push and pound with clenched fists in order to be felt, and he dared not stop the fierce rhythm of his voice until their replies had reached that fevered pitch of satisfaction. Yes, Lord—grind out the unheated tenements! Merciful Jesus—shove aside the low-paying boss man. Perfect Father—fill me, fill me till there's no room, no room for nothing else, not even that great big world out there that exacts such a strange penalty for my being born black.

It was hard work. There was so much in them that had to be replaced. The minister's chest was heaving in long spasms, and the sweat was pouring down his gray temples and rolling under his chin. His rich voice was now hoarse, and his legs and raised arms trembled on the edge of collapse. And as always they were satisfied a half-breath before he reached the end of his endurance. They sat back, limp and spent, but momentarily at peace. There was no price too high for this service. At that instant they would have followed him to do battle with the emperor of the world, and all he was going to ask of them was money for the "Lord's work." And they would willingly give over half of their little to keep this man in comfort.

Etta had not been listening to the message; she was watching the man. His body moved with the air of one who had not known recent deprivation. The tone of his skin and the fullness around his jawline told her that he was well-off, even before she got close enough to see the manicured hands and diamond pinkie ring.

The techniques he had used to brand himself on the minds of the congregation were not new to her. She'd encountered talent like that in poolrooms, nightclubs, grimy second-floor insurance offices, numbers dens, and on a dozen street corners. But here was a different sort of power. The jungle-sharpened instincts of a man like that could move her up to the front of the church, ahead of the deacons' wives and Ladies' Auxiliary, off of Brewster Place for good. She would find not only luxury but a place that complemented the type of woman she had fought all these years to become.

"Mattie, is that your regular minister?" she whispered.

"Who, Reverend Woods? No, he just visits on occasion, but he sure can preach, can't he?"

"What you know about him, he married?"

Mattie cut her eyes at Etta. "I should have figured it wasn't the sermon that moved you. At least wait till after the prayer before you jump all into the man's business."

During the closing song and prayer Etta was planning how she was going to maneuver Mattie to the front of the church and into introducing her to Reverend Woods. It wasn't going to be as difficult as she thought. Moreland T. Woods had noticed Etta from the moment she'd entered the church. She stood out like a bright red bird among the drab morality that dried up the breasts and formed rolls around the stomachs of the other church sisters. This woman was still dripping with the juices of a full-fleshed life—the kind of life he was soon to get up and damn into hell for the rest of the congregation—but how it fitted her well. He had to swallow to remove the excess fluid from his mouth before he got up to preach.

Now the problem was to make his way to the back of the church before she left without seeming to be in a particular hurry. A half-dozen back slaps, handshakes, and thank-you sisters only found him about ten feet up the aisle, and he was growing impatient. However, he didn't dare to turn his neck and look in the direction where he'd last seen her. He felt a hand on his upper arm and turned to see a grim-faced Mattie flanked by the woman in the scarlet dress.

"Reverend Woods, I really enjoyed your sermon," Mattie said.

"Why, thank you, sister—sister?"

"Sister Michael, Mattie Michael." While he was addressing

his words to her, the smile he sent over her shoulder to Etta
was undeniable.

"Especially the part," Mattie raised her voice a little, "about
throwing away temptation to preserve the soul. That was a
mighty fine point."

"The Lord moves me and I speak, Sister Michael. I'm just
a humble instrument for his voice."

The direction and intent of his smile was not lost to Etta.
She inched her way in front of Mattie. "I enjoyed it, too,
Reverend Woods. It's been a long time since I heard preach-
ing like that." She increased the pressure of her fingers on
Mattie's arm.

"Oh, excuse my manners. Reverend Woods, this is an old
friend of mine, Etta Mae Johnson. Etta Mae, Reverend Woods."
She intoned the words as if she were reciting a eulogy.

"Please to meet you, Sister Johnson." He beamed down on
the small woman and purposely held her hand a fraction
longer than usual. "You must be a new member—I don't
recall seeing you the times I've been here before."

"Well, no, Reverend, I'm not a member of the congregation, but I was raised up in the church. You know how it is,
as you get older sometimes you stray away. But after your sermon, I'm truly thinking of coming back."

Mattie tensed, hoping that the lightning that God was surely
going to strike Etta with wouldn't hit her by mistake.

"Well, you know what the Bible says, sister. The angels
rejoice more over one sinner who turns around than over
ninety-nine righteous ones."

"Yes, indeed, and I'm sure a shepherd like you has helped
to turn many back to the fold." She looked up and gave him
the full benefit of her round dark eyes, grateful she hadn't put
on that third coat of mascara.

"I try, Sister Johnson, I try."

"It's a shame Mrs. Woods wasn't here tonight to hear you. I'm sure she must be mighty proud of your work."

"My wife has gone to her glory, Sister Johnson. I think of myself now as a man alone—rest her soul."

"Yes, rest her soul," Etta sighed.

"Please, Lord, yes," Mattie muttered, giving out the only sincere request among the three. The intensity of her appeal startled them, and they turned to look at her. "Only knows how hard this life is, she's better in the arms of Jesus."

"Yes"—Etta narrowed her eyes at Mattie and then turned back to the minister—"I can testify to that. Being a woman alone, it seems all the more hard. Sometimes you don't know where to turn."

Moreland Woods knew Etta was the type of woman who not only knew which way to turn, but, more often than not, had built her own roads when nothing else was accessible. But he was enjoying this game immensely—almost as much as the growing heat creeping into his groin.

"Well, if I can be of any assistance, Sister Johnson, don't hesitate to ask. I couldn't sleep knowing one of the Lord's sheep is troubled. As a matter of fact, if you have anything you would like to discuss with me this evening, I'd be glad to escort you home."

"I don't have my own place. You see, I'm just up from out of state and staying with my friend Mattie here."

"Well, perhaps we could all go out for coffee."

"Thank you, but I'll have to decline, Reverend," Mattie volunteered before Etta did it for her. "The services have me all tired out, but if Etta wants to, she's welcome."

"That'll be just fine," Etta said.

"Good, good." And now it was his turn to give her the benefit of a mouth full of strong gold-capped teeth. "Just let me say good-bye to a few folks here, and I'll meet you outside."

"Girl, you oughta patent that speed and sell it to the airplane companies," Mattie said outside. " 'After that sermon, Reverend, I'm thinking of coming back'—indeed!"

"Aw, hush your fussing."

"I declare if you had batted them lashes just a little faster we'd of had a dust storm in there."

"You said you wanted me to meet some nice men. Well, I met one."

"Etta, I meant a man who'd be serious about settling down with you." Mattie was exasperated. "Why, you're going on like a schoolgirl. Can't you see what he's got in mind?"

Etta turned an indignant face toward Mattie. "The only thing I see is that you're telling me I'm not good enough for a man like that. Oh, no, not Etta Johnson. No upstanding decent man could ever see anything in her but a quick good time. Well, I'll tell you something, Mattie Michael. I've always traveled first-class, maybe not in the way you'd approve with all your fine Christian principles, but it's done all right by me. And I'm gonna keep going top drawer till I leave this earth. Don't you think I got a mirror? Each year there's a new line to cover. I lay down with this body and get up with it every morning, and each morning it cries for just a little more rest than it did the day before. Well, I'm finally gonna get that rest, and it's going to be with a man like Reverend Woods. And you and the rest of those slack-mouthed gossips on Brewster be damned!" Tears frosted the edges of her last words. "They'll be humming a different tune when I show up there the wife of a big preacher. I've always known what they say about me behind my back, but I never thought you were right in there with them."

Mattie was stunned by Etta's tirade. How could Etta have so totally misunderstood her words? What had happened back there to stuff up her senses to the point that she had missed the obvious? Surely she could not believe that the vibrations coming from that unholy game of charades in the church aisle would lead to something as permanent as marriage? Why, it had been nothing but the opening gestures to a mating dance. Mattie had gone through the same motions at least once in her life, and Etta must have known a dozen variations to it that were a mystery to her. And yet, somehow, back there it had been played to a music that had totally distorted the steps for her friend. Mattie suddenly felt the helplessness of a person who is forced to explain that for which there are no words.

She quietly turned her back and started down the steps. There was no need to defend herself against Etta's accusations. They shared at least a hundred memories that could belie those cruel words. Let them speak for her.

Sometimes being a friend means mastering the art of timing. There is a time for silence. A time to let go and allow people to hurl themselves into their own destiny. And a time to prepare to pick up the pieces when it's all over. Mattie realized that this moment called for all three.

"I'll see ya when you get home, Etta," she threw gently over her shoulder.

Etta watched the bulky figure become slowly enveloped by the shadows. Her angry words had formed a thick mucus in her throat, and she couldn't swallow them down. She started to run into the darkness where she'd seen Mattie disappear, but at that instant Moreland Woods came out of the lighted church, beaming.

He took her arm and helped her into the front seat of his car. Her back sank into the deep upholstered leather, and the smell of the freshly vacuumed carpet was mellow in her nostrils. All of the natural night sounds of the city were blocked by the thick tinted windows and the hum of the air conditioner, but they

trailed persistently behind the polished back of the vehicle as it
turned and headed down the long gray boulevard.

> Smooth road
> Clear day
> But why am I the only one
> Traveling this way
> How strange the road to love
> Can be so easy
> Can there be a detour ahead?

Moreland Woods was captivated by the beautiful woman at his
side. Her firm brown flesh and bright eyes carried the essence of
nectar from some untamed exotic flower, and the fragrance was
causing a pleasant disturbance at the pit of his stomach. He marveled at how excellently she played the game. A less alert observer
might have been taken in, but his survival depended upon
knowing people, knowing exactly how much to give and how
little to take. It was this razor-thin instinct that had catapulted
him to the head of his profession and that would keep him there.

And although she cut her cards with a reckless confidence,
pushed her chips into the middle of the table as though the supply was unlimited, and could sit out the game until dawn, he
knew. Oh, yes. Let her win a few, and then he would win just a
few more, and she would be bankrupt long before the sun was
up. And then there would be only one thing left to place on the
table—and she would, because the stakes they were playing for
were very high. But she was going to lose that last deal. She would
lose because when she first sat down in that car she had everything riding on the fact that he didn't know the game existed.

And so it went. All evening Etta had been in another world,
weaving his tailored suit and the smell of his expensive
cologne into a custom-made future for herself. It took his last

floundering thrusts into her body to bring her back to reality. She arrived in enough time to feel him beating against her like a dying walrus, until he shuddered and was still.

She kept her eyes closed because she knew when she opened them there would be the old familiar sights around her. To her right would be the plastic-coated nightstand that matched the cheaply carved headboard of the bed she lay in. She felt the bleached coarseness of the sheet under her sweaty back and predicted the roughness of the worn carpet path that led from the bed to the white-tiled bathroom with bright fluorescent lights, sterilized towels, and tissue-wrapped water glasses. There would be two or three small thin rectangles of soap wrapped in bright waxy covers that bore the name of the hotel.

She didn't try to visualize what the name would be. It didn't matter. They were all the same, all meshed together into one lump that rested like an iron ball on her chest. And the expression on the face of this breathing mass to her left would be the same as all the others. She could turn now and go through the rituals that would tie up the evening for them both, but she wanted just one more second of this soothing darkness before she had to face the echoes of the locking doors she knew would be in his eyes.

Etta got out of the car unassisted and didn't bother to turn and watch the taillights as it pulled off down the deserted avenue adjacent to Brewster Place. She had asked him to leave her at the corner because there was no point in his having to make a U-turn in the dead-end street, and it was less than a hundred yards to her door. Moreland was relieved that she had made it easy for him, because it had been a long day and he was anxious to get home and go to sleep. But then, the whole business had gone pretty smoothly after they left the hotel. He hadn't even been called upon to use any of the excuses he had prepared for why it would be a while before he'd see her again. A slight frown crossed his forehead as he realized that she had seemed as eager to get away from him as he had been to leave. Well, he shrugged his shoulders and placated his dented ego, that's the nice part about these wordly women. They understand the temporary weakness of the flesh and don't make it out to be something bigger than it is. They can have a good time without pawing and hanging all onto a man. Maybe I should drop around sometime. He glanced into his rearview mirror and saw that Etta was still standing on the corner, looking straight ahead into Brewster. There was something about the slumped profile of her body, silhouetted against the dim street light, that caused him to press down on the accelerator.

Etta stood looking at the wall that closed off Brewster from the avenues farther north and found it hard to believe that it had been just this afternoon when she had seen it. It had looked so different then, with the August sun highlighting the browns and reds of the bricks and the young children bouncing their rubber balls against its side. Now it crouched there in the thin predawn light, like a pulsating mouth awaiting her arrival. She shook her head sharply to rid herself of the illusion, but an uncanny fear gripped her, and her legs felt like lead. If I walk into this street, she thought, I'll never come back. I'll never get out. Oh, dear God, I am so tired—so very tired.

Etta removed her hat and massaged her tight forehead. Then, giving a resigned sigh, she started slowly down the street. Had her neighbors been out on their front stoops, she could have passed through their milling clusters as anonymously as the night wind. They had seen her come down that street once in a broken Chevy that had about five hundred dollars' worth of contraband liquor in its trunk, and there was even the time she'd come home with a broken nose she'd gotten in some hair-raising escapade in St. Louis, but never had she walked among them with a broken spirit. This middle-aged woman in the wrinkled dress and wilted straw hat would have been a stranger to them.

When Etta got to the stoop, she noticed there was a light under the shade at Mattie's window, and she strained to hear what actually sounded like music coming from behind the screen. Mattie was playing her records! Etta stood very still, trying to decipher the broken airwaves into intelligible sound, but she couldn't make out the words. She stopped straining when it suddenly came to her that it wasn't important what song it was—someone was waiting up for her. Someone who would deny fiercely that there had been any concern—just a little indigestion from them fried onions that kept me from sleeping. Thought I'd pass the time by figuring out what you see in all this loose-life music.

Etta laughed softly to herself as she climbed the steps toward the light and the love and the comfort that awaited her.

Gloria Naylor's best-selling novel The Women of Brewster Place *won the 1983 American Book Award for first fiction. Naylor has since produced a distinguished quartet of novels:* Linden Hills, Mama Day, Bailey's Cafe, *and, most recently,* The Men of Brewster Place. *A native New Yorker, Naylor says she grew up shy, a quiet, watchful child "in a hothouse of transplanted southerners, colorful and vibrant people who wore their emotions behind a facade of always having to make do."* Etta Mae Johnson, *the title character in this excerpt from* The Women of Brewster Place, *is just such a woman. Naylor, who also writes for theater, film, and television, lives and works in Brooklyn.*

THE SERPENT'S GIFT

AN EXCERPT FROM THE NOVEL

Helen Elaine Lee

Note: This excerpt is made up of sections that do not appear consecutively in the novel.

J ust as LaRue was getting to know Olive, Ouida was having her own summer of discovery. She was finding out about choosing, and about a woman she had never expected to know.

Her kisses were like nighttime secrets, and Ouida swore that her laugh, like the rain, made things grow. Zella Bridgeforth touched her somewhere timeless, held her, compelled her with her rhythms, and Ouida answered her call. She chose her, after all, but the path that led to Zella took her, first, through other choices.

The summer of 1926, the summer they had met, Ouida would later think of as her "swan song." She had swung her corset-cinched body along the streets of the city with long steady strides, smiling but never meeting the eyes of those who paused from whatever they were doing to partake of her radiance. Just divorced from Junior, she was finished, finally, with trying to will their union into rightness.

As soon as she had landed her manicurist job and rented her flat, she had surveyed the range of the possible from the vantage point of her manicurist's table, feeling, for the first time in her life, that she owned the choice. From the spin of options, she made assessments. And she did some choosing.

She chose Johnston Franklin, the middle-aged white man

who stopped in the shop on his business trips from Louisville. He came in and stared at her while waiting for a chair, and she met his glance, her chin in the air, and kept working. While he sat for his haircut and shave, he asked Alton, one of the barbers, who she was. When Alton didn't answer, Johnston Franklin turned in the chair, his face half-covered with lather, and addressed Alton with a demanding look. Alton turned away and stirred his soap, assessing the cost of defiance. Finally, he said, "I think she's married, sir. Least that's what I've heard."

Johnston Franklin laughed and said, "Well, I'm not interested in her husband. What is her name?"

Alton stirred his soap some more and then answered, "Ouida Staples. Miss Ouida Staples."

Ouida had noticed the exchange and could see Johnston Franklin coming her way out of the corner of her eye, but she refused to look up. She sat at her table humming while she polished and arranged her instruments, the edge of his gold fob, a crisply creased pant leg, and the tip of an expensive shoe just within view. Finally, when he realized that she wasn't going to look up at him, he sat down and ordered a manicure. She took his hands and began her task.

"I understand your name is Ouida," he said, "and that's an unusual name." She lifted her eyes slowly, as if it was an effort, assessed his face in an instant, and returned to his hands. The barbers watched to see what she would do.

"And how *are* you today, Ouida?" Johnston Franklin tried again.

"Oh, I'm just fine," she answered with a hint of insolence as she lifted her eyes, "sir."

"Well . . . I don't recall seeing your lovely face in this establishment before . . ." Ouida kept filing, silently.

"I come in here every month or so . . . here on business,

quite regularly, and I will certainly make it a habit to visit this establishment more often." She filed his nails silently, thinking how soft and pale his hands were.

"Well . . ." he ventured, "this town sure is different from my home . . . it's the city, all right, and I do like, now and again, seeing something besides trees . . . of course, this town doesn't compare to New York . . . now that's a different story, that's the real city. Have you ever been to New York, Ouida . . . Miss Ouida?"

She shook her head, and kept working on his nails. And receiving neither information nor interest, he jerked his hand away as she was finishing up, paid his bill, and left. He returned the next week, and the next, watching her from the barber chair, and when he was finished being shaved, he came up to her and leaned over her table until she met his eyes. Matter-of-factly, he said, "It would be my pleasure if we could spend some time together . . . tonight, perhaps."

She looked at him, her head tilted, and measured the choice. She saw a square pink face, not so different from many she had seen, well fed and well tended, and even though it wasn't a face that moved her much, she thought she could look into his restless moss-green eyes for a little while. It was a face that held the promise of things she couldn't afford, and their delivery with a kind of homage.

She glanced over at the barbers, Alton and Regis, who watched the whole thing unfold and waited for her to resist sweetly, and their expectations bred defiance. The other barber, Flood, never looked her way.

"Not tonight," she answered as she stood up and went to tend to some other job, making him wait until she returned to tell him when.

It was a timeless play, the choreographed conquest of strange exotic prey, and Ouida was willing to play it for a time. It was a variation on a role she knew, and even though she was familiar with the script, she liked to think that it was she, in fact, who controlled the hunt, fooling the hunter into thinking things moved along by his design. She figured she could learn something about the rest of the world from Johnston Franklin, about the places he visited that she had never been. She liked the challenge. She liked the gifts he brought. And she liked his liking, too.

Their first night of sex, Johnston Franklin had undressed completely and was waiting for her in the bed when she came in from the bathroom, and she had stood, fully dressed, and looked at him. "Well, you certainly are direct, Johnston-Franklin. You get right to the point."

She found herself calling him by his full name, even in bed. And after they had sex he talked to her of his business trips, of meetings and sales and the shops and restaurants he had visited. It was as if just being around Ouida made something in him loosen and spill out, the things he held separate from the rest of his life. Eventually, he started discharging the details of his day, his aspirations and his self-doubts, as soon as he saw her, and he talked all the way through undressing, right up to their first embrace.

He was captivated by her beauty, and her knowledge of its power, and he had seen it in the way she made him wait that first day he saw her, and had wanted it for his own, sensing there was something, some kind of magic, that she knew. He wanted to know it, too.

He wanted to know about the way she lived life up close. While he heard things and looked at colors and shapes from somewhere outside of himself, he could tell that when Ouida did something, she was right in the middle of it. He asked her to reveal to him her eye for things, and he asked her to give him the rich details she saw. "Tell me a texture," he would say, as they lay in the rich linen of his hotel, and she would begin to describe some fabric she had seen.

"Silky, like a river in sunlight, and purple, with flaws that aren't flaws, but just the way of the cloth. And it feels purple, Johnston Franklin. You know how purple feels? Rich, with a grain that's both kind to and hard on the fingertips. Now it is your turn," she said, lying back on the pillows. "Tell me about the trees you have at home."

"Okay . . . well . . . let's see," he said and then stopped. "I can't," he protested, but she continued to prod him. "Okay, okay. The trees in my front yard are oak trees. They are live oak trees."

"Live oaks," she said.

"Yes. Live oak."

"Well, that doesn't mean a whole lot to me, Johnston Franklin. Are they shaped like fat stodgy men, or lithe like young girls? Are they dark, and do other colors show through in spots? Are they sheltering, or does the rain get past the leaves? And what does the bark feel like to the touch . . . does it stand away or cling to the wood?"

He leaned back against the pillow and tried to imagine them. "They're shaped . . . like oak trees are shaped, I guess. I never noticed. And they're green . . . and brown, like I suppose most trees are."

"Well, how does the trunk feel?" Ouida asked.

"They are like . . . they're live oak, that's all. I don't know what else to say," he stammered, as she shook her head and argued.

"I know what you call them, Johnston Franklin, but what are they like to you?"

"We had them put in a long time ago . . . they're what everyone has . . . and they're old . . . and big . . . and they have leaves, like all trees. I don't know what else to say. I don't know, that's all I see."

Ouida looked at him, propped on her elbow, and then slid down under the covers and went to sleep.

Johnston Franklin visited weekly for several months, but Ouida began to withdraw from him as she felt him trying to hold her closer and closer, like a butterfly in a Ball canning jar. Waxed paper stretched across the top. Breathing holes punched through.

The last time they met, on one of his regular forays from his wife and family, he held onto her as she got up to leave, and demanded to know where she was going. Ouida pulled her arm free and gave him a decimating look as she got her things to leave. When she glanced back to look at him for the last time, she saw a child whose fingers held traces of the black and orange dust of captured butterflies.

When it was just about finished with Johnston Franklin, Ouida chose the barber, Flood, who drew her with the economy of his attention, and looked at her from underneath his eyes. The other barbers flirted with her all the time, and played at asking her out. "You shore is one fine-lookin' woman," Alton would say, leaning on the arm of his chair as he waited for his first customer, shaking his head. "When, just when, are you gon' marry me?"

"After she marry me and I leave her," Regis answered, "'cause you know a woman fine as she is don't mean nothin' but trouble. I prefer the ugly ones, truth be told, 'cause that way you're glad when they leave you."

She laughed at them playfully, and said, "You two are just no good. What about that devoted little lady of yours at home, Alton?"

"She would understand. She know I just married her 'cause I was waitin' on you."

Flood never joined in the joking, and he barely even smiled. Ouida didn't even know if he was married, and as she wasn't looking for a husband, she didn't care. He never looked her way when Johnston Franklin came to the shop, and he never shaved him or cut his hair. He prepared all of his own lotions and tools, neither accepting nor offering help. He traveled solo, with a hardness about him that she wanted to work soft.

When Ouida had passed between barber chairs one afternoon in search of towels, and brushed against his arm, he hadn't started, or looked at her, but she had seen the muscles in his forearm tense as he gripped his comb. After that she found reasons to go by his chair. Knowing that she would have to go after him, and thrilled by the pursuit, she brought him a cup of tea one morning and left it on the counter behind his chair. He let it sit all day, never thanking her and never drinking it. She did the same thing the next day, and the next, until, holding the cup with both hands, warming his palms, he lifted it to his mouth and drank. And as he lowered the cup, he looked at her with desire, and a trace of contempt.

The next evening, she waited until Alton and Regis were gone, and she and Flood were left to lock up. Fiddling with his scissors and combs, he slowly cleaned up his chair and the floor around it, while she arranged and rearranged her manicurist tools, unable to speak. He went for his coat and hat and headed for the door. As he reached for the doorknob, she spoke.

"Flood?"

He stood with his hand on the knob and his back to her and then he turned, and she said nothing as he stood at the door waiting for her. They walked to her flat, and as soon as they got inside the door, they tore at each other's clothes, and took each other on the bare floor, as if it couldn't be helped, as if it had to be that way, the hard urgency a hurting they both wanted to feel. As soon as it was over, he dressed and left without saying good-bye, and Ouida didn't think of the risk she had taken until it was too late.

At the barbershop, things didn't change on the surface, and Ouida knew little more about Flood than before. What she did know was that the heat, the tension between them would make him return, and she waited for him to come to her again. At times she wondered if she had dreamed it, until a week later, she had stood watching him after Alton and Regis had left, and he looked at her and grasped the back of his chair tight, until the leather squeaked. She knew he wanted her again; and again, he waited at the door.

In their fevered loving, Ouida saw Flood surrender, silently, to something in her. She wanted to be the one who reached him, against his will, the one whom he couldn't help but come back to, the one who excavated his pain, his need, and for a time, she was willing to exchange peace for the intensity of the fight. Again and again, she tugged on the one string that joined them and she reeled him in.

When this was no longer enough, Ouida had tried to push it further, to find out who he was, but the two of them were stuck in a moment in time, repeating again and again the same act, moving nowhere. By the time she heard Zella's call, she was letting go of what she had, and didn't have, with Flood, and she chose Zella, rain voiced, in whom she met herself.

The first time she saw her, Zella was standing on the corner waiting for a streetcar as it began to shower, and from the barbershop window Ouida watched her digging in her bag for something to shield herself, cursing as her hair got wet. As soon as she had pulled out a newspaper to cover her head, she had tossed it down and stood there laughing as her head got soaked. Ouida glanced up and saw her as she was putting her instruments away, and moved to the window to watch as Zella lifted her arms and face to the rain and shook her head, opening her generous mouth to taste the falling water.

The next time she saw her, Zella had come into the shop for a haircut on the weekday allotted for colored customers, and Ouida had watched her enter and approach Alton's chair, struck by the way she moved with authority over space. She was tall and slender, and a few years older than Ouida, almost thirty. Her skin was copper-colored and her hair was a mass of dark ringlets, but it was her large flashing black eyes that were remarkable, one smaller than the other. When she walked over to Alton's chair and sat down, he came around to face her and declared, "Now you don't need a shave, and I know you not even thinkin' 'bout cuttin' off all that pretty hair, so just what are you doin' in my chair?"

Zella frowned and gave him a look that was a challenge. "You cut hair, don't you," she stated, rather than asked, and Alton nodded. "Well," she said, "I suspect you cut it like your customers ask you to, is that right?" and Alton nodded again. "Then I suggest you get busy with your scissors and crop mine just above my cheek. Right about here," she said, gesturing with her hand.

Alton argued with her for a while, but he gave in when Zella said, "Why is it that colored folks feel every bit of our hair ought to be on our heads! If we were as concerned with what's in our heads as we are with what's on them, we'd be a lot further along."

At that, Alton had to laugh, and he took up his scissors. He shook his head as her hair fell to the floor, and exclaimed what a shame it was the entire time, and after Zella looked at the finished product in the mirror, she got up, paid him, and left, nodding to Ouida on the way out.

"Well," Alton said, as she was leaving, "girl, bet' not mess with that one. I know her peoples, and she ain't quite right. What I mean to say is . . . she ain't normal."

When Ouida stared at him, wanting to know more but afraid to ask, he continued, "I know she'd like a sweet young thing like you all for her own. Her kind, they like that."

"Now that's a lovely woman," Zella said to herself once she was outside. She turned back and caught Ouida's eye through the window, and there was between them a moment of recognition, whose power made them turn away.

Ouida went to the family house that evening and stayed the night, and Vesta sat on the edge of her bed working lotion into her face while Ouida was brushing and plaiting her hair. "Vesta, I met someone who's different," she ventured, unsure of herself.

"Different . . ." Vesta replied. "What does that mean?" And Ouida paused. "I don't know. Different, somehow. I don't know how to explain it."

"You gotta do better than that, Ouida," Vesta said. "It's late and I'm not up to reading minds tonight."

"Well . . . she gets her hair cut short, and at the shop," she began, to which Vesta raised her eyebrows. "I don't know, she's kind of not feminine, but she is feminine after all." Vesta just looked at her.

Ouida told Vesta what Alton had said and then she stopped brushing and asked, "What do you think, Vesta? You know anything about these things?"

Vesta didn't and so she shook her head. "I've heard of people like that, but no, I don't know at all about that sort of thing. I can say, for sure, though, that it sounds like trouble to me," and then she finished up with her face, turned her bed down, and curled up facing the wall. But she lay there in the darkness considering what Ouida had said, and it was a long time before she fell asleep.

The next time Ouida saw Zella, two weeks later, she had thought about what Alton and Vesta had said and she was ready for Zella's greeting, but not for the way she made her feel, like a dry part of her was being watered. "Rain," she whispered to herself, "rain."

After her haircut, Zella sat down at Ouida's table and said, "I think I'm due for a manicure." In fact, she had never had a manicure, but something in Ouida's response to her glance had pulled her there, and she had to see what her voice sounded like.

"My name is Zella," she opened, and Ouida responded, "Ouida . . . Ouida is my name."

They smiled and Zella asked her what kind of name it was and where she got it. She said, quietly, "It was passed down. Or so my mother said." As Ouida worked on Zella's hands, she noticed how strong and worn with experience they looked and felt, and she wanted to know where those hands had been.

Zella began to feel the need for a weekly haircut or a manicure, and she and Ouida found themselves sitting for hours talking while she surrendered her fingers to Ouida's, and felt something in her tear loose. Each time she left she told herself on the way home that she was risking her heart foolishly, that in the end, she would be destroyed. She knew, somehow, that Ouida had known only men, and she told herself that she could never have her and that she had to stop going. But she always found a reason to return.

She stayed one time until the barbershop closed, and the two of them kept on walking down the street toward Ouida's flat. They stopped to buy fruit and when they got to the flat, Ouida made tea and offered Zella one of her chipped cups, and then they sat in the nook she had made next to the kitchen with her cerulean-blue chairs, telling about themselves until their hands, both reaching for the teapot, touched.

"Say yes," Zella whispered.

"Yes," Ouida answered. "Yes."

They sat in the last light of the day as it thickened and

became gold, entering through the window, coming down to them, meeting them. Lowering itself into their laps, the golden light thick with all that the day had held. Light not merely for seeing, but for touch. For love.

It was almost dawn again. Almost light, but not yet, not yet. Zella rose from the bed and went to the icebox to get a pear. She sliced it into wedges and removed the seeds, and little beads of juice stood out on the cool inner surface of the fruit. She knelt beside the bed and said, quietly, "Close your eyes."

And she turned a wedge of the iced fruit, turned it, to Ouida, and the open cool innerness of the wedge met her lips. Ouida sank her mouth into it, giving in to it, and Zella fed her, after she was spent, but not really, not quite, not yet, as the fire rose in her again, mingling with the ice-hot wetness of the fruit, into an ache that had to be quenched even though it was getting light, pale light, pale and thin and tinged with blue, thin, but not yet, not yet, and it had to be now, even though there would be time for it all again and again and again across the years, it must be now and now and now. . . .

When her period had been late for a week, Ouida told herself it would come, that she had never really been regular. When a month had passed, she shifted between panic and denial, trapped and without the inkling of a route toward help. When she saw her naked profile in the mirror one morning, she could no longer hide.

Stepping into her panties, she caught a glimpse of herself, and let them drop as she straightened up. She looked from mirror to flesh, and touched slowly, with fingertips first, and then with her whole hand. She returned to her image in the mirror and then backed up and sat down on the edge of the bed.

She sat there for an hour, stunned by the reality that was,

somehow, hers. She was hit by a wave of disbelief, even three years after her death, that Ruby was not there, and as she thought of what to do about it, she knew that she needed Zella's help. She waited until they lay in bed that night, their legs entwined, to ask. It was then that she spoke of her other night visitor.

"Zella, you know that luggage with my monogram, that I said my uncle sent me? And the organdy hankies in my top drawer?"

"Un hunh," Zella responded, half asleep with her face in Ouida's neck.

"Zella, listen. I have something to say," she declared with quiet urgency as she nudged her arm.

Zella raised up on her elbow and looked Ouida in the eye, a pinpoint of dread dilating in her stomach.

"Well, they didn't . . . they didn't." She looked away, and it seemed that she actually aged in the time it took for her to turn back to Zella's face. "I didn't get them from my uncle at all."

Zella stared at her, unwilling to help her finish what she had to say. She tightened her jaw and braced herself against the coming blow, as Ouida finished. "The white man brought them. The one from Louisville."

Zella was too stunned to absorb anything besides Ouida's last syllable, resounding over and over again in her head, "Ville . . . ville . . . *ville.*" And then she felt the tip of rage as Ouida finished.

"Zella, it's been two months since my last period. I need your help."

Zella looked at her, mutely, as the confession came out in a rush, and rose from the bed. And as the numbness faded, the full range of her feelings passed through her. She turned away from Ouida, who sank into her pillows silently. Zella paced the kitchen floor and then sat, facing the window. Hours later, she came to bed.

She stayed, as she knew she would, and reached to turn off the light. They faced opposite directions, their backs not touching. During the night, Zella turned to look at Ouida's sleeping face, emptied of stress but pale and tired, and wondered how she had let herself love so, against the one rule she knew about never getting close to women who love men. She studied the face that she had trusted with an anger that had chilled into something distant and analytical, searching for hints of dishonesty in what now appeared to her to be a mask.

How could the person beside her be so foreign, and yet so known? How did it happen that way? It all seemed a message to Zella of what she could not have. She turned to look at her over and over and asked how Ouida could do this to her. And then, somehow, in an instant, as she studied the face that seemed altogether emptied, she felt that what was happening was happening to them, and accepted the love she felt.

When Ouida woke the next morning, Zella was sitting at the table fully dressed, drinking tea. She had stayed. When Ouida saw her there she felt a surge of panic, but as she came into the kitchen, she saw a cup of tea waiting for her. She sat down, and they looked at each other silently. Zella spoke: "Ouida. What do you want to do?"

Ouida shook her head and said, "Before we talk about it, I have one more thing to tell you. So that it will be clean." She looked straight into Zella's eyes and said, "There was another. There was the barber, Flood."

Zella looked at her, from what seemed like far away, knowing somehow, through her jealousy, that whatever else Ouida had been doing was about something other than love. And so she nodded, and pointed to the cup of tea. As Ouida sat down to drink, Zella set out the choices: the one, crazy, that she felt her way toward in darkness, and the other, reckless, the terror of which was known.

Zella told her later how she had counted up three windows and stood staring for ten minutes. She left, got a block away, and then came back. She stood at the curb looking up, pulling her coat close and wondering how she could climb the stairs, and how she could not.

She had gone first to her aunt Mandy, who ran a boardinghouse for young women. She knew not to say the word abortion, and formed her question carefully.

"Where can a girl who's in trouble get help?"

Her aunt smiled slightly, relieved that the rumors she had heard about Zella were either untrue, or had only represented a phase. There was an awkward pause, and then Zella spoke.

"Not me, Aunt Mandy. I'm asking for a friend."

Mandy's smile faded, and she lowered her eyes, ashamed, and told her how to find out what to do without really asking.

Zella had memorized the address, and had gone there after work. She looked up at the window and finally opened the door, moving toward the third floor with decisive steps. She stood facing the grimy yellow door while she got her instructions in order, and knocked. The door opened as far as its chain would allow to reveal the face of a small black woman with piercing eyes.

"I'm here about the goods. About getting them unloaded. WB sent me."

The woman's eyes moved down from Zella's collar to her feet, and then back up again, taking in her tailored clothes and polished shoes. She stopped at her face and spent a good bit of time there, and when the anguish in the eyes told her that it was love that had brought her there, love and desperation, she decided that it was not a trap.

"The goods are your'n?" she asked, roughly.

"No. My friend's."

The door closed for a moment, while she removed the chain, and then she grabbed Zella's arm and pulled her across the threshold.

"Sit down while I tell you what to do."

Zella dwarfed the slim wooden chair and looked around the room. Bits of old rugs were pieced together to cover the floor. The place smelled close and the windows and shades were drawn. The strange, rough woman stood in front of her and shook her finger in her face.

"You go, after dark, tomorrow, at seven at night, to where the Old Stone Road and the street without no name meet, and you make you a right turn. Go to the big elm tree at the next fork in the road, and there will be a black car waitin' for you. Now you tell the man in the car that you come 'bout the cargo, and give him the money in your envelope. He'll take you to the place."

She finished with the most important part. "If you ain't got the money, don't come."

Zella rose and left the room, her eyes meeting the stranger's long enough for her to see something else beneath the harshness of her way. The small gnarled woman touched her arm before she closed the door, and then, alone again, she muttered to herself, "Lord watch over you, child."

Zella descended the stairwell, the grim green walls marked with fingerprints along the banister, and wallpaper that stood away from the walls at the corners and baseboards. She stopped at the foot of the stairs and touched the wall as she tried to make out the pattern. Faded almost to smudges were traces of spring bouquets.

She went next to withdraw the money from the bank and took the streetcar to the Marquis, where she waited until Ouida finished doing a manicure and pulled her aside. As she explained the plan, Zella couldn't help looking at Ouida's stomach, bound tight with a laced corset. She gently tucked a lock of Ouida's hair back in its chignon and left. The next step was to borrow a car.

They met that evening at Zella's flat, and said nothing of the next day. Zella ironed and folded a stack of clothes and tried not to think of the coming day. She tried to bury her anger in order to give Ouida strength. She had never really thought, when she allowed herself to consider it, that she, alone, could have Ouida; she had always been afraid to ask her to define her feelings, afraid of things against which she had no power, things so different from her. She had felt, somewhere inside, that she couldn't have her because Ouida was connected to something else, and at the same time she knew that she did, she did have her, and that whatever else there was that Ouida belonged to, the thing that bound the two of them was different, and was strong.

At work the next day Ouida's hands trembled so much that she could barely finish her first manicure. She kept having to excuse herself and go to the tiny makeshift space with a toilet and sink that they made for her in the men's barbershop. She sat on the edge of the utility sink and tried to get calm, but she felt as if she had to keep a careful distance from the center of herself. She felt as if her life had gotten mixed up with someone else's.

She mumbled to herself and returned to her table. Alton kept coming over to ask her if she was all right.

The horror stories she had heard came back to her in snatches as she waited for a customer or held a strange, white, uncalloused hand. She thought of the stories she had heard of butcherings in dirty rooms and bleeding from careless hands, and she imagined the profound shame her mother would feel. And she returned to the thing becoming inside of her, not knowing how to think of it, but knowing that it couldn't be.

She remembered the day Vesta's family had moved down-stairs, Eula sewing by candlelight when the light bill couldn't be paid, eggs for dinner and run-down shoes. Ouida had just begun to shape her life, and she couldn't give that up. For a man who wasn't willing and whom she didn't want? For all kinds of isn'ts and might-be's. Zella had offered to raise it as her own, had said that they could do it together, but she couldn't even see her way clear to think about that.

She knew that she would have to risk her life. Her hand strayed to rest on the almost concealed roundness of her stomach, and she tried to put aside her fear.

Zella picked her up at five o'clock, and they drove through an empty landscape caught between winter and spring, bleached of color. Pools of dark watery ice swallowed weather-worn bits of grass, while other patches were still dry from freezing.

Ouida sat clutching her pocketbook, looking straight ahead, until they came to the fork in the road, and she lowered her head. It was dark now, and they got out and went to the window of the other car, and Zella stepped forward and repeated the code words she had been told to say. The man took the envelope that Zella held out, looked inside, and opened the back door from the inside. They climbed in, and Zella took Ouida's hand.

They rode in the dark for forty-five minutes, going in cir-cles, Zella thought, and pulled up next to a shack surrounded by pools of mud and gravel. Ouida would never lose the sound of the tires coming to rest on the rocky side of the road.

As they were led inside, a man asked, "Which one?" Zella and Ouida looked at each other and Ouida stepped forward. He pointed to a door and Zella started to follow, but the dri-ver stepped in front of her and said, harshly, "Un unh, lady.

You can't go in." As Ouida walked down a filthy hallway, she heard a scream, and stopped for a moment to look back at the door behind which Zella stood, clutching her handbag, before she moved on.

As she came to the end of the hallway, Ouida looked around for something that reminded her of a doctor's office, and then she realized that this was where she had been headed all along. The man who had met her at the door told her to undress, and handed her a sheet. "Put that over your bottom half," he said, making no move to leave. She stood and stared at him until he left the room, and when he came back, she was standing in front of the table wrapped in the sheet, holding her clothes in front of her. He took the clothes from her and motioned for her to get on the table. He took her feet and put them into loops of rope that hung from the ceiling. And he never washed his hands.

As he parted her and felt inside with his finger, she sucked in her breath and tried to go somewhere else. Then there was cold metal pushing in, and a pain that she would never be able to describe, as he began scraping with the curette. The entire time that he was with her, he chewed on a cigar.

And she focused on the grimy lightbulb that swayed above her, wrapping herself in her cries.

She could hear him messing with a can or bucket, and the sound of metal against metal as he put his instruments in an enameled basin. He took her feet out of the loops of rope and stood over her for a moment and said, matter-of-factly, "Some bleeding is normal." He shook his head then, and said as he went through the door. "It's over. You can get up now."

She struggled to get up, as Zella came through the door to help her dress. They had left a cloth and some pins on the table, which Zella helped her pin to her underclothes and pull on.

The whole way back to their car, Ouida rested her head on
Zella's shoulder and concentrated on getting home. No words
were spoken as they got out of the man's car and into their own.

She had soaked through the pieces of cloth they gave her
before they had gone fifteen miles, but Ouida told Zella not to
worry. "He said there would be blood." But Ouida remembered a night of blood-soaked hands, of blood on the moon,
and reeled with fear. Zella stopped the car twice to change the
cloths and tried to stay calm.

Ten miles later, Ouida began to whisper, "It's not right, Zella,
it's not right," and Zella looked back over the seat and felt a rising panic. She pulled the car over and grabbed at the newspapers
on the floor of the backseat, arranging them under and around
Ouida to soak up the fevered blood, chanting one of Tennyson's
verses they had both been made to memorize in high school.

" 'It little profits that an idle king . . .' Say it with me,
Ouida, come on now . . . 'By this still hearth, among these
barren crags . . .' " Zella recited.

Ouida kept up for the first few lines, as Zella tried to start
the car over and over, missing her timing with the clutch.

" 'I cannot rest from travel, I will drink . . .' "

Ouida whispered, anchoring herself with the long-
remembered words. But she heard rushing water in the distance somewhere and, looking for the source, she raised
herself up and then slipped further and further down as her
head fell back to the seat.

" '. . . alone, on shore, and when . . .' "The water rushing,
she knew she heard it, and she turned around, searching in
sunken darkness around her, and heard the faint whisper of
Zella's voice.

" '. . . have suffered greatly, both with those who loved
me and . . .' " She heard the water, and she could hear Zella.
And then she let go.

Zella managed to get the car started, and raced back to the city, going over and over their options. She knew that they could not go back to the shiny black car where the road divided, and that even if they could make it back there, they would never be able to find the shack again. She picked up the verse again, reciting now for herself. " '. . . To rust unburnished, not to shine in use . . .' "

Ouida found herself turning round and round in search of the water that she heard, and then saw the mouth of a tunnel, which she entered, alone, no longer linked to Zella's voice.

She followed the water sounds through the dark tunnel, feeling her way along the sides of the passage with her hands, and came to a little cave, carved from the side, a hole almost, half underground but with an opening above, which seemed to blossom into itself, jeweled green and soft with the moistness of moss and unruly grass, water spilling down over the edges of rocks, once jagged, and now eroded smooth. The earth, wet and heavy, held the blooming place like a secret, and at its opening, Ouida stood.

Zella had almost reached the edge of town, speeding as she continued reciting. " '. . . as though to breathe were life . . .' "

Ouida yearned to sink her fingers into the clay, to touch the tangled roots it hid, to feel it against her and the water raining, beating on her skin.

She stood at the mouth, stunned by its dark and wild beauty. By its secret. And she reached out her hand, to find, between her and the water, a set of iron bars.

She wanted the place, needed it, and thrusting her hands between the bars, she tried to reach it, tried but couldn't reach, but tried reaching and reaching.

Zella had to think of a doctor who would accept her explanation of a miscarriage and take the risk of helping them. The only

name she could come up with was Dr. Miles, a family friend. As
she drove, she focused on reaching the safety of his house.

When they got there, he told her that he couldn't. Just that
he couldn't help, and she had pushed her hand into his closing door and refused to leave until he gave her the name of
someone who could. She ran back to the car and drove to the
address, her foot shaking so violently above the pedal that she
almost couldn't drive, unaware until she got there that he was
not a doctor, but a veterinarian.

And he had tried to help. When Zella had knocked at his
door, he had answered with a dinner napkin still tucked into
his collar. "Yes, may I help you? What's wrong, child? Don't
just stand there, tell me what's wrong."

She took him to the car, where Ouida was stretched out on
the backseat, surrounded with bloody newspapers, and he
stood on the sidewalk looking up and down the street. "Help
me get her inside."

Once they were inside, he told her what kind of doctor he
was, and Zella just stood there and looked at him with her
mouth open.

He gave her some medication and told her to go home, afraid
to send her for a doctor. "What I do in this office is one thing, but
I cannot allow you to go to a hospital. They will know exactly
what you've done." Before they left he asked if they were sisters,
and Zella's silence was the only answer she gave.

Ouida woke in a hospital days later, to the sound of a door,
shutting? Opening? She wasn't sure. In the quiet of the night,
it seemed as if it was the only sound there was.

Reborn in the still blankness, and unsure, Ouida found herself, again and again, waking to the sound of that door.

She returned from the memory shaken, stunned with the
past's consumption of the present. The memory would revisit

her, a month later . . . a year later . . . in that plateau of the day that has been left unclaimed by tasks. And every time she woke from it, she recognized the smell of rich wet earth.

———

Helen Elaine Lee, born in 1959 and raised in Detroit, was educated at Harvard College and Harvard Law School. For almost a decade, she practiced law in Chicago and Washington, D.C., and wrote fiction on the side. The balance shifted in 1994 with the publication of her richly textured first novel, The Serpent's Gift, a saga of an extended family group that endures prejudice and tragedy, and manages, in Lee's words, to "pull light out of darkness." Currently an assistant professor of writing and humanistic studies at the Massachusetts Institute of Technology in Cambridge, Lee is close to completing her second novel, Water Marked.

AFRAID OF THE DARK

Valerie Wilson Wesley

Reena," David said softly. No one called her that but him. Her name was Irene, but he had always thought that the softness of "Reena" fit her better. She turned to face him, and for a moment the old warmth flashed in her eyes. But it disappeared as quickly as it came.

"How have you been?"

"All right," she said. There was a sadness in her voice that hadn't been there before. Had he put it there? he wondered. She waved at someone across the room and, turning back to him, said, "It's been a while, hasn't it, David?" The scent of her perfume took him back to the times they'd made love in his small, dark place on Valley Street, where her smell had lingered in the sheets long after she'd left. The dim lights in the crowded room highlighted the rich chestnut color of her skin. He had tried more than once to capture its warmth on canvas. But he never had.

Their eyes met briefly, then hers moved to a man across the room, the one she had waved to. Her smile to him signaled that she would be back in a moment, and that this man to whom she spoke was of no importance. It told David what he already knew—he had waited too long. He felt angry, then jealous. He was immediately ashamed of both feelings. He had no right to either.

"Are you still painting," Reena asked, "or have you gotten a job?" She said it with a bitchy edge that hadn't been part of her when he'd known her. Had he taught her that, too, he wondered, leaving his bitterness in her as silently as he'd once left his seed?

"Painting is my job, Reena. You know that." He said it quietly, and wasn't sure whether she heard it over the din of the music. But he had told her that so often when they were together, it almost didn't matter now.

She changed the subject. "How is Gerald these days? Still up to no good?"

David studied her with disbelief. How could she not have heard? The numbing sadness that had been part of him since his brother's death swept over him again.

"He's dead, Reena. He died last summer of a stroke." Her own sadness was fresh now as she grabbed his hand and held it with a tenderness he hadn't known since she'd left him. "I called you a couple of times, but I couldn't seem to catch up with you." He said it lightly, as if it hadn't hurt. But the truth was, he had never needed anyone as much as he'd needed Reena back then.

Gerald wasn't supposed to die at forty-five. The eight-year gap between them had seemed to narrow as they got older, and they had shared so much. David felt even now that there was so much more he could have learned from his brother, so much more laughter they should have shared, women they should have discussed, stories they could have traded.

Reena glanced across the room at the man she had come with. David avoided looking at him. He had always been possessive of her, and he didn't want to find that look now in another man's eyes.

"I left some messages on your machine," he said.

"I didn't return them."

"Why?" he asked, but he knew the answer.

"You know why," she said evenly.

A familiar pain seeped into his chest. His eyes shifted to a woman in turquoise whose dress clung so smoothly it was almost musical. Reena watched him.

"Still can't keep your eye on one woman at a time," she said with an amused smirk.

Other women had been a problem in the four years they'd been together, but only once had he done more than look, and she had forgiven him for that. She'd known how much he loved her. Even after all this time, he couldn't recall a woman that he enjoyed touching more than Reena. Her tenderness had freed concealed parts of him, and there was a fervor in their love-making that neither of them had previously known.

When he thought about it now, David realized that his father had had as much to do with his decision about the baby as anything else. He had thought that he had finally reached the point where he was indifferent to him, and it had been a welcome absence of feeling. But when Reena had told him she was pregnant, his father's ghost and all that it brought with it had come marching back.

He'd been happy at first, as happy as she was. That had been clear to both of them.

"What should we do?" she'd asked, trying hard to contain her excitement. They had been together long enough to be invited to baby showers and children's birthday parties. Her younger sister had three sons, and Reena carried their pictures around as if they were charms. She was thirty-four years old, and she couldn't pass a child without making some fond comment, or see a baby without wanting to hold it.

"I don't know," he finally said, with a perplexed giggle. It was the most honest thing he could say.

For a week or so, her excitement had been contagious. David had pulled out an old photo album and turned the pages, studying this uncle's nose, that aunt's lips, his own baby self. Names came to him—Jamal, Warren. Or maybe Gerald, after his uncle.

That night he awakened at five and realized that he hadn't told Gerald about the baby. Gerald would just be getting home from his night shift as a security guard, David knew, and because he couldn't go back to sleep, he had decided to go see him.

They'd sat on Gerald's couch sipping gin and orange juice, Gerald's version of a breakfast drink.

"You'll have to stop painting and ask Bernstein to take you on full time," Gerald said as he lit a cigarette. David just sipped his drink.

"How the hell did she manage to get pregnant?" Gerald demanded suddenly. "You've been living together damn near four years, and now she's getting pregnant?"

David, stunned by Gerald's outburst, shrugged and looked past his head, through the filmy gray windowpane to a tree beyond. The tree had begun to sprout buds. It was nearly springtime; David had almost forgotten it.

"I ran into Pop yesterday afternoon," Gerald said, changing the subject.

"Yeah? What's he up to?"

"Same old shit." They both laughed. "We talked for a minute about old times and, you know, what's he doing, what he's going to do, what he always wanted to do for us."

"Yeah," David said. "The usual shit."

"Yeah. Pop's not looking so good, man. Looks like he's about to croak."

"Well, man, you know what they say. Such is life."

Gerald splashed some vodka into his brother's now empty glass. Then his refilled his own.

"To Pop," Gerald said. They clinked glasses.

"Bastard," David muttered under his breath. After that they drank in silence, each of them thinking about their father.

It was a pact between them: They never discussed their father's ways—his temper, his cruelty—even with each other. The silent pain bound and trapped them. They alone knew how deeply it cut, and that it had never healed.

"Hey, man," Gerald said finally. "I meant to ask you about the Lockspur show. I couldn't make it over there, but I heard it was slammin'."

"I sold the big one, bro'. The big one. Three grand. I couldn't believe it when Lockspur handed me that check. There was a write-up about it."

"I saw it. You know I'm going to read anything they have to say about my little brother." Gerald lifted his glass in a mock toast. "Our family name might be up in lights despite the rest of us, you jive little nigger." He gulped his drink and hugged David. "Go for it, baby. Tell the world to kiss your talented black ass!"

David hugged Gerald back. He noticed tears glistening in the corners of his brother's eyes, but Gerald quickly blinked them away. David hugged him again, tighter, not wanting to let go. And then he'd gone home to Reena.

"How'd you get pregnant?" he asked her that night after dinner, as they were cleaning up the kitchen.

"I don't know," she said lightly. "I suppose the same way women have gotten pregnant since the beginning of time."

"Why didn't you put in your diaphragm? We've been living together four years and nothing like this ever happened before."

Reena tore a piece of aluminum foil off the roll and carefully placed it around a glass bowl containing leftover potatoes.

"It was a mistake. It happened. I'm pregnant," she shrugged. "Nothing is one hundred percent sure."

"Well, it's a mistake that I don't feel like paying for for the rest of my life!" He hadn't meant it to sound like it did, but he hadn't stopped himself either. Reena recoiled as if he'd slapped her.

"Do you really feel that you would end up paying with your life for a child we would have?" she said quietly.

David noisily scraped leftovers from his plate into the trash. He avoided Reena's eyes.

"I know how much it would mean to you. I know how much it would mean to me. Maybe at some point we can have kids . . ."

"Are you telling me to get an abortion?" Reena asked, her voice incredulous, her head tilted at a funny angle, like a child asking for the truth about a lie she had been told.

"We can have kids at some point . . ." he repeated.

Reena snatched his plate away from him. Fiercely, she squirted dishwashing liquid on top of the dishes in the sink and turned on the water. When she spoke again, her voice was perfectly controlled. "David," she said, "I will be thirty-five years old in November, and I'm pregnant and want to have this child. We've been together for four years. How can you ask me to kill it?"

He moved angrily away from her. "It was a mistake, damn it. You said so yourself. Reena, don't romanticize this thing. We're not kids. We're not playing house. We have control of our lives. We weren't planning a baby. Neither of us is ready."

Reena faced him and touched her still firm stomach. "Part of you is growing inside me, and I can't forget that. It may have been a mistake to begin with, but half of us who are here are mistakes . . . I mean . . . we could . . ."

"I just told you I don't want to have it!" David burst out. There was an impatience in his voice he hadn't meant to put there. But it was there now and he was glad of it. "I just told you I can't deal with it, not the money, not the dependency. None of it!"

"I don't want to wait!" Reena screamed. She hadn't raised her voice since they'd begun talking and now it was almost welcome. "I don't want to wait. Wait? Wait until you've sold more paintings? Wait until you're established? How long will that be, David?" She lowered her voice. "Three years? Ten?"

She searched his eyes for an answer, an affirmation. She reached out to touch his shoulder and then his cheek with the soft, moist palm of her hand. "David," she whispered. "People manage. They get by. They have children and they take care of them and they get by. The same way my parents did, your parents did . . . "

David hurled his glass into the sink; its splintering fragments clattered against the porcelain sides.

"Well, then have it!" he shouted. He glared at Reena, who stared back at him, her eyes surprised and frightened. He wasn't sure where his anger had come from so suddenly, but it shook him violently, like a spasm, pouring from his mouth, rising from the very deepest part of his being. He grabbed her by the shoulders and shook her as hard as he could. "Have it, goddamn it! Have it!" he yelled. "Be like the thousand other women with one or two kids trying to scrape together on chickenshit. End up like your sister. End up like my mother!"

He had never touched her in anger before, and it frightened him as much as it frightened her. He thought of his father then, and the rage that seemed to come from nowhere and the jagged wounds he had put upon his mother's face on drunken Friday nights. He thought about the time Gerald hit his father, before he left home for good, and how after that he had been alone for the beatings. He forced his hands to his side, but he'd shaken Reena longer and harder than he knew, and when he let go of her, she fell backwards against the table. He was still angry. He didn't want to see the fear in her eyes—like the fear in his mother's eyes—and so he left the house without looking at her.

He spent the night at Gerald's. They finished a fifth of scotch and a dime bag of weed, and he fell out on the couch.

He couldn't recall the last time he had done that. He called a woman he had slept with before Reena moved in and spent the next two nights with her. When he came back home to Reena, the woman's perfume still clung to him. He told himself he didn't care.

"I made an appointment at the clinic to get a D&C on Thursday," Reena announced as he came in the door. "Will you be there at four to pick me up?" Her voice was firm, with no warmth or feeling. He nodded that he would.

David arrived at the clinic at three-thirty. He read magazines three months old and stared into the faces of the women who came and went. Neither he nor Reena spoke in the cab on the way home. When they got back to the apartment, he asked her if he could fix her something to eat. She just looked at him like she didn't understand what he was saying.

They were together for another week, and then one morning, Reena packed up her things and moved out. Six months after that, Gerald died. That had been more than a year ago. This evening, this place, with the music too loud and too many people jostling them, was the first time David had seen her since then.

David tried to think of something more to say but couldn't. Reena smiled at him, pleasantly, noncommittally, but David couldn't smile back. When her friend motioned to her from across the room, David kissed her on the forehead the way he used to and watched her move away from him.

He went to get a drink, then walked over to the woman in turquoise who moved like music. They started talking, but in the middle of their conversation, he couldn't remember what he was saying; he excused himself and went to get another drink. When he came back, the woman was with another man, so he stood against the wall, talking about the

Knicks to someone he had played ball with in the neighbor-hood earlier that summer.

It was dawn when he finally left the party. Walking down the stairs to the street, he realized that it was much cooler out than when he had come. Wind from the river sent a chill through his body, and he pulled his lightweight jacket tight. But he couldn't stop shivering.

"I'm drunk," he said to himself as he sat down on the stairs. Waves of nausea and self-disgust shot through him. The chill wouldn't leave. He held onto himself then, holding and hugging his own trembling body as Gerald had held him when they'd been boys sharing a closet made into a room, and he'd been afraid of the dark.

———•———

Valerie Wilson Wesley's short story "Afraid of the Dark" was the last she wrote before starting her best-selling Tamara Hayle mystery series, which features a hip, tough African American sleuth who is also a single mother. Wesley herself is married, the mother of two grown daughters. She studied philosophy at Howard University in Washington, D.C., and earned a master's from Bank Street College of Education before switching to journalism. A graduate of Columbia University's Graduate School of Journalism, she later became executive editor of Essence magazine. Her books include five Tamara Hayle novels; a young adult novel, Where Do I Go From Here *(1993), for which she received an American Library Association Best Book citation; and a picture book for children,* Freedom's Gifts: A Juneteenth Story *(1995). Wesley is currently at work on* Charmed, *a nongenre novel, and her sixth mystery.*

WEST COAST
EPISODE

June Jordan

Eddie hung a light globe with the best electric
tape
he could find in
five minutes

then he left the room where he lives
to meet me
            (in Los Angeles)
Meanwhile the light globe fell and
smashed glass everywhere
            (the waterbed
            was dangerous
            for days)
but we used the paperbag that hid
the dollar-twenty-nine-California-Champagne
to hide
the lightbulb
with a warm brown atmosphere

and that
worked really well

so there was no problem
except
we had to walk like feet
on broken seashells
even though

the color of the rug was green
and out beyond the one room
of our love
the world was mostly
dry.

——◆—◆◆—◆——

June Jordan pursues themes of justice and tenderness. Of her latest collection, Kissing God Goodbye *(1998), one critic wrote, "June Jordan is a poet for whom political conviction exists in the same universe of moral effort as love—erotic, familial, and humanistic . . ." The award-winning author of more than two dozen books, the poet is also a clear-sighted essayist and dedicated activist. Her credits include such acclaimed works as 1994's* Technical Difficulties, *a volume of essays and reflections, and* I Was Looking at the Ceiling and Then I Saw the Sky, *an opera set in South Central Los Angeles, for which Jordan wrote the lyrics and the libretto. A New Yorker born and raised, Jordan is currently a professor of African American studies at the University of California at Berkeley. "West Coast Episode" appears in* Haruko/Love Poems, *a cycle of poems written over the course of twenty-two years, in which Jordan explores how love can bridge differences of gender, geography, and race.*

ODE TO
ARETHA

Evelyn C. White

he last time I talked to Aretha Franklin we exchanged a few words about Coretta Scott King. It was in the fall of 1981, after Aretha had given a spine-tingling concert at Radio City Music Hall in New York City. By telling the security staff that I was Martin Luther King's daughter, I had gained entry to the backstage room where the Queen of Soul stood in a muted black tuxedo and fluffy pink house shoes.

I stood at the outer edges of the love-drunk throng that circled Aretha and waited patiently for my turn to pay homage to the Queen. Aretha politely greeted each admirer as she puffed languidly on a menthol cigarette. Although gracious, she definitely gave the impression that she would rather have been in a setting more in sync with her shoes. Rising like luscious brown dinner rolls from the tube top she wore under her tuxedo jacket, Aretha's breasts, like her feet, seemed to be begging to go home.

After a few minutes I was ushered to the front of the crowd by a towering Black man who proudly introduced me to Aretha as "Martin's daughter." Taking a deep drag on her cigarette, Aretha smiled demurely, looked me in the eye, and gently asked, "How's your mother?" Festooned in a yellow bandanna, a paint-splattered sweatshirt, and bright red parachute pants, I met Aretha's gaze and calmly replied, "Fine." Before she received the next person, the Queen of Soul turned back toward me and said, "You look different, but then again, it's been a long time."

It's been nearly thirty years since I first heard the electrifying shouts and moans of Aretha Franklin. Since then, I've bought just about every album she has recorded, seen her perform live whenever I could, and filed every scrap of paper bearing her name that I ever found. And while I would never engage in such tomfoolery today, I am not ashamed to fess up to the schemes I concocted to meet Aretha—all in the spirit of reexperiencing a past that so strongly informs my identity today. I am willing to reveal my passion for the Queen of Soul because she has always been willing to open her heart and let listeners feel her joys and pains. In a culture where Black women are taught to numb, blockade, detour, stifle, dismiss, and ignore our feelings, Aretha Franklin has shown us how to open ourselves and be free. Her expansive and unbridled bosom says it all.

One of my most vivid childhood memories is of my mother and her friends sitting in our living room talking about Aretha. The scene is Gary, Indiana, in the late 1960s. Back then, Gary was a flourishing steel town flanked by the sand dunes of Lake Michigan on one side and the hip grandeur of Chicago on the other. The perpetually burning furnaces at the mill released a fiery orange smoke that enveloped the city and ultimately became Gary's most famous landmark. But we were not worried about air pollution, toxic waste, or protecting the environment back in those days. As a child, I loved looking up into the shimmering orange haze the steel mill had painted against the blue sky. It was like finding dreamsicles in heaven.

For Blacks fleeing the hardships of the South, the mill provided a pathway to their dreams. With the hearths going full

blast twenty-four hours a day, 365 days a year, the mill offered
steady jobs for Black men without high-school, let alone college, diplomas. On the paychecks they brought home from the
mill, the men in my neighborhood were able to keep dinner
roasts on the table and car notes for Ford Galaxies and Chevy
Impalas paid. Their labor bought Easter clothes, *Ebony* sub-
scriptions, hula hoops, chemistry sets, and piping-hot bags of
popcorn from Sears. Thanks to a strong economy, the term
"female-headed household" was nonexistent during my childhood years. An "absentee father" was a man who worked hol-
idays or a double shift at the mill.

It was during the late-night hours when the menfolk were
at the mill that I recall my mother and her friends gathering
to talk about their lives in spirited and sensual conversa-
tions during which they often shared their feelings about
"Sister Ree." While other neighborhood women dropped in
from time to time, the group that usually came to my house
included: Mrs. McCann, a large, fun-loving mother of ten,
Mrs. Henry, a salty-tongued woman whose right side had
been paralyzed by a stroke, and Mrs. Smith, a Seventh-Day
Adventist who had a shiny black myna bird named Duchess
that mimicked every word we said.

With regard to Black music in the late 1960s, The Word
was definitely Aretha Franklin. In soulful arrangements that
blended her gospel roots with the driving funk of rhythm and
blues, Aretha released a series of hits for Atlantic Records that
put the "H" in holler and the "G" in get down. Along with
the James Brown tune "Say It Loud! I'm Black and I'm
Proud," Aretha's "Respect" had become an anthem of the
Civil Rights movement. With its plaintive and sassy lyrics, the
song had also emerged as a bold commentary on relationships
between Black women and Black men. Twelve years old when

it was released, I remember feeling a sense of triumphant ela-
tion whenever I heard Aretha belt out "Respect." "Here's a
sister who ain't taking no mess," I'd think to myself as Aretha
wailed. Her impassioned, soulful licks and sly innuendos
about sexual pleasure made me feel good about myself both
as a Black American and as a young girl about to discover sex.

My feelings about Aretha were validated by the voices I
heard as I stood pajama-clad in the hallway, eavesdropping on
my mother and her friends. With the ink-black darkness of the
bedrooms at my back, I'd lean against the furnace room door,
my right ear pressed against its slats. I would pitch my left ear
out toward the living room where an amber pool of light put
a loving glow on the words that drifted back to me.

"Girl, have you heard Aretha's new record?" That was
usually the voice of Gerri McCann, who lived three doors
down in a red house that was the closest to the highway
entrance if you were driving to Chicago. Her proximity to
the big city and the fact that she had more children than any
other woman on the block gave Mrs. McCann an earthy
"worldliness" that both attracted and intimidated me. I
thought she was cool because one afternoon when I was visiting her daughter Yvonne, Mrs. McCann put Marvin
Gaye's "Hitchhike" on the record player and danced—her
fleshy body flailing wildly around the room. But she also
unnerved me because I figured a mother who would "shake
it" in front of neighborhood children was liable to say or do
anything—like ask me in broad daylight if my period had
started or if I was wearing a bra.

Her question hovered in the living room air for a minute as
my mother and her friends geared up for the conversation.
"Girl, I heard it on the radio just the other day, and I went
right to the record shop and bought it," Mittie Smith would

say. "You know Aretha can't sing unless she's in pain. She must really be in bad shape 'cause this song is just too tough."

"We . . . ll, I re . . . ad in *Jet* that her hus . . . band beat her up," said Mrs. Henry, whose Mississippi drawl crawled heavily since her stroke. "I wish a nig . . . ger would try to go up . . . side *my* head. I'd knock him o . . . ut."

"Myra, you know you ain't got but one good arm left," my mother would say, prompting affirming guffaws from Mrs. Smith and Mrs. McCann. "You best be trying to keep it."

With that the whole group would fall out in a burst of laughter that rolled down the hallway, accented by the clinking of ice cubes in their Bacardi-filled glasses. "They're having fun," I'd think to myself happily. "They're having a good time."

It was thus through the prism of Aretha Franklin that I first came to see my mother and her friends as Black women with lives outside of cooking, cleaning, taking care of husbands and kids. As I stood in the hallway, held by their conversation, I realized they had feelings, opinions, and interests in matters outside of their homes. I came to understand that the women who laughed and cussed about their thighs getting stuck to our plastic-covered sofa had not always been mothers and wives; I began to see glimmers of them as young women who'd once dressed up and stayed out late finger-poppin' at parties. I pictured them as being bashful, raucous, giddy, vulnerable, and timid. I also imagined their aspirations and dreams.

Years later, I realized that my innate physical and emotional desires for women were likewise being shaped by the moments I spent bearing silent witness to the interactions among my mother and her friends. I longed for the sister love that filled our living room.

One night they were talking about "Ain't No Way" and that high note Cissy Houston hit ("and held, baby") singing background. Then the discussion shifted to a topic that nearly caused me to blow my cover in the hallway. As usual, it was Mrs. McCann who got things rolling: "Sometimes, when Ezra and I are screwing, honey, it feels so good. I just wanna scream."

"Girl, I know exactly what you mean," Mrs. Smith quickly added.

Screwing? Ezra? That was Mr. McCann, a tall, light-skinned man who was always smiling and appeared totally nonplussed by the fact that he had a dozen mouths to feed. Caught off guard by Mrs. McCann's comments, I immediately flashed on the box of small silver screws my father kept in his toolbox. With his maroon-handled screwdriver he'd twist and grind the screws into place as he fixed broken pot handles or assembled Christmas toys. I was deep in thought about the matter when Mrs. McCann began to pant and make mock sighs of pleasure. I got the picture. I'd seen enough Troy Donahue movies to know exactly what they were talking about.

"Sex," it dawned on me with such force that it seemed as if I'd bellowed the word out loud. "Mrs. McCann is talking about doing the nasty."

Once I got over the shock of hearing this mother of ten talk dirty, I was mesmerized by the conversation which, other than the initial comments, I can only remember in muted tones and impressions. I do know that I was not ashamed, embarrassed, or upset about the words or images that drifted from the living room down the hallway to me. I sensed no hurt or pain in the sentiments my mother and her friends expressed about sex. On the contrary, I remember the ease, excitement, and openness with which they talked to each other. They shared an intimacy and closeness that defined Black sisterhood for me for life.

The "Ain't No Way" sex conversation was also important because it distinguished my mother and her friends from Donna Reed, June Cleaver, and the other television moms who'd been a part of my upbringing. Like many Black children of the era, I secretly longed for a family that was as ordered, polite, and stable as the Cleavers and the Reeds. I wanted a dad like Ward Cleaver who carried a briefcase and wore a suit and tie to work instead of a blue work shirt. I wanted a perfectly coiffed mother who peeled potatoes wearing high heels, a dainty apron, and a tasteful strand of pearls.

But after the "screwing" discussion I began to see the shallow emptiness in the lives of the white television mothers. The "perfect" TV families against which many Black children unfairly measured their own, lacked the warmth and spontaneity of the homes in which they were raised. I could not imagine June or Donna uttering a syllable about sex, let alone using the delightfully graphic terms and descriptions that rolled so easily off Mrs. McCann's tongue. The sex conversation made me feel proud of my mother and her friends for being passionate and sensual women. Standing in the hallway, I was happy to hear them talk about desire and their appreciation of husbands who, in the words of Aretha, gave them their "propers" when they got home from the mill.

Of course, on the flip side of passion there is the possibility of heartache. And the Queen of Soul has always given Black women an effective remedy for romance gone down the tubes.

Despite her well-documented history of man trouble, Aretha is never downtrodden, pitiful, or defeated when she sings. Take "Don't Play That Song for Me," her signature tune about a troubled love affair. Far from playing a victim, Aretha delivers an assertive, power-packed directive making it clear that she doesn't want any part of the smooth-talking man who did her wrong. Calling her lover on his false pledge of devotion, she counters his every declaration of love with a soulful reminder that he lied. Even in pain and heartbroken, Sister Ree stays in charge.

Truth is, regardless of the turmoil in her love life, Aretha's artistry makes it impossible to feel sorry for her. You just can't imagine her depressed, blowing her brains out, or overdosing (à la Billie Holiday) over a man. Not the Queen of Soul.

Setting a healthy model for other sisters to follow, Aretha opens her mouth, sings about her misery, and gets it out of her system. And when she's finished shouting and screaming, you know Aretha is heading straight for the kitchen. You can picture her at the stove in her fluffy pink house shoes, puffing on a cigarette as she checks on her pot of greens. Heartbreak notwithstanding, she's made it clear that no man is going to stop her show.

My mother died just as Aretha was hitting her disco phase. The McCanns moved to Chicago. Two of Mrs. Henry's daughters got murdered, and Mrs. Smith's husband went to his shoe repair shop one day and never came home. When I cajoled my way into that dressing room at Radio City Music Hall, I was searching for a path back to cherished childhood memories. More than anything, I wanted to recapture the warm love and joyous laughter that was shared between four Black women and filtered to me through a soft, amber light. I hope that Aretha and the King family don't mind.

A nationally recognized lecturer on feminist issues, Evelyn C. White is the author of Chain, Chain, Change: For Black

Women in Abusive Relationships *(1995) and the award-winning* Black Women's Health Book: Speaking for Ourselves *(1994). She also coauthored the 1993 photography book* The African Americans *and was the associate producer of the 1996 documentary* I Shall Not Be Moved: The Life of Marion Riggs. *A graduate of Wellesley College and Columbia University's Graduate School of Journalism, White earned a master's in public administration from Harvard University in 1991. She has written for the* Wall Street Journal, *the* San Francisco Chronicle, Essence, POZ, *and* Sojourner, *among many other publications. A visiting scholar in women's studies at Mills College in Oakland, she serves on the board of the Soapstone Women's Retreat in Oregon and the Harvard Club of San Francisco. She is the official biographer of the Pulitzer Prize–winning writer Alice Walker.*

TRUTH OR
CONSEQUENCES

Carolyn Ferrell

1. Look at her. See that mouth? Chapped. Desert dry. Little lip flakes falling on her shirt over her titanic titties growing milk like a gas pump. Broken kisser. That's one of the first signs. She can't do it right anymore. She closes her eyes and leans her back on the janitor's closet door, but it's just not like it was before. It does not taste like daydreams. It's like something savory left behind, over the roof of the mouth. Something from the good old days. You know how when snakes lose their skin? Well, it's like that.

2. It mainly happens in the ninth grade of life.

3. The teachers start attending you differently, asking hard questions to prove that your brain isn't dying away. It does so happen. The brain cells lead a precarious life, with only certain variables affecting their fleeting status. Alcohol, weed, too much television with the lights off, little unexpected bundles of joy in your oven. You can start to forget things, even things like your mother's maiden name. You can't sign a damn permission slip to go to the Museum of Natural History in New York City. Your handwriting's all off. The teachers then profound you, all for the sake of those dying brain cells. They

want to save you. But then they tell you: The capital of Vermont is not Vermont City. It is not Vermontville. Give me the square root of 3. Name a Founding Father. Can you recite the Preamble without looking? And what is the meaning of this line of poetry: "Whoever you are, we too lie in drifts at your feet?" The teachers swear they are doing you a favor, that they are resuscitating you from a world of hanging darkness.

4. Her face is breaking out. Pimples don't just come in one by one, they attack like an army, and her face is the fucking Civil War. There is nothing she can do about it either. We open the *Worlds of Biology* textbook and learn all about how pimples form, about the layers of grease on the epidermis, the hair shafts, the oily deposits. We are disgusted. But she just reads it all seriously and takes short notes and writes Jude Jude Jude in the margins and draws horses in a sunny meadow every now and then and looks out the window at the chickadees sparking the snow with their feathered feet and trustworthy faces. They say to her: Join us.

5. It only happens to girls who have interesting fathers.

6. We can't run in gym class anymore, but Miss Foster makes us anyway. It's the law in New York State, she says proudly. We have to do laps just like anybody else. We have to climb the balance beam and try to pull ourselves up on the rings. If we can't run fast enough, we are hit in the backs with the kickball and that makes another out for our side but who cares not us because we are dying because our backs are the absolute unhappiest places on earth. We wear the sweaty red pinneys that smell of hurtful nonsense appetites: cornstarch straight out the box, eggs and peanut butter, sugar in mashed potatoes. The clean ones are given to girls who can really run

and sprint, the girls with floating bodies. The bright side is: We don't have to do military sit-ups. We don't have to throw *or* catch the medicine ball.

7. I meant, it only happens to girls with *interested* fathers. The kind that look over the shower curtain or who ask a daughter like LaShawn Anthony to take a walk with them early Sunday morning in the bushy park where there are places to sit down and talk and decide on her future and what-not. There is nobody around in the park. Nobody sees her clamp both of her hands on the back of her bra, trying to keep the hook in place. Nobody sees the look in her face when her lap becomes a pillow for a hungry head. Trees slash the sky, brooks whimper along the ground, pebbles plague like mothers underneath her feet. When it is over, she might sit there and admire the lace of the overhanging willow branches and see herself in every cranny, a blue escape route. Or she might go home and eat breakfast with the others and forget and feel like the clouds in the sky above are made of cement or glue or forgotten prayers. She stares out the window for a long time, wishing she were far from here, perhaps in the bright lights of New York City. That's where things happen. Not in the dirty sand bay beaches of Long Island. The truth is, she might have a wee wee in her pee pee, in which case her mother, her grandmother, her aunt and her cousin beat her on the back with a hairbrush till she is carpet-red. She screams the living daylights. They call her Backslider, Whore, Shit Head. She screams. Off in another place, her grandfather and her uncle sit in the kitchen over grits and butter and wonder what the world is coming to. The Jamaican neighbor ladies walk over with a folding card table and greasy dinner biscuits in gravy as their offering and they ask, Yes Lord, Why Our Children Must Punish Us So? Then they deal out the first hand.

8. She likes to pretend that nothing has changed. That she is still sugar, she is still a crystal girl. Last fall it was Viola Jenkins with her nerve. Viola was going so far as to try out for Homecoming Queen, so she put her name on the ballot along with the shoo-ins: Desiree Demarco, Charlene Capers, Tiffany Thompson-Williams. She went around telling people how friendly and good-hearted she was, what all she did for the school (class treasurer, radio-club president, home-economics monitor), but hell no. Do you think we cared? There were those months she did not come to school, when her brother came in and got her out-of-school suspension homework and retrieved her report cards for her aunt and her grandmother at home. Now she was back and trying out for Homecoming Queen, she had even written her name on the ballot. We laughed. In the hallway, Charlene Capers asked her, So how you going to count Little Marvin? What activity he is? He come under chess club? And we laughed even harder. The result was that later, through grapevines and hard hallway stares and little tappings of the heart, Viola got into a fight with Charlene Capers and broke the girl's collarbone with her own little hands. In Science 9, Desiree told folks Viola could've smothered Charlene to death with her titties. We laughed. We knew. You can't change fate.

In November, the Homecoming Queen was Lilac Wilson. Viola was back at home, with the next one. At the football game and ceremony, Lilac's mother walked around with Lilac's bouquet of roses and baby's breath and her diamond crown in her gloves. She cried, The Lord Have His Mercy, Good Things Come to Those Who Wait.

9. They fall asleep everywhere. It's embarrassing as sin. In class, on the sidewalk, in the Long Island Rail Road waiting

room. Me and Lulu had planned to go all the way to New York City, but then we didn't have the fare and the conductor looked at us like trash. After he kicked us out, we walked to the Night-Night Store at the Massapequa Station instead, and we bought some things with mad sugar in them: miniature donuts, grape athletic punch, Now and Laters. Lulu said she needed sugar to help her keep her eyes open. She said she felt like the walking dead. Her belly looked like a spare tire and sank down into the sidewalk with every step. She was wearing Gene's sneakers, the ugly ones people call Skips. She only had money for the Night-Night Store.

We found a place to sit on the curb and then I told Lulu about the money I was planning on getting, all fifty-five bucks in cash money, and how I was going to the beauty shop in town to get my nails done, how Mrs. Wilson there could work wonders even with the ends bitten off to the beginning, and how I was getting what they call French tips, how I would wave them this way and that. I would get noticed. Lulu asked, How you getting that money? I looked down. The truth is always loud and clear to someone in the background. She opened up her can of punch. She said, I don't plan on getting fat till the absolute end. But you. *You don't need to get fat— ever.* You don't have no reason to get yourself noticed. You better watch the fuck out.

Lulu glared at me and waited. She wanted me to agree with her. I made up a crazy story. When this happens, my palms sweat but there is no other way out of the grave I am digging with my tongue. I told her that the money would be a gift from my uncle Todd. That he always brought me gifts when he visited from Jamaica. That he once brought me a coconut doll, and another time it was those sugarcane candies. I told her this time he gave me money. It wasn't all a lie. I did have an uncle Todd. Lulu rolled her eyes and blew these perfect rings out her mouth. She said, If I had money for every time I got money, then well, I just don't know. She looked hard at me again and tossed the empty can in the gutter grate.

The night was full of early fireflies confused by the parking lot headlights. A smell of old beer embraced me and her, making us feel warmer than we should have in that pre-summer air. But it wasn't all a lie. In reality I once had loved my uncle from Jamaica. I used to sit on his crossed leg and play horse. I remember him now in the kind of light you remember rosy things, not in the gray lens of your everyday misery. I said to Lulu, When I was little and cute, I told everybody I was going to grow up and marry Uncle Todd, you know how those things are. A girl's voice in a girl's heart. And he used to tell me, You won't have long to wait, baby girl.

In reality he first used to bring one girlfriend over from the island with him, an old lady, and then he brought another one, this one having blond-dyed hair and a monster-size ass. She wore African and her name was Carrie. She spoke to us in songs. We could listen to that voice all day, and she wouldn't be saying much of anything. Then one summer on his visit my uncle started taking out my sister's junior-high friend Samantha, seeing her behind our backs, and even though she was only in ninth grade, boom boom they got married. She found this bridal gown in the thrift shop of St. Martin of Tours and she loved looking at herself in the mirror, her brown relaxed hair, her crooked teeth. Todd told her the lights in her eyes reminded him of the sparklers of Spanish Town.

They had lied about her age in New Jersey and got married. When they returned my sister didn't want to speak to Samantha. She made Samantha give back her autograph book, and when Samantha started showing, my sister used to dump a bucket of cold water on her head whenever she came to our door. My sister would wait by the upstairs window with the mop bucket. You could hear the ice cubes sloshing. Meanwhile my mother told my father, You bring that cradle-robbing bastard back in here, and you can count your days left living.

I would see Samantha on the street now and then looking huge and hurting and hunted. I never knew why he gave up Carrie. Samantha would tell me lies, like her and Todd were planning to move to St. Albans Queens or Cambria Heights or Flushing. She was nothing like Carrie. As for me, Uncle Todd would catch me on the way home from school and stroke my braids in front of the Village Courthouse. The way he looked at me was like a tranquilizer. He always had the same soft words, the same soft baby voice, even after he married Samantha. You won't have long to wait.

Lulu snored. Her head was leaning against a car door. I felt myself fuming. Her lines and lines of cornrows, whitened with lint, had come aloose. I was getting ready to leave her ass there in the parking lot of the Night-Night Store and walk home by myself. How can you just have an athletic grape punch and here you be snoring. I got about ten steps away when she came to and ran up to me and grabbed my arm. I know why he gave up Carrie, she whispered. It was like she had just had a dream. Her breath was stank and heavy, and the spare tire began to move like a ghost. She said to me, Sarah! Do you know how many times *my eyes* looked like the sparklers of Spanish Town? And *here I am*.

10. Sometimes they get religion. Michelline Hamilton's mother made her become a Jehovah's Witness and ask the Holy Father for forgiveness before the one meal she was allowed to have every day: lunch with milk. She also had to walk from door to door in North Amityville with her baby brother Carl and ask ladies if they had a moment in their busy day to spare,

if would they be interested in discussing the Word of the Lord. He can provide us comfort in our most derelict times. Do you know that the Lord created all things, great and small, and that we must accept His glorious deeds? The Lord is in every little crevice of our broken lives. The ladies at Jefferson Estates smiled, the ladies along Albany Avenue offered her to come in and take a nap. We are His servants. Why do we go astray? Only the Lord can answer us. In July she had to wear a white suit, in October she had to wear a brown suit, to match the leaves on the ground. Her feet grew two sizes bigger and flatter. The Lord leadeth me to still waters. Where are those still waters? Her older sister Maya, who didn't belong to any church except the Church of the Heathen, laughed when she told me their mother forced Michelline to wash out her dress suit every night, to get out that horrible child smell that was coming off of Michelline's skin. She laughed when she told me that their mother beat Michelline's back and shoulders with a pancake flipper, that she made her cut all that beautiful black hair off her head. Their mother said, You don't have any fear in me, well baby you gonna have some fear in the Lord.

One time she broke Michelline's wrist with that flipper. Her older brother Jackson smacked her in the face on a regular basis and told her to stay away from his basketball friends. Then one time they had to rush her to the doctor's because she fainted, only to find out it was a heart ailment, probably there since her special condition had come on. Michelline got some vitamins, and her doctor told her to drink one cup of cold black coffee every morning, but her mother said, Damn doctors don't always know the truth of things, and then Michelline was back out there, the sun hot even for November, knocking on the doors, looking the ladies of the house in the face, asking, Can the Lord answer your questions today?

11. It is true that some of them do actually get hitched. It happened to Mary Evans and to Mindy Bray. Mary had hers in a church, with bridesmaids. Mindy Bray did it behind closed doors at her uncle Marion's house, the one who always smiled at us from the living-room curtains. I don't know how she did it, but Mrs. Bray found a big enough wedding gown, and shoes, and a garter belt. They made up the living room all fancy, with party garlands and tablecloths and matching forks and matchboxes that read: To the Darling Couple May All Your Wishes Come True. Someone made turkey and ribs. They say Mindy was a hell of a sight. Buster had no choice but to fall in love with her, is what they also said.

Mary Evans walked down the aisle in the same dress she wore every day to school. Her mother Mrs. Evans said, You ain't but going to do this but once, so there's no need to be buying anything fancy or maternity. *You are not doing this again.* And by her look Mary Evans knew what her mother was saying to her. It shook the house, the pavement, the lawns in the neighborhood.

Mary Evans did have her hair done up fine in the neat dreadlocks, the twisted kind, the ones streaked with gold amber, the ones that aren't funky and loose. Mrs. Walker, a guest with her fourth wineglass, sighed, Bet Willa is happy her girl got that Scotty. Mrs. Johnson, diet cola, answered, These girls will stoop to anything these days. I hate to see a good boy going down. Mrs. Walker confirmed, He been down further than that, and Mrs. Johnson giggled, You bad Ernestine.

On the other front Mindy Bray ran away from home three weeks after the wedding and her babyfather didn't really want Little Bust so it looked up to Mrs. Bray to take the baby on. He turned three, and no Mindy. He turned five and the babyfather told everyone Mindy was working 42nd Street in New York

City. He knew, he had seen it from the school bus window on the trip to the Museum of Natural History. Strutting her stuff under the Neon Lights of Broadway, twirling her pocketbook. Mrs. Bray told him to stop that lying or else. Then Little Bust turned six, and then the babyfather moved to Roosevelt a few towns over, to sell things where nobody knew his face.

On the other front Mrs. Evans cried at her daughter's wedding. The groom cried. They served chips and salsa, and later a cake filled with alcoholic cherries. Mary Ann Evans name was now Mary Ann Wilson. Her mother-in-law wouldn't look at her. She said of her son, One out of three ain't such a loss.

Everyone went downstairs in the church basement and smoked. The feeling was, life had a million doors to it and there were no tigers. The groom went to college. Mary Ann had the next baby in the spring.

12. Actually, it can happen anytime. Just ask George Wilkins, Sim Blackstone, Charles Washington. Girls are not alarm clocks, not by any stretch of the imagination.

13. Todd took me out for an ice-cream sandwich. I was feeling suddenly ancient, suddenly ripe. I asked him, What about your wife? She going to be jealous? He replied, She is a thing of the past. Then he told me to put out my cigarette. Didn't I know I was too young to smoke? Give me some sugar instead. You better stop, I said, but it came out all schoolgirl. I felt my hair sag in the cold May sun. I went with him.

He had rum raisin, the flavor that only people in love eat. He swung his arm around my neck and said, Do you know your eyes call to mind the lights in Atlantic City? His arm was like a crane. I felt it lift me into a world of hunger and fleet. Little Samantha was a thing of the past. I began to desire him.

14. Some mothers do have understanding. Cherie Simone's mother was even happy for her. She made Cherie's brother's room into a nursery and took Cherie out for baby clothes after school. She cooked Cherie pizza and macaroni and cheese and German chocolate layer cakes and salt pork with greens. She looked at her daughter with eyes like yards of love.

Forsythia Grant's mother was the same. She put Forsythia up in front of the gospel choir so the little girl didn't have to strain her neck. She forced the cheerleading coach to keep her on, till things got too tight. Forsythia's mother drove her daughter to the beach, to Sunken Meadow on Long Island Sound, and told her that this was her future, all laid out in front of her like eternity. Forsythia could see straight through to the land on the other side, it was Connecticut, it wasn't no eternity, but then her mother told her to shut the fuck up and imagine.

Jaycee Crawford's mother adopted the baby as soon as it came and called it Jaycee's late-bloomer brother. Jaycee looked shamed. At first she did not want to touch the stroller, or the stove that heated the bottles. She grew out of that in time, though. Her mother had told her to love her brother. So Jaycee learned to tie his booties, his shoes, his galoshes. She even went to his graduation from kindergarten into first grade when he was eight and already writing his name and said, It's not too many girls can be proud of their little brother like me. And they said he wouldn't learn, and here he is going into first grade. What the hell were they talking about?

15. In my reality my uncle Todd rode the loop-de-loop and practiced the hammerhead saw on me. He bashed my bumper cars. The noise was as quiet as the thin sound swirling from a water-coaster splasher. You go down in a log built for two and you think you drown, but you don't. You survive. He swept my shreds into the twisting sky.

I would be lying down. My bed would be made of feathers and crusts. No one at home. The doorbell would ring. Who was it? Todd wouldn't let me go downstairs and find out. Close your precious eyes, he told me. I got sugar honey in my ice bucket for you.

The folds of my legs would come undone, the linings of my arms would unravel and ravel back again. If only you knew. What the hell are you crazy people staring at? Get the hell back into your classes. If only you knew.

I used to keep my eyes closed. That was so schoolgirl. The fear: this can't be happening to me. The joy: is this happening to me? An older man. My girl-woman dreams. These thoughts were way before Todd introduced me to the pills. Green, this is Sarah. Sarah, this is Red. Get ready baby girl.

Then there were the liquid sidewalks that forbade my feet from ever touching the ground, and all those eyes in the willow branches I could see from my bedroom window. Where was my sister all this time with her cold bucket? After a few weeks, when I started missing junior bowling league and Long Island All-State Girls Chorus practice, I started to keep my eyes open wide. Todd wore pants that jangled with change and strange keys. They slid off him like a seal's back. You're all mine. Get ready, baby girl.

With my eyes open I dreamt. In the corner there would be a tombstone marked: True Wisdom. My mother's heart split open into sheaves as if a garden rake were going through it. She raised a kitchen knife but we knew she wouldn't harm a fly, no matter if it was Godzilla's fly. Stop talking that nastiness, I do not want to hear it. I do not want to hear it. But wasn't she the one who was against Todd in the first place? She went back to after-breakfast drinks, playing bridge, volunteering at the Hollywood Baptist Church Sunday School, no eating. She was her own ride.

16. Later, the nurse at the clinic asked me, Are you sure you're all right? You don't have to go through with this, you know, honey.

I'm sure. It's just that I keep hearing things.

What kinds of things? she asked. At that very moment the chair underneath me yelled, I'll kill you if you go through with this! You have no idea how I'll kill you!

Nothing really. Let's get on with it.

Well, said the nurse, maybe you need some more time. I'm going to steer you over here and you can take a look at some more literature. The literature is usually what decides it.

And she handed me these rags I had not seen in the main waiting room. She was a secret soldier in God's Army. One of them said: The Lord is a hospital with plenty of patience. The other one said: Whoever you are, we too lie in drifts at your feet.

17. If you think you can be happy after the ninth grade, think again.

18. If you think you can be happy in the tenth grade, when all the wind blows over, well, let me give you a cigar. It's a few things I'd like to change, but life is always a coaster. You can get on the express train to New York City that leaves every couple of hours from the Long Island Rail Road, but you know in your belly, this is the way things are.

———•·•———

Born in Brooklyn, raised in Long Island, and now living in the Riverdale section of the Bronx, Carolyn Ferrell is the author of the award-winning collection Don't Erase Me *(1997). Her* stories catch in their bright, hard light the humor and the pathos of life for urban adolescents, marked by grinding poverty, too little love, pregnancy, AIDS, and violence. "When I was in junior high," Ferrell says, "I was saddened and intrigued by the very young girls who'd become pregnant. I wanted to know the real story behind their situations. I was intrigued by reactions of other children and adults, by rationalizations made by everyone, by signs and symbols of pregnancy, by official and unofficial stories, and by the silence surrounding the girls. I've never stopped thinking about those girls." In "Truth or Consequences," Ferrell unsparingly reimagines their lives. The former director of a South Bronx family literacy program, Ferrell now teaches at her alma mater, Sarah Lawrence College. Recently, she and her husband, a psychologist, became parents of a son.

EVERY TIME MY LIL' WORLD SEEMS BLUE

AN EXCERPT FROM THE NOVEL
Liliane

Ntozake Shange

Eye-hand coordination is what takes so long. Just look, not watch, the figure. Let my hand move along the same lines as my eyes. Let my hand go where my eyes go. At this rate I may be finished drawing this young man, maybe, next year, when twin full moons hang outside my window. This is not the most ethical of experiments. I don't have any idea who this young man is. I am indulging in anonymous sexual stimulation. Does that make me as venal as that stoop-shouldered Greek deli delivery man I stood behind at the Rite-Aid counter? His face couldn't have been more than two inches away from some sleek girlie magazine centerfold. Made me wonder, if this was one of those scratch-and-smell bonuses I'd heard about at an antiporn meeting not too long ago. So, here's this grown man with his face up inside this centerfold. From where I was standing, all that was visible were two ankle-height boots with very very high, come-fuck-me heels fitting into both of his hands, like in the circus when acrobats balance flying women in their hands. Then, two equally parallel legs creep from his rather stubby fingers to his forehead, so he looks to me like a fellow growing tawny calves and suede boots from his skull.

He must have felt my eye disclaiming his behavior as the activity of a healthy adult. He dropped the magazine, featuring the legs that belonged, it turns out, to a smiling white woman holding her backside open where the staple was. He jumped back, looked up at me, smiled. With aplomb, I said, "Sir, you've dropped your magazine." He replies, "Oh?" I point directly to the stapled anus, "There." Blushing, the deli man brushes his hand across his mouth, mumbles, "I'm finished."

Eye-hand coordination. Eye-hand coordination, that's what makes a certain kind of painter. This guy is definitely not going to be a painter. He's still looking at his magazine, now.

There's this place, a spot, on the mid–West Side where I used to meet a fella who stayed with me off and on. Well, I used to see him. I stopped going out with him because he had this terrible habit of wearing my shirts to meet me. Now I am virtually sure he wasn't a cross-dresser or something, someone who just adores putting on women's clothes. I think he was one of those men who was working on himself, you know. The man of his times not afraid of his female side, his softness and all that. I'm not against any of that, but I'm not sure that men's consciousness-raising groups in the forest with animal skins and drums is the path to their female side. Plus, I resented him, his name was Alex, for that matter. I can find no good reason for him to constantly show up in my clothes. It's amusing before making love, I guess; to exchange things, roles, scents. Yet I can't help thinking that he's actually not investing his own money, the time it takes to find these particular garments, that . . . Well, they look like me.

Maybe Alex imagined wrapping me around and about him when he slipped those wiry arms in my sleeves. The wildest thing I can conjure up is that when he put my pants on that was some simulation of fucking. I don't know. I just got aggravated when he'd casually appear with none of my hips or bust and look perfectly adorable. Alex could probably have walked all over Manhattan naked if it wasn't against the law, and come to meet me, too. Oh, whatta husky cherub he was: eyes so deep I could wake all up in them; lanky, wiry brown taut like wound hemp. Maybe he wasn't such a bad idea after all. He could've worn my shirts so he'd be closer to me. Now, that could be interesting, a fellow with a fetish for me. Maybe Alex didn't actually have anything to wear, hummh.

Anyway I met him at this place that had one of the deepest jukeboxes, had the greatest B.B. King, The Orlons, The Cadillacs, even The Five Satins. For fifty cents I could enter any rollicking summer of my life, any New Year's Eve, every teenaged dream and take Alex with me. I probably was too hard on him, expecting familiarity with a past I didn't share or refer to, unless some ditty by Ruby and the Romantics or Mary Wells grabbed me up.

I can't exactly say what Alex did with a lot of the time he had on his hands. He was gone a lot, on the road a lot with this rock band or that avant-garde group. He wasn't a musician, I was boycotting musicians at that time, but I didn't quite find my way out of "the industry," you know what I mean? So, Alex did lights, sound, road management, that sort of thing. Thank goodness I am not a groupie. Never was. But I don't feel in charge of what I'm doing now. I am not able to move this pencil off my paper, nice heavy-grained paper I searched for yesterday, knowing I would come here today to draw this man I don't know and then take all that I drew from and of him home with me again.

What baffles me is that this is the same table I would sit at to wait for Alex, always-in-my-wardrobe Alex, yet there's none of him around me. All I manage to do day after day is to go look at art: Julian Schnabel, Brice Marden, Jennifer Bartlett, "The Nigger Drawings," and I end up here looking for him. How, you say, can I obsessively seek out a man of whom I have no knowledge? I know the nape of his neck from ten feet, how his braids fall over his shoulder blades, the angle of his chin when he laughs, the curve of the delts and the arrogance of his posture, his ease among friends. I just look at him. I watch and my hands do the rest. I keep coming back on some ritual of expiation. I've burned no candles, strewn no flowers, asked no questions. And this is a place to ask some questions. Lemme tell ye, if there's some dirt to be had, dug up or fabricated, we are in heaven. From the bathroom to the bar is a nest of intrigue, seductive badinage, and income-appropriate drug trade. Remarkable insights offered from all quarters. That's not including the men's room. I have some friends, rather acquaintances, who pass through. Nadia who must be one of the most beautiful women in the world: deep copper like wildflower honey, a laugh like a million snuggles, the libido of a Great Dane in heat. She was a professional backup singer, Frankie Valle, Lou Rawls, John Cougar Mellencamp. She had all the looks, the voice, and the coke. A couple of high-living Guadaloupeans gave the place a twinge of sophistication. Otherwise, it was straight-up industry profilin' or procurin' of pussy, or cocaine, whatever made you happy. Name that tune, baby.

It's not that no one paid me no mind. I sent any number of evil "don't sit your ass down here" looks at men who were gracious, good-looking, well nourished, I always pay attention to that. All I wanted was to draw this man with the braids who sat just beyond an arch that separated the serious diners from the middling drug-booty cruisin' set. He always had a full meal. I found something exciting in that. What he wanted to eat. The muscles he used when he raised his fork to his mouth and set it down, how he pulled brown bread with raisins apart and spread real butter. I am telling you this from inference. I can't see his face. Never tried to. What would be the point? I come every day. I sit right here and wait. He comes every day and sits right there. I draw as much of him as his time allows, before he's surrounded by these women who've made an art of themselves. When the curls and busts start to hover, I pick up my things and take the local train home. That way it takes longer to leave him. I don't like wanting anything too much, that's just my way. In a fit of independence one evening, I think Little Willie John was singing something, I bounced off to the ladies' room with my friend, Nadia. We must have stood outside those two itsy-bitsy stalls all of a half hour before these girls couldn't anybody hardly see if it wasn't for ALL them eyelashes and bags coming ahead of them, came falling right down in front of us. We could have laughed, I guess, but we were getting ready to powder our noses, too. I swear I've spent as much care and energy examining Nadia's nose for traces of white powder as I spent seeing to myself. I had lived with a junkie once who was adamant that being a junkie didn't mean one had to look like a junkie straight off.

Well, Nadia and I got right lit up. I forgot about my other obsession. I even told Nadia, there was a guy right outside who'd give Teddy Pendergrass or Reggie Jackson a run for they money outside this very door. But we didn't budge. Stayed up in that mirror like goddamned Snow White's step-mama. Oh, Jesus, talk about some *peligrosa* foolishness.

Somehow Nadia and I managed to stumble and giggle our way back to the café itself. She was in amazing suede shorts that made me reconsider the significance of thighs. No matter, we came screeching and hooting bout stuff that was nobody's business into the rush of the late supper crowd as opposed to the early morning crowd which was a boisterous collection of educated hoodlums. We hushed abruptly. That's how folks were looking at us like we should hush. We did.

I looked up by the arch to fine dining and he was gone. He

was gone. But I don't know who this guy is. Nadia thinks I
made him up, he exists in my mind, she says. I'm having a
panic attack. I go to my notebooks. There he is. There he is
again. He's real. I've got him right here. I look up. Heads of
Sly Stone–looking muthafuckahs get in my way. Jerri-Curl and
Luther Vandross types block my view. *Boyz,* early in the scene,
put they nasty-lookin' sweatshirt-hooded heads in my way. I
don't know what he looks like. I mean, only I know what he
looks like. He's disappeared. I can't breathe. I can't find him.
I push the cognac Nadia's brought me aside. I decide to search
for him. He could not have left. He means too much to me.
He cannot be gone.

Trying to get niggahs busy chatting up a girl to get out of
my way is almost a lost cause. I think their feet grow in my
direction when I'm not looking for them, but somebody else.
Trip bitch! their feet proclaim. I keep looking in men's faces.
Other men I don't know. I don't know his face, either. I should
walk backward, looking for his braids. I know his braids,
black twists they are really not braids at all. They come down
his back like a black surf; like black string cheese. I know this.
I should go backward. He would never have left me. I take
him home every night. I take him home with me.

I sleep under a six-foot incarnation of his braids in bronze.
This is not funny. I'm not in control of this. I can't stop myself
from laughing. I need to find this guy I don't know. Yeah.
Everybody does, they say, "I don't know his name, but I'll rec-
ognize him." "Right!" "Baby, you sure you not talkin' bout
me?" "Look close, now."

Why everybody look so seedy? Everything so stink and
nasty? The place deserted, still fulla these no-count syco-
phants. What else to do, but find the music. Go directly to

the jukebox, Liliane. Find a melody, Lili. Go get you some music. I brush by smells of bourbon, musk, weed, and sweat. Any other time I'd at least check out a silhouette, but not now. I get to the jukebox, temporary Promised Land. Thank you, Jesus. Lemme see. Lemme see. Lemme see. Yes, The Shirelles, "Blue Holiday," Barrett Strong, "I Apologize," and Willie Colon, "The Hustler." For me. I dedicate all this to myself. Nadia is rubbing up behind me like she's bout to pee on herself. "What in the hell do you want, Nadia? He disappeared. He's outta here and you, you sposed to know every goddamned thing and you don't know who I could be talkin' bout."

"Now. Hold your horses, Miz whatchamacallit. . . . All I said was I couldn't place nobody quite how you explained. Sound like Gabriel and his horn on a Concorde jet or something."

"I don't make fun of you like that," I stammered. Well, what difference did it make. I've got my drawings, got my bronze braids, and I ain't got my feelings hurt.

That's not quite true. I'd grown dependent on this set of shoulders. That's not like me, to give up so much to a man's guardianship. I'd worked with fire and peculiar mixes of metals to fashion myself a canopy in his image. I was bashful, demure even, when I pictured myself before him. And we know I don't know who he is. Well, the crux of it is that I wanted a technologically proficient Third World man to enter the twenty-first century with me. I know, I know a barbarian when I see one. I know I'll know the King of Kings, when it's that time. I know this boy ain't the Apocalypse, but you can't hear it? Oh God, whenever I see the line from his elbow to his earlobe, Carla Thomas jumps all over my ass talkin' bout, "Gee whiz." Is this the real nature of pornography? Have I lost my mind and any sense of integrity a feminist has to have to be taken seriously?

There's a possibility that no one can tell. He's not like a tattoo or scarification, I mean.

Can you tell by looking?

"No."

"Nadia, shut up. He could take you to his house and bring you back in six weeks and you wouldn't know."

I'm going to down a magnum of Perrier & Jouët in my black satin teddy and the lace panties with the open crotch. I'm gonna stay home and draw drawings of the drawings of him that I've got. I'm not going to come out of my house until there are some hip black people in outer space. I'm not going to play me some Ruth Brown records, eat hominy grits with brown oyster sauce and do all the things I been told make a woman feel like a woman should.

I'm going to the telephone that's not a direct line to the coke man, so I can see if this guy who sorta likes me is busy. This is so crazy. I know I gotta do some reality work here. Call a man you know, Lili. Don't go all the way on out there, darling. Call Alex, see if he wants to wear some of your clothes, while you walk round naked. All right. Don't call Alex. Be a class A lunatic and sleep neath them metallic dreadlocks hanging over your bed. Nothing kinky there, huh? I am trying to let my tears fall in my snifter like Courvoisier got the best of me. I want to ask Nadia to take me to the ladies' room again. For a quick toot or two. I want to stand. I liked what his beauty brought out of me. Eye-hand coordination and all. I'm thinking maybe the rush from the enigma he is is sufficient. That'll get me through, you know. Right on cue, some sideman plays The Isley Brothers, "Love the One You're With." I feel my *survivor* kick in and take a deep breath. She lets me run my tongue over my lips. Chastises me for gritting my teeth, helps me tilt my chin with insouciance. Now, we ready? she asks.

When I raise my eyes and feel all that defiance burning behind my lashes, I'm struck dumb.

He's walking toward me.

He's smiling at me.

His braids fall over his chest too. I'd never allowed for that. I'd never imagined seeing him face-to-face.

I'd never meant to ask his name.

I'm losing my breath, he's lifting off the ground.

He's whispering my name, "Liliane, Lili, Lili." I know I don't know this man. I steal up on him in the late afternoon in a studio musicians' hangout. Nobody, only Nadia knows me, here. I never said anything to him.

"Lili," he takes my mouth in his and I lose any semblance of anatomical realities. How, how, how, could such a man know me already? I am staring, an imbecile, *une idiote joyeuse*. I'm managing to smile. I can't help myself.

I am touching the rafters of my dreams when all of a sudden The Isley Brothers' sideman's selection "Shout" blares all round me in a twirling swish of me in his arms in this den of iniquity that was clearly Eden. I should think so, I said to myself, trying to steady myself from a true swoon'n' faint.

"Yeah, *sí*. Liliane."

"The artist?"

"Yeah, most of the time, yeah."

"I haven't seen you since you let all those blackbirds free out some tower you built in Port-au-Prince a couple of years ago."

"You mean, the birds with messages from the first free Africans in the New World."

"Well, baby, they weren't the first free ones . . ."

"The first ones freed by their own armed struggle."

"Right . . . I gave you a message to put on one of them. Don't you remember?"

I am feeling my face get red, so red I'm going to explode. I can't say anything. I am talking to the man I've even been taking home with me every night, a man I don't know. He says he's been in one of my projects. And how he has, every sinew, contraction, and gesture. Yes.

"Liliane, are you alright? Can I get you something?"

I still can't say anything. I just shout for a colored joy, a gritty pelvis-born glee rises up outta my throat and I haveta smile to let it out.

"Oh, pick me up and kiss me again. Then we can talk all night long."

"You sure," he says with a twinkle in his eyes would make a guy with eyes in the back of his head jealous.

"Oh yes," I say.

"You know what my message on the free-flying bird said?"

"No, of course not. They went out in the sky around the world tied up in our dreams and desires to be found like anything else that's sacred."

"My message said, now I wrote it out by hand, now, my message said, 'I want to see this woman again without machetes and barbed wire so close.' "

"C'mon, now."

"Seriously, I thought about that a lot. You sending them birds anywhere they wanted to fly with whatever wishes anybody brought you. I never thought I'd run into you again, though."

"I've been . . . Could you put here, here, your left hand by my cheek. Yeah. Humm. I've been trying to draw this."

"What?"

"This feeling, your hand from this angle, there."

"Lili, I'm not sure I'm gettin' all this. Go slower."

"No, you don't want me to go slower. I'll get too confused.

Just let me tell you the truth."

"Well, okay, but everything's alright."

"No. Everything is not alright. I've been drawing you. Every day from right over there. Eye-hand coordination. I was working on. I practiced getting you just right. I sleep underneath braids, huge bronze braids like yours, I made from drawings of you I took home every day. And I never said hello to you or asked how you were feeling."

I'm every shade of purple now. I am crying. He lifts my chin. I do not look at him. I cannot.

"What's wrong with that? You're an artist, right?"

"Yes. I was perfecting eye-hand coordination."

"Fine. That's good."

I feel his forearm tween my waist and my ribcage, lava, a house music triple-threat bass mix.

"Yeah. Now all you gotta do is kiss me again. Then tell me your name, so, I know how to say, please do it again. . . ."

"Thayer."

"Thay—" I want to have a decent conversation, but his tongue is all up, back in my mouth so all I can do is remember drawing with my heart. My hands are swept up in muscles, Aretha's wail is coaxing me off my feet.

> And I ain't never, no no,
> Loved a man the way that I/I love you.

But that's me, Lili, sayin' "Kiss me once again. Thayer, don't you never, never, say that we're through, cause I ain't never loved a man the way that I've, I've drawn you."

———•◦•◦•———

Dramatist, poet, and novelist Ntozake Shange was born Paulette Williams in Trenton, New Jersey, in 1948. A graduate of Barnard College, she went on to earn a master's in 1973 from the University of California at Los Angeles. There, she took the name Ntozake ("she who comes with her own things") Shange ("one who walks like a lion") and began to turn personal and political angst into powerful literature. She combined poetry, music, and dance with her idiosyncratic use of language to create for colored girls who have considered suicide when the rainbow is enuf. *The widely celebrated "choreopoem" opened on Broadway in 1976. It was awarded an Obie and nominated for Tony, Emmy, and Grammy awards. Shange has since published two poetry collections,* Nappy Edges *(1978) and* From Okra to Greens *(1984); a second choreopoem,* The Love Space Demands *(1991); and three novels,* Sassafras, Cypress & Indigo *(1982),* Betsy Brown *(1985), and, her most recent,* Liliane *(1994), from which this excerpt is taken. The latter novel is a portrait of an artist through her relationships with her therapist and her lovers. Shange now lives in Houston.*

MOON
PENITENT

Diane McKinney-

Whetstone

The moon was a dot in the sky as Cartha watched her husband, Raymond, come home. He was a capable accountant but fairly impotent when it came to her needs. The deep needs nestled in her softness like that spot the size of a dime that the doctors had assured would be easy to shrink. She thought about the spot, and the dot of the moon against the navy glazed sky as Raymond laughed his way onto the porch.

A stranger with him. *Always bringing someone home to fix things,* she thought. The dishwasher hose, the motion sensor on the upstairs deck, the timer on the gas grill. This one was as tall and thin and dark as the space surrounding the moon. His shirt was a baby-blanket blue and made of cotton gauze: a red twisted licorice stick protruded from the pocket of the blue gauze like an upturned drill bit.

"Babe, meet Cole," Raymond said as he leaned into the porch swing and mashed his lips against Cartha's cheek. "Never believe it, babe. I'm at the gym, stopped at the gym after work, that's why I'm late. Anyhow I'm doing the Lifecycle, complaining to the guys about the damned closet door being off the track, how I got that crap all over my hands, axle grease or whatever the hell it was, when I'd tried to fix it earlier—"

"And let me guess," Cartha interrupted in a voice that

sounded like it wanted to fall asleep. "Cole here is an expert on sliding glass doors?"

"No expert." That's all Cole said. Then he extended his hand to Cartha and smiled.

Cartha thought that his hand was too large for his slender build, and his smile too slow, at least his mouth that took time to catch up with the rest of his face when it smiled. She ignored his hand and stared instead at the moon.

"She doesn't mean to be rude," Raymond whispered as he motioned Cole in through the front door. "Hasn't been feeling well. Otherwise lovely wife, couldn't ask for a better wife."

His voice drifted and Cartha didn't strain to hear. She was angry that he'd brought another stranger home. Not the crackling anger that used to leap like a brush fire when the wind was right, but a muffled one like a low groan covered with wool and pressed deep inside where the dark spot was growing.

She pushed her bare feet against the wooden planks of the porch floor to get the to-and-fro motion of the swing. The air had been still and thick with moisture, but now it moved with the swing and even lifted her hair, weighted down in locked tussles. She at least hoped this stranger would stay until she fell asleep. She couldn't tolerate Raymond's cheeriness, his monologue about how uncanny that he should run into this guy at the time they needed him most.

She did fall asleep, waking only when she felt Raymond lift her tiny, sagging body from the swing. She kept her eyes closed while he carried her up the stairs and pressed her gently into bed and covered her feet with the white down comforter. The ceiling fan clicked predictably as she listened again to Raymond cry.

The moon was a small crescent and reminded Cartha of the jewelry the Fifty-second Street vendors sold on green felt-covered tables in front of Hakim's Bookstore. She could

smell the incense and oils, almost taste the lemon pound
cake she would buy from the Cookie Jar when she still had
her appetite and could swallow well. She stared at the moon
and thought about the city—how long it had been since she'd
barreled through its caverns on the train. Raymond insisted
she not drive in, even when she'd still had the strength to
drive. "They'll stalk you," he had threatened. "Car like ours
they'll kill you for, stuff you in the trunk like a rag doll."

She pushed her bare feet against the porch to move the swing
to the beat of Raymond's voice in her head. She wondered
where he was anyhow. Wondered if maybe the carjackers had
gotten him, stuffed him in the trunk every night this week, as
late as he'd been. She stopped the swing when she heard footsteps. Thought that she would try to pull together enough
strength to greet him standing up for a change. But she was
tired. And then it wasn't even Raymond making his way up the
steps. Nothing like him. This figure was taller, darker. This was
the one who'd fixed the sliding glass door.

"Raymond's not here," she said quickly, as if her weak
voice had the power to stop a determined man in his tracks.

He did stop though. They all did. When they showed up a few
days after they'd made right whatever Raymond had said
leaked, or hung wrong, or was cracked or frayed or confused
(one had even told him that wiring gets confused), they'd stop at
the sound of her voice, in deference to her frailty, she thought.
This one, Cole, leaned slightly in a bow, showed his palms as he
did, said, "I don't mean to disturb you, Cartha—may I call you
Cartha?" And not waiting for a reaction, slipped into the chair
across from the white wicker swing where Cartha sat straight
and still. "I just left Raymond at the gym. Said he's got to go back
to the office—high-powered account he's on. So I just thought
I'd come by and check on you, you know, sit with you a while."

She scanned his shirt as he talked. This shirt was cotton

gauze and naturally wrinkled. She moistened her lips when she saw the red twisted licorice peeking from his shirt pocket. Her favorite little-girl candy. She wanted to ask for it, wanted to stretch and break it into bite-sized bits that she could chew on for a while, but it would take too much work. "Did he send you?" she asked instead.

"He didn't send me. He told me you're sick, though. I hope you don't mind."

"That he told you, or that you just popped over here unannounced?"

"I like your hair." Cole ignored her question as he sat forward in the chair and leaned his arms against his knees. "It's very political. First thing I noticed about you the other night."

"No politics. Just too tired to comb it. It's all I can do to wash it." She watched his face. He didn't believe her; she could tell by the way his eyebrows came together in a V. Raymond had believed her; after she'd patiently twisted each wisp of her hair to nudge it into locks, he'd offered to get someone over there to fix it up for her. Now that they'd left the city, he'd told her, she couldn't just let it grow wild like those Jamaican Rastas. And when she'd insisted that she didn't have the strength to keep it up, he'd relented, said it would be okay only until she was able to start going out again.

She leaned slowly against the swing back and started a gentle to-and-fro. "So you noticed my hair, so I noticed your hands." She watched his eyebrows curve up in a question.

"What about my hands?" he asked as he extended them into the moonlight and almost touched her to-the-floor dress.

"Too large for the rest of you."

"They are. I know they are."

"From shooting up?"

He nodded. "I should have known you would know. Your husband told me that you're smart. Quite, quite smart."

"Not all that smart. I used to be close with some people who did that, when I lived in the city. Raised in the city, you know."

"Well, this must be hard for you. Living way out here. You miss it, don't you?"

"What's to miss? Drive bys, guard always up, half-dead men soaking up the rank steam from sidewalk vents." She said it with determination. Kept her saucer eyes wide-open. Raymond used to tell her he knew when she was lying because her baby-doll eyes went to slits. She didn't want this Cole to think he understood her. Next thing he'd think he knew her well enough to ask her how it felt to die.

"And you like your hair. I noticed that about you, too." He said it as if he'd just read her mind.

"I noticed your eyes smile before your mouth."

"Meaning?"

"Meaning your reaction's sluggish, meaning you're still shooting up."

"Well, I admit it," he laughed softly. "I did it before I came over here the other night, only because I would be working, helps me concentrate."

"And tonight?"

"I'm not working tonight. Like I said, only came to sit with you a while."

"Ritalin's cheaper."

"What?"

"If you really want to concentrate. Ritalin's cheaper. Thought shooting up went out with disco, anyhow." She turned to stare at the crescent moon. The moon relaxed her. And so did his presence on the porch. She thought that if she looked at him right now, his face would be opened in a smile. She'd noticed that about him, too: He had an expansive face that widened when he looked at her, as if to give his face more room for drawing her presence in. The wicker creaked as she shifted her weight on the swing and the fluffy white seat pillows exhaled softly. "So you came to sit. So you sitting."

The moon was half full and hanging low as Cartha stilled the swing and fought the sleep that was covering her softly like the dark cotton air. Raymond was late—had been late every night that week. He'd be late again tonight, he told her. Big account. Very big. So big he might have to work all night long. Might as well pack a change of clothes just in case. Would she be okay? he'd asked. Should he call the hospice and arrange for someone to stay the night? She insisted not. She liked the quiet. But this quiet was irritating as it pranced through her head and almost mocked her in this single house on the private road. The house that Raymond had promised would be perfect for raising children far away from the decadence of city life. She imagined him at his late-night desk with his spreadsheets and Mont Blanc pens, working with sterile, passionless intensity to maintain their lifestyle. It was easier for her to imagine him that way.

She fell asleep on that image until later, much later, she felt herself being lifted from the swing. She kept her eyes pressed shut so she didn't have to hear the litany of "Sorry I'm late, babe." She let her head roll away from his chest the way someone in a deep sleep would. Her locked hair dropped and swayed and pulled at her scalp as he moved up the steps. She hated this part. The way he'd just let her head hang and bob like she was already dead. The cramp she'd get in her neck while her head bounced roughly as he took his time up the steps, punishing her with heavy, erratic foot stomps. By the time he got to the bedroom, it felt like he would just cast her off in disgust and toss her on the bed, or even hurl her against the scalloped wooden moldings that framed the wall. But then he'd soften. Maybe from the vanilla-scented candles she'd burn, the ones that she'd bought on South Street when she'd had her palms read. His humanity would return and he would place her gently down.

Except tonight these footsteps were lighter, these arms stronger. Tonight he cradled her head, protected it with his arms, moved his fingers through her scalp as he carried her up the steps. Tonight she felt his heartbeat as she nestled her head against his chest and then the texture of his shirt against her cheek. The cracked softness of cotton gauze. Tonight he stopped midway up the stairs to press his mouth against hers. She kissed him back with lips that were fleshy and full, the only part of her that still had a fullness to it. She smelled the licorice on his breath, tasted it, opened her mouth wider to draw in more of the taste, to swallow it up.

She was wide awake by the time his slow, soft footsteps navigated the winding hallway into the master bedroom. He eased her delicately on the bed and she kept her eyes shut and almost held her breath as he walked into the bathroom and let the water gush into the porcelain sink. She pictured the lather from her soap melting into the blackness of his hands, and then there was silence as the rush of the water went still.

That's when she heard it—the urgent smack of rubber against skin. She knew what he was doing then. She pictured him holding one end of the rubber tourniquet between his teeth and the other with his free hand as he tightened it around his arm until the erection in his vein pulsed. The swish of matches struck in succession—three, four, she counted them and wondered if they still used bottle caps and bent spoons. She heard him suck his breath, lightly. She knew he'd just plunged it in, probably for the thousandth time, and now the blood was bouncing in the syringe like a bright red tide when the moon is full.

As he walked back into the bedroom, his footsteps dragged slightly, the way Cartha had noticed his smile dragging the week before. She wondered what he'd fix now, since he'd insisted he only used drugs when he was working. She was about to ask him, challenge him, tell him to get his high ass out of her house. But she wanted more to feign sleep, keep her eyes closed on what he was doing the way she used to with the people she'd been with before Raymond.

Her feet were cold and she wanted to push them under the white down comforter. At least Raymond knew to cover her feet. She rubbed them together; it sounded like a burst of static had just whooshed through the speakers of the built-in sound system. She could smell the soap mixed with wintergreen alcohol as he neared the bed. Her feet were like ice blocks and she was about to sit up, snatch the comforter open to cover her feet. But right then he took her feet in his hands.

His hands were warm and he stroked the soles of her feet and covered them with his hands. At first it tickled and she almost giggled. She hadn't giggled in months, since the time she'd smoked a joint to kill the effects of the chemo. Then he used his thumbs and pressed against her feet and she was far beyond giggling. The repeated press of his thumbs, the velvety feel of his fingers as he stroked her feet from her instep to her heels, her toes to her ankles. It was every pleasure she'd ever felt lassoed from the beginning of her life, roped in, and then centered right there in the soles of her feet that he touched. She wondered if death would feel this good.

And then when he moved from her feet and blanketed her body with his, she thought she would die if she didn't cry out. She had to make a sound from the back of her throat, and then another, until it was a continuous stream of a sound as he touched that spot that had grown all these months unrestrained; the chemo, the radiation, hadn't touched it. But his heaviness did. The familiar heaviness reminded her of the people she'd been close with who'd shoot drugs and then couldn't do anything with their heaviness. Cole couldn't either. So he just rested still against the spot. She imagined that the spot was being consumed by his stillness, bursting into sparks like a firecracker on Independence Day, and then fizzling into nothingness.

The moon exploded into the night with its fullness. It seemed to take up a whole side of the sky; not even the stars could compete as Cartha bounced on the swing and hummed "Heat Wave" the way she thought Martha and the Vandellas would. She crossed her legs and smoothed at her shorts splashed with bold purples and reds and felt good about the dinner she'd prepared for Raymond tonight. Her locks were piled high in a roll on top of her head and she felt like a queen as she pushed her sandaled feet against the porch floor and got the swing going to the beat of the song. Tonight she would tell Raymond she wanted to go back to work, just a couple of hours once or twice a week for now. No, she'd insist, her hair wouldn't be a problem. They were so glad to hear her doctor's report, that the spot was finally showing signs of shrinking, they'd take her back however she'd choose to come. They were good that way.

She jumped to her feet when she heard Raymond's footsteps on the porch. She ran to him and hugged him and kissed his neck. Her chin mashed the knot of his handmade silk tie. His Polo by Ralph Lauren cologne was strong and stung her nose and made her sneeze. "Thought you switched; you know that cologne bothers my allergies."

"Sorry, babe," he said as stretched his arms and pushed her gently from him. "I thought now that you're better, you could handle it. My favorite, you know that, but if it still bothers you, I won't use it any more. Promise, babe."

She could feel his thumbs pushing against her bare arms as he held her. She shrugged her shoulders to make him move his hands and then adjusted the straps on her deep purple tank top. "Well, loosen your tie," she said. "We can have wine out here, then I'll throw the vegetables in the steamer. Salmon's grilling. Made your favorite herb sauce, too."

"It's so good to have you back, babe," he said as he undid his tie and slipped off his shoes and propped his feet in the white-cushioned wicker swing. "I was just telling the guys how much better you've been the past week; that lab report did miracles for you." He rocked the swing and the chain squeaked. "Chain sounds too tight," he said as leaned his head against the chair back and closed his eyes. "Need to get someone over here to take a look at it."

"What about the guy who fixed the sliding glass door?" Cartha said it with restraint as she turned to go in the house to get the wine. She could hear the wicker breathe and the swing creak as Raymond readjusted his propped feet and nestled himself deeper in the chair. "You ever hear from him?" She fought to keep an even tone.

"Heard he overdosed yesterday or the day before." Raymond's voice drifted like he was falling asleep. "Not sure when. Wasn't like he was a friend or anything. Just somebody with a habit who maintained equipment at the gym."

Cartha had stepped inside the front door. She leaned against the marble foyer wall to steady herself. The wall was cold and smooth and unyielding. *No!* she shouted inside her head.

She groped her way into the kitchen, tried to focus her eyes through tears that were hot and thick. She thought she should cut the peppers. They were red and yellow and orange. She'd gotten them from Genuardi's earlier. The smoke from the salmon grilling on the back deck was dark; she thought she should turn the salmon. She remembered then that she'd come into the kitchen for the wine. She managed to get back out on the porch with a modicum of composure. Raymond had fallen asleep with his feet in her swing. She banged the wine bottle against the wicker-bound glass table. Pushed at his feet, tried to knock them off the swing. He stirred and shifted and smiled in his sleep.

The porch was too small. Suddenly, with Raymond asleep with his feet in her swing, she looked at the moon in its climax. Wished its light would perforate the porch air and outline Cole's frame, and he would step out of the dark like a cutout doll coming to life from the page. And he'd lean toward her, holding a licorice stick. Red and sweet and strong. But the air was flat and still. No forms moving through it.

"He wasn't just someone with a habit," she said through her teeth. "And fix the swing your own damn self." Raymond shifted and snored as she walked off the porch and took the long way around to turn the fish on the grill.

Diane McKinney-Whetstone always knew she would write novels, but she bided her time as a publicist for the U.S. Forest Service until her twins were ten. Then in 1996, she hit her literary stride. Her exquisitely crafted first novel, Tumbling, *enthralled critics and won numerous awards. Her second novel,* Tempest Rising, *was published two years later. Like the first, it tells the story of a fiercely loving African American family struggling with the dilemmas of modern life. She wrote "Moon Penitent" between novels. "It's an unusual love story," she reflects. "The idea of these two wounded people providing a sanctuary for each other haunted me for a long time before I wrote it down." McKinney-Whetstone teaches fiction writing at her alma mater, the University of Pennsylvania. She lives just outside Philadelphia with her husband and their twins.*

OCTOBER
BROWN

AN EXCERPT FROM THE NOVEL
Rattlebone

Maxine Clair

W e heard it from our friends, who got it from their near eyewitness grandmothers and their must-be-psychic neighbor ladies, that when she was our same age, our teacher, Miss October Brown, watched her father fire through his rage right on into her mother's heart. In a fit of crazy-making grief, October Brown threw herself at walls and floors and cursed the name of God, apparently not mere blasphemy but mutterings that could cause limbs to crimp and men to yowl like jackals. The story went on that immediately thereafter, Satan himself had made a visitation to October Brown, and from that time until the year she became our grown-woman schoolteacher, the burnt brown of her left cheek was marked by a wavery spot of white: a brand, a Devil's kiss.

We put this together with what we already knew, which was that a patch of bleached skin meant death was on the way; the white would spread. When it covered your entire body you died.

I doubt that any of us fully believed every part of the story, but we were so seduced by the idea of it that before the end of the first day of school we buzzed with frenzy—a frenzy contained, because we imagined that a woman surrounded by

such lore would have to have a bad temper, a flash fire that
could drive her from her desk to yours in a single movement,
dislodge you by your measly shoulders, plant you hard on the
hardwood floor, tell you in growling underbreaths of wrath to
stand up straight and say whatever she wanted you to say, and
then crumble you in the mortar of her black-eyed stare.

Intuition is the guardian of childhood; it was keen in us,
and we were right. Before we knew what current events were,
she asked us who Wallis Warfield Simpson was and we sat.
Attention shot through our arms and nailed our fists to the
center of our desktops. Not a single hand went up.

Our eyes dared not follow her as she got up from her desk and
moved around the room in a slow prance, falling back in her
double-jointed knees like a camel with each step, around and
around the room, asking "Who was Edward the Eighth?" speeding up while a few eyes shifted, a few feet shuffled under desks.

"Who knows or thinks they know?" she asked, and she
was back at the desk again.

"All right, then, who was George the Sixth?"

We were still again, still until she whumped her *Thorndike
International Dictionary* onto her desk and we grabbed our
elbows.

"Look at me."

We looked.

"Who was George the Sixth?"

We looked, and the blue *Thorndike* flew over our heads
and crashed into the back wall between two sixteen-paned
windows. One corner pane of glass, weakened by BB shot
some winter or summer before, fell to the radiator and shat-
tered on the floor.

"Tomorrow I will ask you again."

My mother said that that was the nervy part of Miss

Brown coming out, the Negro woman-teacher part of
October Brown "trying to put some sense into y'all's pick-
aninny heads," she said.

"Tell your parents you will be learning French this year.
Tell them to send a note if they want you to be excused from
this part of your education." She went on: "These books are
old, but the rules have not changed. These books are special.
Each one of these books belongs to me personally. You cannot
buy one of these books or replace one, so govern yourselves
accordingly." Then she said to John Goodson, "Pass these
books out as far as they will go and share with your neighbors."

Never mind that the Kansas City curriculum did not
include French, never mind that the Superintendent of
Elementary Schools made threats against her for it. *"Qu'est-
ce que c'est?" "C'est le pupitre." "Qu'est-ce que c'est?"
"C'est la lumière."*

The unblemished side of Miss Brown shone on Wednesday
afternoons after recess. "Class, put your heads down," she
would say, and down went one overhead row of lights as she
hushed her voice and read to our lowered heads about the
time when everything was blacker than a hundred midnights
and a lonely God stepped out on space, batting his lightning
eyes, and made the world, made us out of mud by the river,
and she read to our sleepy heads about boys going down a
river on a raft, read to us in wherefore language about a boy
and a girl, star-crossed, killing themselves accidentally and on
purpose. She read aloud to herself and our curious heads listened, sneaking peeks of her perched on the side of her throne,
legs wound round each other in long grace, her face a still,
dark well of molasses, and death-kissed. Her coal-black hair
carried all the life smells of her; parted in the middle, it hung

in crowded crinkles to the shoulders of her shoulder-padded, to-the-nines dresses.

Those dresses. "I wouldn't wear nothin like that, but she got tiny hips," my mother said. They were draped at her waist or flounced, crepe with sequined dragons and peacocks, glittery butterflies, dresses that shone like the sun in the drab circle of dark clothes dark girls wore at the rear of the classroom, the place to which we gravitated at lunchtime, the back of the room where she graded papers, spread her napkin for her peeled boiled egg, peeled red tomato, her peeled-and-opened-like-a-flower orange on a white china plate aquamarine-trimmed. We nibbled, crust first, our baloney sandwiches and tried to match her spread on the waxed paper inside our fold-over-tuck paper pouches.

For all of us, staying at school for lunch meant being away from home all day, playing jacks, telling Hank Mizell stories. Hank was our recognized criminal who had stolen a dollar of the Defense Stamp money from Miss Brown's drawer and smuggled it out in his shoe. No one had told. Loyalty was hero-making, and from that day on, he was invincible.

But my mother said the Mizells had money enough to do anything they felt like doing. "Don't go gettin any notion in your head that you can do it too," she said, cross at me for no reason at all.

By a happenstance unclear to me then, my mother had steadily grown a baby inside her, aggravating my father in the process.

"What you think I am, Pearl, made of money? You better get your head out of the clouds and get some more ironin in here or somethin."

Whenever they talked, they talked about the baby. When ever they didn't talk, it was about the baby too. For me they had only silence.

If you've ever tasted the after-rain clay dirt on a Kansas summer afternoon, or if you've ever secretly wanted to, you may
understand why I was often tempted to eat a stick of chalk. It
held the smell of that clay dirt. But if you had seen the over-
grown girl that I was, standing dumb at the blackboard one day,
sucking a stick of chalk, it might have seemed peculiar.

"Irene, what is wrong with you? Are you ill? Don't hunch
your shoulders, answer yes or no," Miss Brown said.

I couldn't answer.

"If nothing is wrong, write your sums and be seated," she said.

That morning I had awakened to heat in my father's voice.
"How many times do I have to tell you, Pearl? Stuff costs
money! Since when can't you wash diapers? We didn't have no
diaper service for Reenie."

And my mother's heat when she told him, "Don't start
nothin with me, James. I'm the one havin this baby. Who got
the last pair of shoes that come in this house? Answer me that.
Who's all the time wearin me out about how his papa used to
eat steak every Sunday?" My father tromped up the stairs. My
mother tromped right behind him, not letting up.

They were on opposite ends of the same track, and I knew
from time and again that they would both speed up, bear
down until they had only inches left between them, then they
would both fall back and rumble until silence prevailed. Later
my father would bring home orange sherbet and my mother
would rub his back and they would both be laughing.

But this time, before the rumble melted away, I heard
what sounded like the whole house falling down. My father
hollered out like he was using his last breath and ran down
the steps. I flew to the top of the stairs. He was picking her
up from the bottom, all the while praying, "Mercy." He
yelled for me to call the home nurse on the phone, but when

he saw that I couldn't move, he carried my mother to her bed and ran to call the nurse himself.

"Reenie, you wait by the door for the nurse," he told me, but I could not leave the foot of my mother's bed. Covering her with a quilt, he asked her "*please*" to be quiet, but she went right on nonstop about all the things she meant to order from the catalogue for the baby, all the places I could stay if they had to leave me alone. When the home nurse came, she told my mother and father that I should be sent along to school, but my father let me stay at home until they left for the hospital.

Certain that my mother's fall was preface to disaster, I stood there at the blackboard with the chalk in my mouth, sucking on the fact that one or the other, mother or baby, would die. I tried to focus my grief on the loss of the hump in my mother's belly but, unsure of my power to choose, I bit down on my mother gone.

"Irene, put the chalk down. You'd better sit and work on your word problems. What's the trouble?"

None of this escaped my friend Jewel Hicks, the pink-ribboned, talks-too-much, needs-her-butt-beat jewel daughter of the on-our-party-line Mrs. Hicks.

"Her daddy made her mamma fall down the steps and her mamma's going to have a baby."

Wailing is the sound you make to straighten out a tangled throat so that you can breathe, and to spill tears from boiling eyes so that you can see your "Come on, Irene" way out into the hall. Our janitor pushing his T-broom nodded, "How do, Miss Brown" in the dimness of the hallway, and the cedar-sawdust-muted click of her high-heeled shoes comforted me as much as her arm around my shoulders all the way to the girls' rest room while I cried myself into hiccups.

"Now listen. No matter what happens, you are going to be

all right," Miss Brown said. "You're a crackerjack, you're smart, and you can be strong even when you're afraid. But don't worry, your mother will be fine, the baby too, your daddy too. "

When I got home from school that evening, my father had a guess-what lift in his voice and a halfway smile on his face.

"Of course your mamma wouldn't leave you and me like that," he told me. "And to boot," he said, "she got us a brand-new baby boy." I was the happiest girl in the Rattle-bone end of Kansas City.

A few days later a baby came home with my mother. It was a tiny, raw-looking thing, writhing, gagging. At sudden times it drew up, spread tiny fingers, and grabbed at the air, shuddered as if it were falling. It squealed and fussed, and dirty clothes grew in mounds on the back porch. It slept, we listened to *Damon Runyon* and *Let's Pretend* with our ears stuck to the sides of the radio. It was the-baby-this, the-baby-that; it was practically Thanksgiving before things got back to normal.

By Christmastime Junie was sleeping all night and my mother had gone back to taking in ironing, ironing bushels of clothes. My father found masonry work indoors, all of us busy and tickled to be busy. A week before Christmas the Montgomery Ward truck pulled up in front of our house and we were immediately giddy. I knew some of the catalogue orders had to be mine. The driver brought several boxes to the door and my mother—"Step back, Reenie"—took them quickly to her room. Watching to see if that was all, I saw two men rolling a gleaming-white surprise down the plank to the sidewalk. I yelled so, my mother came running, then danced a piece of jitterbug when she saw it. "Westinghouse" it said. "Westinghouse!" I yelled. They sat it in the middle of the front room. "We needed it," my father said, grinning when he came home and my mother hung on his neck.

The double-wringer washing machine was a Mizells-ain't got-nothin-on-us kind of thing, but I was even more ecstatic over my first store-bought, stitched-down pleated skirt, and knee socks to match. We were definitely coming up in the world.

Winter always arrived before the sun was very far south in the sky, so that a white Thanksgiving was as unremarkable as jon-quils ice-sheathed at Easter. A blizzard, though, was a drama that threatened to bring the house down. With a perverse exhilaration, we compared it to what we knew as ultimate devastation: the Atom Bomb.

Slate-gray clouds rumbled across the sky and exploded in needles of sleet. Then the all-day-all-night snow-wind screamed, whipping snow from place to place, unpredictably laying blank the railroad tracks and the cemetery, our out-posts and borderlands, corners where we turned for home.

On the day of the storm, stuck at school, we were put out about the fact that here we were, eight years old, and still had to wait for somebody's mamma to walk us home. In blizzards of previous years, the room mothers had always come bring-ing rainbow sandwiches—potted meat, cheese, and sweet rel-ish layered on bread and cut into thin fingers—piled high on a platter for us to come up and take, one sandwich at a time. I remembered being secretly relieved to link my arms into two others and be part of a dark brood in make-do headgear that followed William's mother to the early light of our own porches, where we were handed over to our own mothers.

Jewel's mother swept in and bundled up her sweet one; Hank's uncle came to take everyone who lived on Wynona. No sandwiches arrived, though John Goodson's father did bring vanilla wafers. Pancakes of snow slid down panes of glass, then dribbled into the double-cardboard pane and dripped onto the radiator. I watched.

This once was the only time my father ever came to school, and he didn't merely show up; he kicked the classroom door hard from the outside. When Miss Brown opened it, my father stood snow-weighted in his black-and-red mackinaw and hunting cap, holding an orange crate lined with an army blanket. "Hi," he said to her. He was grinning. She turned away without speaking, without finding anything to do with her eyes.

"The room mothers sent this—there's enough chili in there to feed all y'all," he said.

Miss Brown shook out the blanket and lifted my mother's canning pot from the crate, then boxes of crackers, Dixie cups, streamers of paper-wrapped, figure-eight wooden spoons. O happy day! Single file, we got our cups filled and sat down to eat wherever we liked.

At the back of the room Miss Brown spread my father's mackinaw on the radiator, steaming and burning wool. My father sat big on top of the last desk in one row; Miss Brown sat smaller on another, across the aisle, facing him, and they talked while we ate our chili.

She peeled her orange, dangled her legs in the aisle. She held it out to him, a flower offering on a china plate. He shook his head no. She ate one section, cherry-slick fingertips into cherry-red lips, so proper. My father talked. He reached for a piece of her orange. She talked. She talked. He talked. Leaning over, she laughed and her heavy, live, crinkled hair fell forward and covered her face. She looked eyes-through-hair at him. She snapped straight and threw the mass of hair back, held it back with both hands, spreading elbows angel-winged out into the air. Letting go of her hair, she shook it into place and crossed her legs, talking, talking.

Smiling, she touched the many-colored, parrot-appliquéd shoulder of her dress. Smiling, my father showed teeth all around white. A pretty dress. Black, crepe, French. She arched herself, swung her legs, girl on a swing. When my father stood up to go, he slid his arms into her holding of his mackinaw. She held the door—"Bye, James"—for us.

No matter how fast he walked, I kept one step behind him, deep in his footprints down Sherman Alley and out Lenexa. Though he carried the box, he never slowed down. I passed him on the run into the narrow path of our street and tried to run, feet stinging, home. After all the rush, I had nothing to say to my mother, who sang to me her rendition of Nat King Cole's "Sweet Lorraine" over my feet, cold in the basin.

If winter seemed definite, desperate, then spring seemed timid, capricious, like an innocent girl feigning wisdom. One day you felt a near-balmy wind, or sensed an almost-perfume from crocuses, saw the perhaps-violet six-o'clock sky and you guessed it was spring.

I was mostly indifferent to it. Something had invaded our house. I watched my mother's belly.

"Don't be ridiculous, girl, I almost got my waist back," she said.

That wasn't it. Still, a no-name, invisible something had settled on us. For instance: I saw it in the way nothing suited my father.

"Pearl, can't you think of nothin to cook but neckbones? The stuff tastes like homemade sin. Ain't we got nothin sweet but pound cake?" he would say.

He was impatient with Junie—"Keep that boy quiet or git him outta here." Or careless with my mother's feelings—"You look like who'da-thought-it in that dress." Or he was absent, playing whist somewhere late at night with people my mother called God-knows-who.

I heard it in the way my mother said "Reenie, be quiet" or

"Talk up, girl" or "You shoulda been through cookin by now.
Play with your brother." She'd stay behind her bedroom door
for hours, and come out with her eyes puffy.

She cried, she said, for my grandmother who had died
when I was four. She cried, she said, for my uncle who was in
Korea. For Junie's rash, the burn on her ironing hand, a hole
in my sock. For nothing, she said. "Nothin is wrong."

But it was there.

Too early, before bird-twitter one morning, I heard my
father's brogans shuffling, my mother's voice breaking in ways I
held my ears against. Doors and drawers slammed, their voices
peaked and sprawled, jabbed through the floor and walls.

When my father's heavy boots thundered all the way to the
front door and down the walk without sounding even for a
second like he was turning around, I ran to my window. In a
morning light that was like gray gauze, I saw him swing a large
suitcase into the cab of his truck.

I could barely hear my voice ask why. My mother could
barely say, "Just for a while."

Counting the days, I tried living the fantasy of my father
away on a trip. But evenings, just before dark, when all the
neighborhood seemed to settle inside kitchens and I sat alone
at our table watching my mother—her whole dinner between
two slices of bread—stand at the window and eat slowly into
night, I knew that my father was gone.

At first he stayed away, but eventually he took to stopping by
to bring money or groceries or just himself for us to see. My
mother always got busy in the kitchen or upstairs and left me to
wonder out loud why and where and how much longer he would
be wherever he was living, and who was fixing his dinner.

"Wait now, Reenie," he said. "That's for me and your
mamma to talk about." But he told me that no matter where
he lived, when school was out, he would still take me with

him to pick wild greens and he would still teach me how to tell the good mushrooms from the bad ones. It was relieving to hear, but the end of school was like eternity, something I could not imagine.

On Sundays my father ate dinner with us. After dinner, when he fell asleep on the divan with Junie in a snoozing bundle on his chest, my mother and I watched, ostensibly sewing and doing homework, but watching what could be if we could somehow fasten up the life we'd had together.

Then one morning I took a shortcut through the hollow and when I arrived at school early, I saw a blue flatbed truck just like my father's pulling away from the curb and Miss Brown going into the building. I thought to call out, but the man in the truck was wearing a felt hat with a brim, the kind men wore to church. My father had only a hunting cap. Besides, I reasoned, my father had to be at work long before I had to be at school; it could not be him.

At about this time, school seemed pointless. Easter came and went and not even my new linen pleated skirt could cheer me. I relinquished my crackerjack seat and gave up my friendship with Jewel, so when we made our annual school jaunt to the Nelson Gallery of Art in three church buses with room mothers and teachers keeping a lid on our bubbling enthusiasm, I must have been ripe for the new taking-over of my mind.

In the days that followed, I took to drawing. For no reason I drew trees. Naked winter trees, charcoal black on white paper. Trees with no buds, no leaves. Trees whose roots went down to the tip of nothingness, trees held in place only by the space on the white page. "Spring fever," Miss Brown said. I drew fragile roots and branches in the margins of incomplete homework, badly done test papers.

"Tell me what's gotten into you, Irene," she said. I studied

less and drew more trees, and she slashed the trees with red
X's, asked me about my falling-asleep-with-my-eyes-open
look. I drew more and she made me redo the work neatly. I
drew black trees instead of redoing my work and she kept me
near her desk and monitored my papers, asked me none-of-
your-business things about my mother and father.

It rained. It rained more. And on one of those rainy afternoons that we stayed in for recess, Miss Brown left the room.
Hank Mizell, digging through the bowels of the supply closet,
came up with the box of Kotex Miss Brown reserved for intimate female catastrophes. With all eyes coaxing, he splashed
red tempera down the middle of one napkin. Miss Brown
opened the door at just the right time to catch him in the not-
even-a-prayer position of placing it on her chair.

"Out!" She grabbed for his arm. He dodged.

"You better not touch me," he said.

She grabbed again, faster this time, and caught his arm.

"I said out of here!" And she pointed to the door.

"Get your hands offa me, you black sidditty bitch! My
mamma said you're a whore." And Hank fixed his eyes on
me. Miss Brown looked at me too, then fixed her eyes on him.

Her look carried such fury we could all feel the silent curse
she singed him with before she spun and pranced head-high
out the door, her smeared Devil's kiss glowing pink. Hank
shrunk and slinked out behind her. I ran to the doorway and
watched them, hen and duckling, down the length of the hallway and into the office.

The next day, rumor billowed that Hank's mother was
coming to school to straighten the whole thing out. Hank
Mizell's family owned the funeral home, and as hoity-toity as
his mother was in protecting their name, she was deaf, mute,
and blind when it came to Hank. We were excited. According

to our Jewel, Hank had told his mother that Miss Brown had slapped him, said it happened on the way to the office, said she made the scratch he was sporting. His mother was coming to take Miss Brown to the Board, Jewel said. The almighty, no-corporal-punishment-allowed Board of Education.

The principal looked pressed. "Who saw what happened between Miss Brown and Hank Mizell?"

Every hand went up.

"Who would like to come with me to the office to discuss it?"

Every hand went down.

More tense, she pressed. "John Goodson?"

"I don't remember all of it," he said.

"Jewel Hicks?"

"My mother said that I should stop telling everything I know," she said.

"Irene?"

I was silent.

"In my office, Irene."

In the office they all sat in a semicircle in front of the principal's desk. On one end Miss October Brown sat erect in an armchair, with both high-heeled feet on the floor, looking through a *Weekly Reader* as though she was alone in the office. She folded the paper and folded her arms. Then Hank Mizell's mother. She wore a whole fox around her shoulders, its beady eyes open in my direction. She held Hank's hand over the arm of her chair. Then Hank, hunched and cramped in his mother's hold. Then the janitor, hunched too.

"Sit down, Irene," the principal said.

I smoothed the pleats down the back of my linen skirt and sat carefully on them.

The principal said, "I want all of you to know that we're

here simply to get to the bottom of this matter. I don't have to tell you that we can do this quickly if each of you will just relate the truth." And she sat down behind her desk.

"Henry, would you like to begin by telling us what happened yesterday?"

"Yes, ma'am," Hank said. His story included being caught out of his seat even though it was recess, being yanked by the arm that was still sore, being frightened enough to swear, and being slapped.

"She slapped me upside my head hard, and her fingernails are sharp," he said. "They scratched me."

Miss Brown crossed her legs and folded her hands in her lap. Hank Mizell's mother looked at the cherry-red nails and sighed the sigh of the wronged.

"Miss Brown?" the principal said.

"First, let me just remind all of you," Miss Brown said, "that this is not the first time Henry Mizell has been guilty of unacceptable conduct, nor is this the first lie he has ever told."

"I beg your pardon," Hank's mother said. "You don't talk like that about my son with me sitting right here. I don't have to be subjected to this."

"Please, Mrs. Mizell, let's let Miss Brown finish." The principal wrung her hands as Miss Brown told her story, which involved her instructions to the class about staying in their seats whenever they were using paint, her shock about the sanitary napkin and the name-calling.

"I did touch his arm to restrain him for a moment because he broke to run," she said. "But other than that, I did nothing corporal to him whatsoever."

The janitor spoke without looking up. "You know," he said, "y'all ought to have some way these children can play inside. They need to run when they been cooped up all day or they gonna get into trouble. The boy was wrong, but look like to me he needed to move around some, and seem like the teacher did too. Maybe if y'all—"

The principal interrupted. "Did you see Miss Brown and Henry in the hallway yesterday?"

"I sho'nuff did."

"Did you see Miss Brown do anything? I mean to Henry."

"Naw, ma'am, I didn't. But you know, these eyes is gettin old and there ain't enough light out there. I think I'da heard him, though, if she really whopped him. Course, maybe he didn't say nothin. Maybe he was scared."

We were all quiet for a while.

"Irene?" the principal said softly. All their eyes turned to me. I watched my hands unfold in my lap and smooth my pleats. I looked at Miss Brown looking her I'm-proud-of-you look at me. I looked at the principal, and though my mouth was very dry and my hands very quivery, though my heart was whooshing hard in my ears, I looked her straight in the eye the way people do when they are telling the truth.

"Yes," I said. "She did. " I said level and clear, "She hit him. "

"Irene!" Miss Brown stood up. Her Devil's kiss glowed fire-red as it always did when her temper flared. But she sat down slowly.

"Go on, Irene," the principal said.

"Just before they got to the office," I said, "she turned around and slapped him. I could see them from the door," I said. "I guess she lost her temper because he called her a vulgar name."

"Are you sure, Irene?" the principal said. I nodded yes.

"Well, that's all I need to know to take this up elsewhere," Hank's mother said.

"Mrs. Mizell, I believe we can handle this right here if Miss

Brown is willing to apologize," the principal said. But Hank's mother said, "No thank you, I'm tired of having to come down here every other time somebody gets it in their mind to take their jealousy out on Henry." And she stood up to leave.

Miss Brown picked up the purse beside her chair, stuck it under her arm—"The children are lying"—and headed for the door.

"Please wait," the principal said to Miss Brown and Hank's mother. "Irene, you're excused."

Instead of going directly back to class, I headed for the rest room, where I tucked in my blouse, braided the ends of my braids, and washed my hands in castile. I folded my knee socks all the way down and sat on the cool radiator. A breeze played in the narrow opening of the frosted window, and I raised the window higher to look out.

Spring was unraveling everywhere. Summer was coming when I would go hunting for wild greens with my father, when we would be up in the warm, damp mornings taking his gunnysack with us along the railroad tracks all the way to the woods. Summer was coming when he would show me which was dandelion and which was dock, which was pokeberry and which was nettle. We would bring back morels and truffles for my mother to dip in egg and crackers and fry them crispy brown. Summer was coming and maybe my father would come back. Maybe he would buy orange sherbet every night. Maybe my mother would get her waist back and sew herself a princess-line dress. Maybe she would sew us both one of the new kind of skirts cut on the bias so they flared way out and you never had to worry about keeping the pleats straight.

A native of Kansas City, Kansas, Maxine Clair graduated from the University of Kansas at Lawrence, then worked for many years as the chief medical technologist at the Children's Hospital National Medical Center in Washington, D.C. In 1984 she decided to become a writer and teacher. She armed herself with an M.F.A. from American University, and published stories, poems, and essays in such prestigious journals as Callaloo *and* Story *as well as in the* Washington Post. *Her books include a collection of poems,* Coping with Gravity *(1988); a fiction chapbook,* October Brown *(1992), which won Baltimore's Artscape Prize; and* Rattlebone *(1994), a collection of short stories about African American life in the heartland. "Clair consistently attains the poetry organic to everyday speech while avoiding the quaint, the forced, and the patronizing," one critic wrote of* Rattlebone, *which won the Chicago Tribune's Heartland Prize for fiction, the American Library Association's Black Caucus Award for 1995, and the Friends of American Literature Award. A former Guggenheim fellow, Clair is an associate professor of English at George Washington University in Washington, D.C.*

LOVE IN PLACE

Nikki Giovanni

I really don't remember falling in love all that much
I remember wanting to bake corn bread and boil a ham and I
certainly remember making lemon pie and when I used to smoke
I stopped in the middle of my day to contemplate

I know I must have fallen in love once because I quit biting
my cuticles and my hair is gray and that must indicate
something and I all of a sudden had a deeper appreciation
for Billie Holiday and Billy Strayhorn so if it wasn't love I don't
know what it was

I see the old photographs and I am smiling and I'm sure quite
happy but what I mostly see is me
through your eyes
and I am still young and slim and very much committed to the
love we still have

Nikki Giovanni is an American legend, a beloved literary griot. The poet was born in Tennessee but moved to Cincinnati with her family when she was just two months old. She later attended Fisk University, where she earned a B.A., and did graduate work at the University of Pennsylvania and Columbia University's School of Fine Arts. In the sixties and seventies, her reputation grew and she performed and published her work widely. She has taught at Queens College, City University of New York, and Livingston College, Rutgers University. Her books include Racism: 101, Gemini: An Extended Autobiographical Statement, numerous poetry volumes (including collections for children), and books of essays such as Sacred Cows . . . and Other Edibles. "Love in Place" appears in Giovanni's 1997 collection, Love Poems. The recipient of countless honorary doctorates, Giovanni is a professor of English at Virginia Polytechnic Institute and State University.

ALCESTIS

April Reynolds

In the middle of the night, Alcestis realizes she has spoken much too hastily. He catches her, diaper pins stuck in her mouth, her hand above her head, a stickpin gleaming in her fingers, poised for a single swoop. The small child lies on the table before her, giving the gift of urine. The young boy wags at her side, tugging on her brown khakis, and both children know only one name—Momma. So when Joe-Joe appears at the door, heaving beneath his old blue seersucker suit, she just says yes, yes, and yes again in fear that she will not be able to save the collard greens from the stove, not even thinking, *Now, wait now—*

It is not until late that night that she realizes what she has done, after he lies on top of her, rubbing his hands over her stubbled legs, nuzzling his nose under her armpit, which more than likely smells, since the house ran out of deodorant three days before. They tumble like new lovers and Joe-Joe's breath is heavy and concerned in her mouth, on her shoulders, behind her knees. Given the circumstances, her position as it were, she did not have the time to say, "Wait a minute, let me stay still to think." And so Alcestis must wait until the middle of the night, with Joe-Joe across the bed diagonally, to think to herself, *Just what in the devil is going on?* Her thinking narrows, and she frowns her black ribbon mouth because she knows she can not shake her harried look except on Sundays at church. "So how come now, like this?" she mumbles to herself and to the sleeping Joe-Joe.

Even now she does not think of what she has said yes to, because her nipples tingle from Joe-Joe's mouth. Then Alcestis sleeps, so hard that she does not dream. So sound is her breathing that when Joe-Joe wakes and looks at her in the morning, he thinks that she has already done what she promised. Putting his hand on her chest, he cannot bring himself to cry through his sense of relief, his thoughts that say, *Thank God it is not me*. Joe-Joe is trying so hard not to smile, he cannot feel the steady beat of Alcestis's heart beneath his hand.

Before she wakes and mistakes Joe-Joe's grateful look for love, you must understand what Alcestis has promised and why she must stand by words spoken so often they are cliché.

Ten years ago, Joe-Joe lived with an old woman who called herself Madame (no first name, no last name, just Madame). She was from New Orleans, and for reasons she told no one, she moved to Arkansas, Lafayette County in particular, with three red leather suitcases and a cage full of chickens. She never bothered anyone, never ate in town, and never had a job as far as anyone could tell. And since she came to Lafayette old, and perhaps rich (well, the town reasoned, just where did she get those suitcases and how could she keep those chickens and not barter and trade with a soul?), people found excuses to stop by. And as luck would have it, two months later she cured a small boy of the flu by accident with a fallen vial of gris-gris. They endowed the woman with the name the Old Madame. And they took their sick to her because the real doctor was four towns away.

Joe-Joe's mother had died the same year the Old Madame

moved into town, and soon Joe-Joe ran through all his mother had left him. Joe-Joe was hungry, not doing well with his newly made poverty, but it did not occur to him to get a job (he'd never had one; his mother worked for the both of them until her heart leaped up and quit on her). He met the Old Madame in the woods while he was trying to hunt for rabbit with a clothes hanger. She found him on his stomach in a light gray suit in front of a hollow log with the hanger in his hand. "Oh, son, what are you doing?" she asked him. He looked up at this old woman who stood midcrouch with her hands on her knees. The rabbit took its chance and darted out and past Joe-Joe. "I'm—*god-damn!*" he said as he peeped back into the log. "I was hungry and hunting; now I'm just hungry." Madame smiled at him, showing Joe-Joe her three missing teeth.

"And you come out to hunt in a suit?"

"What man wants everybody to know that he's hunting for rabbit with a clothes rack?" Joe-Joe retorted.

"A man so hungry that he's hunting with a clothes rack," Madame observed. She looked at him, his high ass in those tight pants, the narrow waist, the fake leather belt. "Come home with me. I will feed you," she said.

That was the beginning of Madame and Joe-Joe. It took her a month to bed Joe-Joe—four solid weeks of mustard greens seasoned with ham hock, grits smothered with crawfish and white cheddar, crab cakes with fried quail eggs, everything sprinkled with John-the-Conquer root. Till finally he came to her, tugging on his pants and murmuring, "Oh, Madame, forgive me, I just don't know why. Madame, I just don't know why."

"That's all right, son," she said, "just come here." He had sex with her every day for seven days. She left him alone after that, afraid he would find out that she had drugged him. Madame knew that magic could only do so much. So she let him be, letting him eat her food without thanking her, letting him come into her house at two and three o'clock in the morning smelling of beer and woman twat. She let him do that because the next fall, there she was hunched over the stove fanning John the Conquer in the cheese grits.

This time she did not hold back, and she prayed to Odeah and Ebu with spite on her tongue. Again a month passed and Joe-Joe came to her, waving and reeling in her bedroom door, and when she said, "Come here," he fell to his knees and crawled over to her, grabbed her fat thighs with both hands, and buried his mouth between her legs. He stayed in that position for seven days. The Old Madame loved it so much that she forgot to pray to her gods, and he shook out of his drugged state. He didn't curse her. Instead, he came home early and swept the front yard for the entire year. But to no avail, because she did it to him again the next fall, and he figured out that this was her way of extracting rent, of taking payment when he had nothing to add to the grocery money.

After ten years of hard autumn labor, Joe-Joe meets Alcestis at Bo Webb's Café. She dances alone near the record player, her tall black legs shuffling on the floor, her mouth tied in concentration as she watches her swinging arms.

"Hey, what you doing here alone?" he asks Alcestis.

"Dancing." She watches him without holding her head up. "Ain't you the Old Madame's?"

"I am no one's." Joe-Joe catches her swinging hand, and she laughs because she is surprised and drunk. They dance and dance, bumping the record, coughing loudly to cover the skipping of the song, till Bo Webb's old lady comes out from the kitchen cursing—"My house don't look like no dance hall, so why, so why, so why y'all all here?"—and pushing the men out to the porch with her elbows, and everyone tumbles out, promising to be back tomorrow. Alcestis and Joe-Joe are still together, Joe-

Joe's arm through Alcestis's elbow, threatening to walk her home and she lets him, frightening him, too, with stories of her crazy mother. Joe-Joe does not go back to Madame's for weeks; he sleeps on Alcestis's porch. But then he realizes that he has to go back to Madame's—for his suits and underwear, his toothbrush.

Madame waits for him at the door. "Where you been?" she asks with such concern, Joe-Joe does not lie.

"With Alcestis at her house."

"That momma of hers won't let anything happen."

"Her momma likes me."

"That doesn't mean she is going to let you have Alcestis." Madame assumes Joe-Joe wants to marry Alcestis, and though he has not thought of it before, he realizes she is right.

"I ain't worried about her momma." He walks past Madame into the house. It takes him only thirty minutes to gather all his things.

"Comb your hair," Madame says to him.

"My hair is fine."

"You can't go get Alcestis with a nappy head." Joe-Joe sets his teeth together and reaches for the comb in the Old Madame's hand, not noticing that she has been holding it like a knife. He runs the comb through his hair.

"There. You satisfied?" He turns towards the door and yanks on the knob, walking down the stairs.

"Yes, baby," Madame says to the disappearing back. "I got all I need."

Alcestis and Joe-Joe get married four days after Joe-Joe leaves Madame's house for good. They convince Mable, the town gossip, to ride them all the way to Texarkana. Mable, who keeps her secrets tucked under her dress, drives everyone everywhere, since she drives the only car in town that doesn't have to be anywhere. When Mable asks Alcestis where is her momma, Alcestis says sleeping. She is not lying; one of the things Joe-Joe packed is this tea Madame concocts that he knows will cause the drinker fall asleep quickly, deeply. Mable doesn't say anything when Alcestis gives this fast answer, because Alcestis looks good in her borrowed yellow dress, and Mable knows that unless they find someone in the courthouse, she will have to stand in as witness and maid of honor. *Why stir in shit when I know it will stink?* she thinks. She isn't the one that has to face the momma when they get back.

They get married, Alcestis's dress straining across the chest. Afterwards, Joe-Joe tells Alcestis and Mable that they are not going back to Lafayette County—not just yet. "I got money and connections down here," he tells them. "We have to start on our own." He grabs Alcestis's sweaty palm.

"Right?" he says. "Right?"

"Right," Alcestis says and turns to Mable, wearing a crooked smile.

"Right," Mable says. She is the only one who sounds like she believes what she is saying.

They stay in Texarkana for a year. Joe-Joe works at the Shell gas station, cursing the black grease on his hands that he can't wash out, and Alcestis works at the courthouse, cleaning. Alcestis cries at night and Joe-Joe snores loudly to drown her out.

"Let's go home," Alcestis says one night.

"Yes." Joe-Joe looks up at her. And by the end of the week, Alcestis has convinced a girlfriend at the courthouse to take them back to Lafayette if they pay for the gas.

So everything is okay. Alcestis has dinner with her momma every Saturday night, and she and Joe-Joe are happy. Two more years pass and they have a child, whom they name Eumelus. Joe-Joe has a job at the grocery store and Alcestis stays at home. Four years later they have another child, a boy whose name is Deshawn, whom they call Two-Bit for short. And when Alcestis is not cooking, cleaning, going to the PTA, or running Deshawn to day care so she can look for a job, she takes a deep drag on a cigarette and thinks to herself, *Maybe I'm happy and don't even know it, since I don't have time to think on it.* She does not know that Joe-Joe still sees Madame every week, and maybe if she did she wouldn't care. Or maybe she would.

Saturday night in the midst of red candles, Joe-Joe asks Madame to tell him his future.

"I don't do that kind of stuff," she says to him, pushing the door closed while he stands on her porch.

"Say now, everybody knows Mable sends folks out here when she can't help them."

"Just 'cause she send them don't mean I help them."

"Mable ain't never been confused about where to send people when they need help."

"Who says you need help?"

"I say it. Listen, baby, I just want to know if I am gone be working in the grocery store for the rest of my life. When am I gone get to be my own man?"

"Only you can answer that kind of mess." This is the first time she has not let him in the house, the only time he has come to her and the door has been locked to him. Standing there, he wonders, has he been barred because he has not had sex with her for more than seven years? "If I wanted you, I could have you," she says.

"Then why you being like this?"

" 'Cause I can."

"Come on, baby, don't be like this." He puts his hand to the door, tilting his smiling face through the opening. He pushes the door open and Madame blames her age and weakness. And before she knows it, there she is squatting on her wooden floor, sweat gathering on her lip as she sprinkles his hair on the candle before her. For a while they sit quietly on the floor, then Madame looks at him and says, "Well, what you want?"

"How come I can't get nowhere with my job?"

"'Cause you don't want to."

He thinks to himself, *What kind of shit is this?* but he says, "Well, how can I change all that?"

"Start wanting." He sucks his teeth and says nothing.

Madame laughs and says, "Is this what you came to bother me about—stuff you already know?"

"I thinking. Not every day a man is told his future. Tell me what's gone happen to me."

"When?"

"Oh, shit, Madame. What's gone happen to me now?"

"You will get up, walk out that door, go home to your wife, and sleep."

"Damn, I don't mean right-now future. I mean the future not so close. What's gone to happen in the future that I don't know?"

"You gone die." What she says sits between them like a dead animal, still enough that it could be a play thing. Joe-Joe does not move, and neither does Madame. He decides to respond to the dead thing, which is her voice lying on the floor as if it is play and nothing real.

"We all gone die, baby." He speaks to her as if she is a child, as if she should know better.

"I know that."

"What you talking about, then?" His breath quickens, puff, puff, puff.

"You gone die."

"When?"

"In the future you don't see."

"When?" He reaches across the candle and takes her hand.

"Inside this year." He snatches his hand from hers and throws his arms around his head, because it is the end of October. You cannot hear anything in the room except Joe-Joe puffing beneath his arms. And then his arms fall and he looks up at her.

"How come I'm gone die?"

"Like you said, we all gotta die, baby."

"Bitch. You fat yella bitch," he yells at her and stands, knocking over the candle. He walks to the door without turning around. At the door, he stands facing her, as if he is about to walk in. "You a waste of yella, that's what you are. I know you was ugly even when you was young."

"Maybe."

"What you say to me? What you say? Don't say shit to me, Madame. I ate your twat for seven days, and you turn around and tell me I'm gone die?" He pushes himself out the door and takes off running blind down the dirt road, screaming and screaming, "Bitch, bitch, yella bitch!"

Madame gets up when she can't hear him anymore. Her knees are bad from arthritis, and she makes a note to herself that she has to buy a table for her future customers. She walks to the door and opens the screen, spitting carefully between her feet.

"Shit, I could have told him he was going to say all that, too."

After that Joe-Joe is an angry man. Alcestis asks him what is wrong, why is he behaving this way, and he tells her a lie, so real that he believes it as it comes out of his mouth. "I been having these dreams, these nightmares. Every night, I have the same dream."

"What of?"

"I dream I'm at this restaurant, and this white girl is asking what I want, and I tell her, I want pancakes. And then she says real funny like, them things will kill you. And for some reason or another, I say to her, don't I know it, but damn I got a taste for pancakes today. And then I order them—the pancakes, that is—even though I know as soon as I get that shit in my mouth I'm gone drop dead."

"Go to the Old Madame."

Joe-Joe puts his hands to his face, slumps in his chair, and cries hard, a steady stream. Alcestis puts her head on his lap and thinks that she has given advice so true it takes her breath away, and so repeats it: "Go to the Old Madame. Baby, you know she loves you."

He goes to the Old Madame a couple days later, and he tells himself he goes because Alcestis deserves an answer to his dream.

He does not knock. She does not open the screen door to let him in. "What you want now?"

"You know what I want."

"Ain't no way of getting out what you have to get into."

"There some way."

"None, boy. Now get on out of here."

"You find some way, lady. I done been through a lot with you. You know I have, and maybe I'd tell the people in town what you do to folk when you can't get them the natural way."

"Ain't nobody gone believe that shit, Joe-Joe."

"Ain't they? They sho' believe you can cure folks with dead chickens and spells. I just wonder what all them mommas would think when they find out I spent seven days in the fall for ten years being your I-don't-know-what against my will. I just wonder what all those mommas with all those sons would do when they find out about that. Lord forbid—"

"Son of a bitch is what you are." She says it very slow and does not raise her voice. "You raccoon baby. You smelly, soft dick piece of shit. I wish I had a teacup; I'd shove it up your ass. I got enough of your hair in a sack to make you want to crawl up and nap in my pussy."

"I know you got powers, but how you gone hold off a town full of mad mommas?"

"You give me time, Joe-Joe. You come back here in three days, and no sooner, neither."

"Ms. Madame, you come see me in three days." He moves away from the door. "You always can come see me earlier if you like."

Madame comes to town early in the morning on the third day. She dresses in a white skirt with chiffon underneath and a blouse that peeks a bare shoulder. Joe-Joe's house sits in the midst of town, right next to the grocery store where he works. She walks onto the porch and raps hard on the door. Joe-Joe and Alcestis are asleep. No one answers the door, and she hits it again. Knock, knock, knock. Then Alcestis comes to the door, struggling into her robe.

"Madame?"

"It's me. Joe-Joe needs to see me. He knows what about."

Joe-Joe, too, has woken up and walks up behind Alcestis. Madame sees him.

"You, Joe-Joe. Come with me."

And then they are out the door, Madame in a swish of white, Joe-Joe following her in his bathrobe. Alcestis stands by the door. She shudders, thinking perhaps she should wait for Joe-Joe but decides against it. *Since when has it been this quiet in the house?* she thinks.

Joe-Joe and Madame walk past the town and her house. Joe-Joe wonders where Madame is taking him. "Here, sit here, you." She points to a fallen log and Joe-Joe sits.

"What's all this, Madame?"

"I prayed for you, boy. And the gods look like they didn't

want to tell me nothing at first. Death is hard, Joe-Joe, harder than you think. I can't make death go away. You gotta give something."

"What?"

"You gotta find somebody to die for you."

"Say what?" He jumps off the log and for the first time this morning he touches her. Grabbing her by the shoulders (he does not shout or shake her—just holds her shoulders, and so she thinks that he does this, the jumping and grabbing, all for show), he says, "What you say?"

"Ah, come on, Joe-Joe, what you 'spect? Death just pop up and go away? You know what I realized as I was coming up to your place?"

"What?"

"You ain't got no sense. You ever think maybe it's a good thing you die 'fore them sons realize what a fool they got for a daddy? The only sense you ever had was with that clothes hanger almost twenty years ago and even then you let the damn rabbit get away. You a fool."

"That goddamned rabbit would have been mine if you wouldn't have sallied your fat ass my way."

"If you would have been a real huntsman, then it wouldn't have mattered where I was!"

He takes his hand off her shoulders and steps back from her, shaking his head. "I ain't gone stand here yelling with you about no rabbit!"

"You *are* standing here with me yelling about a rabbit!"

"Fuck you, Madame." He turns away from her, and then takes off into a run, thinking wildly.

He comes home to find his sons and Alcestis asleep. "Wake up, baby. Wake up."

"What, what is it?"

"I'm back."

Alcestis sits up in the bed. "What she say?"

"'Member that dream I was telling you about?"

"Yeah."

"Well, the thing is, I'm supposed to order the pancakes, but now I got to give the pancakes to someone else to eat."

"Joe-Joe, you ain't speaking no sense."

"I know, but you'll see. All I got to do is call my sisters."

"What Pen-Pen and Shawn got to do with anything?"

"Just go to sleep, and if the kids wake up, I got them." She almost sits up again when she hears what he has just said. But then she silently thanks the Old Madame for the sleep on Saturday and slips deeper in the pillows. Joe-Joe gets up from the bed and waits until nine-thirty to call Pen-Pen and Shawn.

"What you want?" Pen-Pen says.

"How come you talk to me like that?"

"'Cause you never call to see how I'm doing."

"I'm dying, Pen-Pen. I'm dying."

Pen-Pen, lying on the couch, yanks upright and takes a pillow to her chest when he says that. "Aw, naw. For real?"

"Come and see me, Pen-Pen. You and Shawn come and see me 'fore I die."

"What you dying of?"

"Don't nobody know yet."

"Joe, I can't just take off from work and leave my kids. If you want Shawn to come, too, who gone take care of my kids?" Pen-Pen blows air into the phone, and begins to scratch her foot with her other hand. "When you need me there?"

"Come now."

"How come now? You don't even sound sick, Joe-Joe."

"I'm still dying. You coming?"

"Yeah."

"Be here by Wednesday."

"I can't do that."

"When's the last time I asked you for something? I'm dying, goddamm it; don't that count for nothing?"

"You really dying, Joe-Joe?"

"I'm dying, baby girl. I'm dying."

"You sho' don't sound sick."

"You don't have to sound like you dying to be dying."

"Damn, Joe. Damn. The least you coulda done was sound sick." And she hangs up the phone.

It is only an eight-hour drive from Dallas on Saturday. Neither sister can afford an airplane ticket, so they bring Pen-Pen's kids to Shawn's husband and take his car. Leaving too soon to pack properly and cook food for travel, they fill the back seat with beer, baloney, and hot dog buns. And so despite where their journey will lead them, sixty miles outside Dallas, they become carefree, laughter-filled and single.

"What you think Joe-Joe up to?" Pen-Pen says. Only four hours into the drive, she has eaten four hot dog–baloney sandwiches.

"Shit, Pen-Pen, Lord only knows." They are both quiet for a while. "Maybe he really dying."

"Maybe he is. Still, he wouldn't of called us to come if that's all there was to it. I mean, when was the last time Joe-Joe called and said he was in trouble and didn't want nothing?"

"He ain't never call to say he was dying."

"Naw, you right about that. I'm just wondering what he up to." They don't speak much for the rest of the trip, but Pen-Pen thinks that besides her presence, and a chocolate cake, she isn't giving a damn thing toward Joe-Joe's funeral.

Congregated in the living room, Shawn and Pen-Pen perch on the couch and Joe-Joe stands against the wall. Being family doesn't make conversation, and it takes fifteen minutes of silence for Joe-Joe to realize that he should ask his sisters how their trip went. Pen-Pen waves away the niceties and says, "I want to talk to this doctor who say you gone die. How he know? He work at the county hospital? Ain't none of them doctors no good. Most of them ain't even doctors yet. Ain't you got no doctor close to here? 'Member those county doctors in Dallas?—like to kill me."

"We got something here, but it ain't no doctor—not no medical doctor, anyway."

Shawn stops cleaning her fingernails. "What he say."

"She say I'm gone die." Both take a breath and hold it, because where they don't have faith in doctors (they all feel that depending on the money you have, doctors can stave off death), they know that the knowledge of death coming from a healer is true, for there is nothing to gain.

"Ain't nothing she can do?"

"She told me something."

"Well?"

"Death just don't go away 'cause you know it's coming. It still come and it still want something. Madame say the only way I ain't gone die is if somebody take my place."

Pen-Pen kicks up from the couch. "See, Shawn, what I tell you? Dirty son of a bitch. That's why you ask us up here, you want one of us."

"Now you wait a minute, Pen-Pen. I asked y'all here 'cause I'm dying."

"You ain't gone ask nobody?" Shawn asks. He turns to her.

"You ain't gone offer?"

"Joe, I got a family—a husband and children."

"I got Alcestis and two boys." He drops his head and looks up again at Pen-Pen.

"Boy, don't you even look at me like you gone ask that question."

Joe-Joe starts to cry. "I'm dying, don't y'all care nothing about me? I'm dying."

"You dying all right, but by my hands!" Pen-Pen crosses the room before Shawn can catch her flying hands. *Pow! Pow! Pow!* Joe-Joe and Pen-Pen plunge to knees and elbows on the floor. Though Joe-Joe has strength, Pen-Pen has fury, and she is winning. She pulls her left knee up hard; Joe-Joe catches it in his hand. With his other hand he slams her head to the floor, and the force of the hit bounces her head upward, and Joe-Joe and Pen-Pen's foreheads clatter against each other.

Shawn rushes towards them, but she doesn't know where to put her hands. Frightened by the solid thud of Pen-Pen's fist against Joe-Joe's stomach, she jumps and lands on Joe-Joe's back, squashing Joe-Joe and Pen-Pen beneath her. "Y'all gone stop?" Shawn screams. Pen-Pen says nothing, since the breath has been knocked out of her. Shawn stands up, Joe-Joe pulls up to his knees, and Pen-Pen sits up on her elbows.

"I'm ready to stop if Pen-Pen gone stop," Joe-Joe says, breathing heavy, sweating, his right eye already starting to swell.

"Pen-Pen, you ready?" Shawn says.

"Yeah." Joe-Joe struggles to his feet and Pen-Pen pulls her left arm back, her fist clenched, and *pow!* Joe-Joe goes down from a sock in the jaw, hitting his head on the coffee table, knocked out.

"You said you wasn't gone hit him," Shawn cries.

"Naw, you said was I ready and I said yeah."

"What we gone do now?"

"He ain't dead," Pen-Pen says, watching his steady breathing. "We should leave before he wakes up."

"You, Pen-Pen, go get some ice."

"I guess that mean we gone stay. Damn, Shawn, damn."

Joe-Joe wakes up with his head in Shawn's lap. "What time is it?"

"It still daylight." Joe-Joe sits up and his head spins. He sees Pen-Pen smoking in the chair. "Ain't nobody here gone get dead for you. Ain't that right, Shawn?"

"Yeah, Pen-Pen."

"Y'all can go home, then."

"You serious?"

"Yeah."

"See, Shawn, see what I say? I ain't even had a chance to get a glass of water." Shawn says nothing and reaches out to rub Joe-Joe's head. "Don't you go thinking nothing else, either. I need somebody to help me drive back to Texas. Let's go now. Right now."

"Ain't you gone get some water from the kitchen?"

"Suck dick and die, Joe. I don't need no goddamned water." Pen-Pen walks to the couch, grabs her and Shawn's coats, then walks across the room to Shawn, yanking her up by the hand so fast that Joe-Joe's head bangs against the floor. "Come on, Shawn."

"We can't just leave him."

"Alcestis help him get up when she get back from her momma's."

Now Joe-Joe is alone. The frantic furious thoughts of a desperate man have taken hold of him. Quickly he runs through all the folks in town, dismissing the young, the family-bound or -made, and the successful, till he figures there are four people that he knows of by name who are old and close to death. He walks out of his house determined, muttering to himself, "The Lord giveth and He taketh away." Joe-Joe comes upon Mrs. Allecto's house, her husband dying of cancer too far gone. She answers the door. "Hello," she says. "I'm so glad you came by." She stands aside to let Joe-Joe pass through the door. "I came to pay my respects, to see if your husband has gotten better," he states. He asks to see the man, and she takes him to the bedroom in the back. *Yes, he is dying*, Joe-Joe thinks.

He kneels next to the man and whispers without explanation, "Would you die for me?"

"You serious?"

"Yeah."

The man turns his head and says, "I got enough of my own dying, don't you think?" Joe-Joe says nothing more and stands up. He goes through the rest of them in a fast, fantastic blur of wrinkled flesh and the smell of rotten teeth. It is almost sunset now. Alcestis waits at home, stirring something in a pot for dinner. And then his mind clicks on it. Why not her? Isn't she the one that loves him most? Hadn't she said something like that before? His steps quicken, one, two, three, and his feet fly down the main street toward his house. He lingers on the porch, his hand outstretched toward the doorknob, and he thinks before he opens the screen door, *I'll cook her dinner.*

She poses not in front of the stove as he thought. Rather, she is changing Deshawn's diaper. Her head snaps up at the bang of the door, and she tries to smile at him through the diaper pins in her mouth. "Baby, baby," he says, "will you die for me?" She spits the pins out in her hand and she almost asks where has his family gone to, but she sees impatience in his hands that clutch the frame of the door. "Yes, baby, yes. Ain't I told you before? 'Member when we first got married—" But she does not finish, since Joe-Joe crosses the room to the table, shakes the pins from her hands, and pulls her fingers to his smile. He throws her hand to the table, murmuring, "I got dinner, don't you worry none. I got dinner."

Now it shines morning. Joe-Joe places his hand on Alcestis's breast, grinning. Alcestis opens her eyes and yawns. "What you grinning at?" His lips fall around his teeth. "Baby?" He does not answer at first. He just looks at her open eyes and her hands as they wipe away the eye snot that gathered at the corners as she slept. Joe-Joe blurts out what flashes in his mind.

"You suppose to be dead."

"Say what?" Alcestis opens her mouth to laugh, but she sees the seriousness. "You, Joe-Joe, what you done done?" So he tells her all of it in one breath, a litany beginning with a log and a rabbit and ending with her at the stove, and her yes—a yes that cannot be taken away. She doesn't even cry, because she knows what sort of husband she has, except she used to think that she was one of the things he was selfish about. She lays her head back on the pillow and stares at Joe-Joe. "Take the kids to my momma's." Joe-Joe scrambles off the bed, calling the children awake. She lies there, left to think alone. *That son of a bitch got me dead.* But then she takes that back, for didn't she say she would do it? *But I didn't mean it like that,* she thinks. *Nobody means it like that, they just mean they love you a lot, ain't that what I meant?* "I don't want to die alone," she says aloud. And then she hears the clattered report of the door and screen closing.

Joe-Joe doesn't know how he curls from Alcestis's mother's house to Madame's. *Maybe she can save me again, by saving Alcestis,* he thinks. His fist lifts and she opens the door.

"You, Joe-Joe, what you want now?"

"I found somebody."

"You didn't."

"Alcestis."

Madame says nothing while looking at him hard. "I can't visit with you now. I'll come by later on."

"You know we ain't got that kind of time. And I ain't going away for you to come to me in three days. You get to talking to whoever you need to talk to and save my wife."

"You killed her." Madame presses her lips and flips her head away from Joe-Joe.

"She ain't dead yet."

"She dead all right. She died right after you left the house. Her arm start hurting something furious, and she tried to get up outta bed, but she couldn't with her arm hurting the way it was. Her heart just broke right in half—she died that way, all alone, clutching the pillow with her one good arm, calling out for your dumb ass."

"Damn it, Joe, you killed your own wife." Pen-Pen's voice snakes out of the door.

"What you doing here?" Joe-Joe steps inside the house and sees Pen-Pen and Shawn seated at a small wooden table.

"Me and Shawn stopped at the grocery store to pick up food for the way back and Madame walked right up us, knew just who we were, and said, 'Come home with me. I will feed you.' So we went right along home with her. But that ain't the point." Pen-Pen pulls a finger up and points at Shawn. "See, Shawn, see?"

"How could you take your wife away from her kids?"

"I asked 'fore I even knew it, Shawn. I didn't think she'd say yes. Didn't nobody else say yes; I didn't think—"

"You never think, you dumb fuck. What we gone do now, Madame?"

Madame looks at Pen-Pen. "You gotta go get her." Pen-Pen laughs, almost. What comes out is a short "Ha!" that sits still in the air. *It's always me, goddamn, goddamn*, she thinks, *it's always me.*

"Me? Why me? I don't even know Joe-Joe's wife."

"Who else?" asks Madame. "Me, I'm too old. I get in that bedroom and instead of walking out, I lay down. Joe-Joe? He the one that put her there; she might not come out at his call. And Shawn ain't strong enough. You the other one; you can get in there and wake death up. We have to go now or not at all," Madame says and sucks her teeth.

"You the strongest, Pen-Pen," Shawn says, and Joe-Joe nods in agreement.

Pen-Pen walks up to the door, not even thinking, *How have I gotten into this mess?* because she knows. Madame's hushed look tells her there can be no other way. They watch her from the middle of the front yard, and Pen-Pen swears they all turn their heads to look the other way when she touches the door. She shakes, a small tremble makes her hands slick, and her fingers shimmy off the knob of the door. *Madame says all I got to do is take her hand and say, "Get up,"* she thinks. She remembers Joe-Joe crying on the way to the house—the tears without sound. Her hand turns the knob of the door and she steps into the coolness of the house, into the absence of sound, which is quite different from someone trying to be quiet. She remembers the man-made silence of her mother's funeral, the shuffle of feet, the coughs behind hands. The bedroom is in the back, so she treads through the living room. The bedroom door stands ajar, and before she steps through she sees Alcestis's foot peeking out of the bedsheet. *Whoosh*, she opens the door farther, looking at Alcestis's hand clutched around the pillow. Alcestis died with her eyes open. Her head bends, facing the window; her legs are parted, half a leg and a foot dangling—or is it reaching?—to the floor.

Her hand stalls before she touches Alcestis. She realizes Alcestis's prettiness. She notices the hairline scar, light gray in death, that peeks out of the corner of Alcestis's mouth and trails off her chin. "Why, I never even looked at her face when she was living." Pen-Pen takes her hand, the hand not around the pillow. "Get up, Alcestis." Pen-Pen's sound seems to beg. Alcestis does not move. "Come on, girl, get up." Maybe Pen-Pen tastes fear, maybe she gropes in anger; in any case, her hands tighten to a vice around Alcestis's wrist and her next words bite: "Get your ass out that bed. Come on, girl. Get mad, get something, just get up." And then she hears it—deep breathing mixed with the subtle sound of phlegm. A spray of sweat gathers on Alcestis's upper lip. Alcestis quietly whirls her head toward Pen-Pen and smiles a nasty, sugary grin. Startled, Pen-Pen's hand almost slips off of Alcestis's sweating wrist, but she does not let go. "Come on, let's get out of here." Alcestis's grin tears wider across her face, and Pen-Pen pulls her up. Her head rolls on her neck, but Pen-Pen won't use her other hand to steady Alcestis's head because of the indecent secret grin and her dead, dead eyes. "Get your feet on the floor." Alcestis arches the foot that dangles off the bed to the floor and slides the other foot off the bed. Pen-Pen pulls hard and Alcestis lurches forward. One, two, three steps and they are out of the bedroom. Pen-Pen leads. They are separated by the length of their arms. Pen-Pen does not turn around since she fears Alcestis's face—and the thought that perhaps if she spins around, now that they are out of the bedroom, and really witnesses Alcestis walking, Alcestis will fly back to death. The screen door looms like a clean bedsheet.

"We here." Their feet waver on the porch. Pen-Pen has turned gray from the fright, and with Alcestis's grin and eyes, they seem like sisters. Then Joe-Joe steps forward, his left hand outstretched.

"Alcestis, baby." She does not answer, so Joe-Joe takes another step, afraid to clutch his wife, who looks to be dusted in flour. "Baby, I'm sorry. I love you, baby. Baby, you hear me?" Alcestis says nothing. One hand clutches the hem of her nightgown, the other wraps like a towel around Pen-Pen's, and that nasty grin stuck in her mouth instead of her voice. Joe-Joe grabs Alcestis around the waist, pulling her away from Pen-Pen's hands. He ducks his head forward and kisses her lips. Alcestis's mouth opens, so what looks to be an indecent smirk opens into a drunk woman's silent laughter. Afterward, Shawn

will swear Alcestis yanked Joe-Joe's lapel too hard, and Pen-
Pen will say no, the fall happened because Joe-Joe tried to
untangle their arms and Alcestis wouldn't let him. Neither one
knows since, in what seems to be either a struggle or embrace,
Madame stoops to her knees, her eyes shut tight, and begins to
laugh and scream—short, harsh—"Ha! You see! Ha! Ha!"
The laughter and words snap out of her mouth, cracking like
pecan shells. In the cacophony, Pen-Pen and Shawn don't know
where to put their eyes. No one sees Alcestis and Joe-Joe swoop
downwards into the dirt. Joe-Joe does not feel Alcestis's breasts
escape her nightgown like river water.

---

*April Reynolds was born in Dallas in 1974. She moved to New
York City in 1997, took a job at American Heritage magazine,
and continued work on* Red Ribbons and the Broken Memory
Tree, *which won second place in the 1997 Zora Neal
Hurston/Richard Wright Foundation, Virginia, writing contest
for best novel in progress. A graduate of Sarah Lawrence College, Reynolds has long been attracted to the classical themes
of Greek mythology. In particular, she was intrigued by Euripi-
des' Alcestis. "I didn't understand it," she explains. "Who was
this woman? Why did she consent to die for her husband when
even his parents had refused him?" To find her own answers,
she recast the tragicomedy in a modern-day African American
context, drawing on characters she might have encountered in
her own southern upbringing. The result is this intricate tale of
Alcestis and Joe-Joe, with the mysterious Madame feminizing
the role of Apollo, and Pen-Pen the role of Hercules.*

WOUNDED IN THE HOUSE OF A FRIEND

Sonia Sanchez

Set No. 1

the unspoken word
is born, i see it in our
eyes dancing

She hadn't found anything. i had been careful. No lipstick. No matches from a well-known bar. No letters. Cards. Confessing an undying love. Nothing tangible for her to hold onto. But i knew she knew. It had been on her face, in her eyes for the last nine days. It was the way she looked at me sideways from across the restaurant table as she picked at her brown-rice sushi. It was the way she paused in profile while inspecting my wolfdreams. It was the way her mouth took a detour from talk. And then as we exited the restaurant she said it quite casually: i know there's another woman. You must tell me about her when we get home.

Yeah. There was another woman. In fact there were three women. In Florida, California, and North Carolina. Places to replace her cool detachment of these last years. No sex for months. Always tired or sick or off to some conference designed to save the world from racism or extinction. If I had jerked off one more time in bed while lying next to her it woulda dropped off. Still i wondered how she knew.

am i dressed right for the smoke?
will it wrinkle if i fall?

i had first felt something was wrong at the dinner party. His

308

*colleague's house. He was so animated. The first flush of his
new job i thought. He spoke staccato style. Two drinks in each
hand. His laughter. Wild. Hard. Contagious as shrines
enveloped the room. He was so wired that i thought he was
going to explode. i didn't know the people there. They were all
lawyers. Even the wives were lawyers. Glib and self-assured.
Discussing cases, and colleagues. Then it happened. A small
hesitation on his part. In answer to a question as to how he
would be able to get some important document from one place
to another, he looked at the host and said: They'll get it to me.
Don't worry. And the look passing back and forth between the
men told of collusion and omission. Told of dependence on
other women for information and confirmation. Told of nites
i had stretched out next to him and he was soft. Too soft for
my open legs. And i turned my back to him and the nites multiplied out loud. As i drove home from the party i asked him
what was wrong? What was bothering him? Were we okay?
Would we make love tonite? Would we ever make love again?
Did my breath stink? Was i too short? Too tall? Did i talk too
much? Should i wear lipstick? Should i cut my hair? Let it
grow? What did he want for dinner tomorrow nite? Was i driving too fast? Too slow? What is wrong man? He said i was
always exaggerating. Imagining things. Always looking for
trouble.*

> *Do they have children?*
> one does.
> *Are they married?*
> one is.
> *They're like you then.*
> yes.
> *How old are they?*
> thirty-two, thirty-three, thirty-four.

What do they do?
an accountant and two lawyers.
They're like you then.
yes.
Do they make better love than i do?
i'm not answering that.
Where did you meet?
when i traveled on the job.
Did you make love in hotels?
yes.
Did you go out together?
yes.
To bars? To movies? To restaurants?
yes.
Did you make love to them all nite?
yes.
And then got up to do your company work?
yes.
And you fall asleep on me right after
dinner. After work. After walking the dog.
yes.
Did you buy them things?
yes.
Did you talk on the phone with them every day?
yes.
Do you tell them how unhappy you
are with me and the children?
yes.
Do you love them? Did you say that you
loved them while making love?
i'm not answering that.

can i pull my bones

together while skeletons
come out of my head?

i am preparing for him to come home. i have exercised. Soaked in the tub. Scrubbed my body. Oiled myself down. What a beautiful day it's been. Warmer than usual. The cherry blossoms on the drive are blooming prematurely. The hibiscus are giving off a scent around the house. i have gotten drunk off the smell. So delicate. So sweet. So loving. i have been sleeping, no, daydreaming all day. Lounging inside my head. i am walking up this hill. The day is green. All green. Even the sky. i start to run down the hill and i take wing and begin to fly and the currents turn me upside down and i become young again childlike again ready to participate in all children's games.

She's fucking my brains out. I'm so tired i just want to put my head down at my desk. Just for a minute. What is wrong with her? For one whole month she's turned to me every nite. Climbed on top of me. Put my dick inside her and become beautiful. Almost birdlike. She seemed to be flying as she rode me. Arms extended. Moving from side to side. But my God. Every night. She's fucking my brains out. I can hardly see the morning and I'm beginning to hate the nite.

He's coming up the stairs. i've opened the venetian blinds. i love to see the trees outlined against the night air. Such beauty and space. i have oiled myself down for the night. i slept during the day. He's coming up the stairs. i have been waiting for him all day. i am singing a song i learned years ago. It is pretty like this nite. Like his eyes.

i can hardly keep my eyes open. Time to climb out of bed. Make the 7:20 train. My legs and bones hurt. i'm outta con-

dition. Goddamn it. She's turning my way again. She's smiling.
Goddamn it.

*What a beautiful morning it is. i've been listening to the birds
for the last couple hours. How beautifully they sing. Like
sacred music. i got up and exercised while he slept. Made a
cup of green tea. Oiled my body down. Climbed back into bed
and began to kiss him all over . . .*

Ted. Man. i'm so tired i can hardly eat this food. But i'd better
eat cuz i'm losing weight. You know what man. i can't even get
a hard-on when another bitch comes near me. Look at that one
there with that see-through skirt on. Nothing. My dick is so
limp only she can bring it up. And she does. Every nite. It ain't
normal is it for a wife to fuck like she does. Is it man? It ain't
normal. Like it ain't normal for a woman you've lived with for
twenty years to act like this.

She was killing him. He knew it. As he approached their porch
he wondered what it would be tonite. The special dinner. The
erotic movie. The whirlpool. The warm oil massage until his
body awakened in spite of himself. In spite of an eighteen-hour
day at the office. As he approached the house he hesitated. He
had to stay in control tonite. This was getting out of hand.

She waited for him. In the bathroom. She'd be waiting for him
when he entered the shower. She'd come in to wash his back.
Damn these big walk-in showers. No privacy. No time to wash
yourself and dream. She'd come with those hands of hers.
Soaking him. On the nipples. Chest. Then she'd travel on down
to his thing. He sweet peter jesus. So tired. So forlorn. And
she'd begin to tease him. Play with him. Suck him until he rose
up like some fucking private first class. Anxious to do battle.

And she'd watch him rise until he became Captain Sweet Peter.
And she'd climb on him. Close her eyes.

> honey. it's too much you know.
> *What?*
> all this sex. it's getting so i can't concentrate.
> *Where?*
> at the office. at lunch. on the train. on planes.
> all i want to do is sleep.
> *Why?*
> you know why. every place I go you're there.
> standing there. smiling. waiting, touching.
> *Yes.*
> in bed. i can't turn over and you're there.
> lips open. smiling, all revved up.
> *Aren't you horny too?*
> yes. but enough's enough. you're my wife. it's
> not normal to fuck as much as you do.
> *No?*
> it's not well, nice, to have you talk the way
> you talk when we're making love.
> *No?*
> can't we go back a little, go back to our
> normal life when you just wanted to sleep at
> nite and make love every now and then? like me.
> *No.*
> what's wrong with you. are you having a nervous
> breakdown or something?
> *No.*

> *if i become the*
> *other woman will i be*
> *loved like you loved her?*

And he says i don't laugh. All this he says while he's away in California for one week. But i've been laughing all day. All week. All year. i know what to do now. i'll go outside and give it away. Since he doesn't really want me. My love. My body. When we make love his lips swell up. His legs and arms hurt. He coughs. Drinks water. Develops a strain at his butt-hole. Yeah. What to do now. Go outside and give it away. Pussy. Sweet. Black pussy. For sale. Wholesale pussy. Right here. Sweet black pussy. Hello there Mr. Mailman. What's your name again? Oh yes. Harold. Can i call you Harry? How are you this morning? Would you like some cold water it's so hot out there. You want a doughnut a cookie some cereal some sweet black pussy? Oh God. Man. Don't back away. Don't run down the steps. Oh my God he fell. The mail is all over the sidewalk. hee hee hee. Guess i'd better be more subtle with the next one. hee hee hee. He's still running down the block. Mr. Federal Express Man. Cmon over here. Let me Fed Ex you and anyone else some Sweet Funky Pure Smelling Black Pussy. hee hee hee.

I shall become his collector of small things; become his collector of burps, biceps and smiles; I shall bottle his farts, frowns and creases; I shall gather up his moans, words, outbursts; wrap them in blue tissue paper; get to know them; watch them grow in importance; file them in their place in their scheme of things; I shall collect his scraps of food; ferret them among my taste buds; allow each particle to saunter into my cells; all aboard; calling all food particles; cmon board this fucking food express; climb into these sockets golden with brine; I need to taste him again.

you can't keep his dick in your purse

Preparation for the trip to Dallas. Los Angeles. New Orleans. Baltimore. Washington. Hartford. Brownsville. (Orlando. Miami. Late check-in. Rush. Limited liability.) That's why you missed me at the airport. Hotel. Bus stop. Train station. Restaurant. (Late check-in. Rush. Limited liability.) I'm here at the justice in the eighties conference with lawyers and judges and other types advocating abbreviating orchestrating mouthing fucking spilling justice in the bars. Corridors. Bedrooms. Nothing you'd be interested in. (Luggage received damaged. Torn. Broken. Scratched. Dented. Lost.) Preparation for the trip to Chestnut Street. Market Street. Pine Street. Walnut Street. Locust Street. Lombard Street. (Early check-in. Slow and easy liability.) That's why you missed me at the office. At the office. At the office. It's a deposition. I'm deposing an entire office of women and other types needing my deposing. Nothing of interest to you. A lot of questions no answers. Long lunches. Laughter. Penises. Flirtings. Touches. Drinks. Cunts and Coke. Jazz and Jacuzzis. *(Morning. Evening. Received. Damaged. Torn. Broken. Dented. Scratched. Lost.)*

    I *shall become a collector of me.*
    ishallbecomeacollectorofme.
    i Shall become a collector of me.
    i shall BECOME a collector of me.
    I shall Become A COLLECTOR of me.
    I SHALL BECOME A COLLECTOR OF ME.
    ISHALLBECOMEACOLLECTOROFME.
    AND PUT MEAT ON MY SOUL.

Set No. 2

i've been keeping company, with the layaway man.
i say, i've been keeping company, with the layaway man.
each time he come by, we do it on the installment plan.

every Friday night, he comes walking up to me do'
i say, every Friday night, he comes walking up to me do'
empty pockets hanging, right on down to the floor

gonna get me a man, who pays for it up front
i say, gonna get me a man, who pays for it up front
cuz when i needs it, can't wait till the middle of next month

i've been keeping company, with the layaway man
i say, i've been keeping company, with the layaway man
each time he come by, we do it on the installment plan
each time he come by, we do it on the installment plan

Sonia Sanchez, born in 1934 in Birmingham, Alabama, moved north after high school to study creative writing at New York University. She spent the next three decades in Harlem exploring a myriad of styles and dialects, mixing poetry with short stories and personal reflections. Now a tenured professor of English and women's studies at Temple University in Philadelphia, Sanchez is recognized as one of the most important African American poets today. Wounded in the House of a Friend (1995) was her first book in eight years. Does Your House Have Lions? was published two years later. Sanchez also writes children's fiction and plays.

THE YELLOW SWEATER

AN EXCERPT FROM THE NOVEL
Good Hair

Benilde Little

I don't know how I knew what I knew. Call it instinct or wisdom, but I had always known that I wouldn't stay in the world into which I was born. Maybe I just hated it so much, I'd unconsciously promised myself to find something else. At college I had envied people who couldn't wait to graduate so they could go back home and find a job, a spouse, a house, begin their life. What seemed so sure and appealing to them was, for me, a Sisyphean task. And the idea that I couldn't do it and didn't want to scared me, made me think there was something deeply wrong with me, that maybe I was some kind of new-breed sociopath who had no consciousness of home. I knew that I wasn't unsentimental—quite the opposite, in fact.

To this day, I can still remember how sad I was when my favorite yellow sweater no longer fit. I had loved to wear this sweater, especially during the first weeks of school. It was hand-knitted cotton and had four covered buttons on it. It made me happy. But in the third grade, I had outgrown it—that was my mother's phrase. She wanted to give it away to some needy child, as she did everything in our house that we no longer used. Even though my arms looked like little fat sausages in the sleeves, I wanted to keep that sweater. I told my

mother it would be a souvenir, like my souvenir Empire State
Building pencil sharpener. But she thought my protests were
nonsense and gave it away. Maybe that's where I learned to part
with things that had become too small, like my life in Newark.
Maybe the idea of wanting to hold on to things was too scary
because I knew that I'd have to let them go someday. I don't
know. I only know that when I finished school and came home
to plan my life and met a guy whom everyone thought I should
marry because my diaphragm failed, I remembered the yellow
sweater, only this time the tight feeling was around my neck
and I couldn't breathe. I couldn't describe it to anyone, other
than Aunt Thelma, who always understood me and would say,
"Baby, if that's what you want to do, then I'm wit cha." My
mother had said I was crazy to pass on this man. "So what if
he's got no sense of humor and he's a little stiff," she said. What
she didn't say, but I was sure she thought, was, He's nice looking and a lawyer. Even Sidney, from my old neighborhood, who
by this time was in drag every day, said, "Girl, it don't get no better than this." I never regretted not marrying him. I would've
suffocated. I would've died.

When Cheryl asked me one day, a few years after I'd had the
abortion, what I really wanted in a man, the only thing I could
think of was someone who gets it, who understands me. Her
own love life was the pits. The guy she had supported through
AU law school who had dumped her was engaged to marry his
secretary. Cheryl was stoic about most things, but after news
that her ex was getting married, she was losing it. I had convinced her to come to New York, where I put her up in my bed,
in front of the VCR. I rented every stupid and sappy movie I
could find. We watched and consumed large amounts of Ben
& Jerry's Heath Bar Crunch and Häagen-Dazs Cookies &
Cream. After a week she was ready to go back home.

I wanted Jack to be that person, the one who understood,

but I was feeling less than certain. He hadn't traveled far enough from home, and unlike Miles, Jack couldn't do levels and seemed to have no desire to learn. I guess he didn't have to, but I began to question whether his world and his scope were too narrow. I was falling in love with him in spite of all of that. He was a rich kid, as I'd first predicted, but he seemed to get me— at least he tolerated my neurotic side, my mood swings. I had gotten past my initial fear of him, and we were now moving toward one year together, and I wasn't sick of him. That was a milestone.

On our way home in a cab after seeing Aretha Franklin at Carnegie Hall, we had that "What do you like about me?" conversation, which invariably leads to "What kind of relationship are we having?" which leads to stuff about the future. Usually I was the one who broached these talks. Most men viewed having a root canal more favorably.

"So, where do you see yourself in five years?" Jack asked as the cab entered the park at Fifty-ninth Street.

"Oh, I don't know, maybe living in London or Paris or in the country somewhere with a house and kids and a dog."

"And a husband?"

"Of course. I wouldn't have a baby without having a husband."

"Really? That doesn't seem old-fashioned to you?"

"Absolutely not. I had a father. I don't want to cheat my kid outta that."

Although my relationship with my father was not emotionally close, I believed in the importance of fathers to kids and hoped for a different emotional situation for my unborn.

"Mmm. Is that you or Mount Holyoke talking?"

"Well, I don't know how to separate those."

The cab pulled into the circular drive of Jack's building and the doorman opened my side. We were at the stage where if we went on a date, it was assumed that we would be sleeping at one or the other's apartment. In fact, we slept together five nights out of seven, and I had my own closet space for a few sets of clothes and two dresser drawers. I even had phone answering privileges.

"If a brother is lettin' you answer the phone, that is tantamount to giving you a ring, okay?" Cheryl had said.

Jack's apartment was a modern L-shaped one-bedroom with den, in Manhattan real estate parlance a two bedroom. The foyer walls were lined with framed sepia-toned pictures of his ancestors, proudly posed, with Romanesque noses and vague Negroid features. The waxed parquet floor was covered with a large Aubusson, and an oversize cognac-colored leather sofa with matching love seat were the living room focal pieces. A rectangular glass-and-granite coffee table was covered with several pine boxes, *AMA* journals, and *Scientific American* magazines. The only nonmedical things he read were Clive Cussler novels and *The Wall Street Journal*. He had a lot of black lacquer—the torchère and the entertainment unit, with its major selection of country and classical CDs. An original Jacob Lawrence and several William H. Johnsons were on the walls, the latter inherited from Jack's grandfather, who had known the artist. His queen-size teakwood platform bed had a matching dresser and chest of drawers. The small white kitchenette with all state-of-the-art appliances was never used, save for the coffeemaker. Jack didn't expect me to cook, which was another thing I liked about him. Often I thought Jack was too good to be true. All the women's self-help with your love life books that I'd consumed over the years had me wondering—if he seems too good to be true, then he is. But just as often, I would think he wasn't good enough, that he didn't have enough edge or enough various interests. He had no interest in reading the credits after a movie. Medicine and adventure novels could get kind of boring.

"You hungry?" he yelled to me from the living room. I was in the bedroom, taking off my navy pants suit.

"I'm a little munchy."

"I'm starvin' like Marvin. I'm gonna order something. What do you feel like, Indian or Thai?"

"Thai."

"Okay. We'll get both."

"No, if you want Indian, I'll eat that, don't get two."

I came back into the living room, dressed in leggings and one of his T-shirts.

"I'm getting both. Now what Thai do you want? Spring rolls and what else?"

It was something that always pointed up our difference. Miles was extravagant to the point of foolishness—he had a Porsche with a car phone complete with call waiting and a fax, plus he carried a cellular. Jack wasn't ostentatious, but he was used to having whatever he wanted. Miles grew up poor, so he was just a kid in a candy store. All his accoutrements were toys to soothe a wound that would never heal. I understood it, but I'd never be able to fix it. With Jack, whatever he wanted he always got, things were nothing to him, and his sense of entitlement was sexy.

"So how about a little appetizer before the food gets here," Jack said as he began nibbling my collarbone. His babylike skin smelled like green and wood. I rubbed his head; his thick curls felt like Persian lamb. I pressed my braless chest against his, and he put his face in my cleavage and inhaled deeply while his hands were on my hips and our bodies were grinding together. His erection was bursting through his summer-weight wool pants. I reached down and undid his pants and pushed his Jockey briefs down to his thighs. He pulled my leggings down and dropped to his knees, putting his nose directly on my clit, rubbing it softly until it began to feel swollen and my legs weak. He pulled me down onto the rug and rubbed my breasts with one hand while he reached into one of the wooden boxes on the coffee table for a condom. He put it on and guided himself into me. The Aubusson was rough against my behind, but I quickly forgot about it. Jack's slow, hard movements made my clit grow fuller and fuller until I exploded. We both did.

The buzzer awakened us, and Jack pulled up his pants to open the door.

"Let's eat in bed," he said from the kitchenette as he put the food on plates and a tray and got a bottle of merlot from his collection. We ate on the bed, feeding each other and drinking wine out of one glass. After we ate Jack had a dreamy, contented look on his face.

"Alice, do you know how much I love you?"

I believed that he loved me, not because he told me, but because of the way he was with me, the way he held my hand when we crossed the street, the way he put his jacket around me when I got cold or held an umbrella over me in the rain. There was a preciousness in his way with me that I'd never had before, at least not to this degree and certainly not with Miles. Jack valued me, and I knew this. Sometimes the thought of it overwhelmed me, made me feel like I couldn't trust it or that there was something wrong with him.

"Yes, Jack," I said finally, "and I love you."

"So what are we doing? I mean, we spend all our free time together. I have shirts at your place, you have stuff here. I mean, I know what I want at this point in my life. I think we should do something solid."

Solid? I thought about that Ashford and Simpson song. But was Jack talking about marriage or living together? I remembered Miles and how badly I had wanted to live with him, even though on principle I don't believe in living together. It's usually what men want to do when they can't make up their mind about you.

"What do you mean by solid?"

"I don't know, just that I wanna be with you. I think we get along, I just think maybe we should do something—"

"Like live together?"

"Yeah or something like that."

"Well, Jack, there's living together and there's marriage."

I knew I was pushing, and I wasn't even sure what I wanted, but I wanted him to be sure and I wanted him to want to do something formal.

"Well, would you like to do something like that?"

I was lying next to Jack with my head on his chest. I couldn't see his face, but I was sure his eyebrows were raised and his eyes practically shut. I felt his heart beating fast.

"Do something like what, Jack?"

He put his hands on my shoulders and brought my shoulders around so that we were facing each other. "Something like get married. I want to marry you."

It was weird. I felt happy, but not the way I had always dreamed I'd feel. I wanted to jump up and down, do cartwheels or something, but that wasn't what I felt. Instead, it just seemed all reasonable and calm, except for the flips in my stomach. I couldn't believe that this gorgeous, successful, smart guy from a very well-to-do family would want me. He could have anybody he wanted, but he was asking me. It was soon, I reasoned. Maybe this was just what he did. Didn't he leave Sherry practically standing at the altar? Maybe I should talk him out of this, tell him that we need more time, but I didn't want to say the wrong thing and blow it completely. This was like finding a great piece at a sample sale that you weren't sure you wanted to buy, but you knew it was a great find for the price and that if you put it down, someone else would swoop it up before it had left your hands. I had to say something, and I had to make it good.

"Jack, I love you and I think I should think about this, just a little. You know, it's a big step, and I had this yellow sweater. . . ."

"Of course we should talk about it, but what's to think about? What about a sweater?"

"Uh, I'll tell you about it some other time. It's just a test I give myself."

We hugged each other and I cried and tried to determine if I was feeling like a sausage.

———

Formerly a reporter for People *magazine and a senior editor for* Essence, *New Jersey–born Benilde Little now lives in the suburbs of New York City with her husband and their young daughter. Her best-selling novel* Good Hair *was selected as one of the ten best books of 1996 by the* Los Angeles Times. *"I wanted to write about the effects of class on black people's inner lives," Little says. "*Good Hair *is about what I call our plantation luggage, because so much of our interior stuff is left over from our past history of enslavement." Little's second novel,* The Itch, *was published in 1998.*

HOW DID
THIS HAPPEN
ANYWAY

Carla Richmond

y scalp remembers the rhythms of many women's fingers. Full palms pressed flat against it when it is freshly razored and alert. The hard edge of a comb scraping parts for braiding. The maddening, itchy, searing, foul-smelling Cream of Nature slapped on my untamed kinks. The bite of the whip-tailed comb working it in. Gentle meandering hands plaiting and unplaiting, slowly massaging from nape to crown, or aimlessly twirling individual locks in deep, suggestive circles. My aunt twisting huge Princess Leia knots. Sitting on the floor, leaning back into the edge of the bed or against the couch, my head caught between powerful, damp thighs, thick fingers working my hair into elaborate designs, two or twenty braids, cutting a rough geography with a wide-tooth comb and thickly greasing each fresh part. My mother clapping me on the head with the brush when I won't sit still. The hiss and *sssssss*snap of Evelyn's curling iron leaving crisp, pray-it-don't-rain curls that she will bouffant and spritz before I leave her salon.

I'm not sure what that has to do with anything, but you wanted to know how did this happen anyway and whose fault it was.

———

You asked me if I've always liked girls.

My first-grade classroom at Queen's College has only a few weak fluorescent lights and no direct sun. Reggie Ingrahm sits behind me. I fix my eyes on a point on the board, seeing none of the lesson scrawled across it, for Reggie entrances me with the incessant motion of her hands. Reggie's hair is the texture and color of hay, chopped short by her mother. She is perpetually amazed by the spring of my precocious naps, which ignore her attempts to press them straight between her palms, yet lock instantly into whatever outrageous shape she desires. I am caught up in the motion of Reggie's hands unraveling my carefully done braids.

Replaiting is not a concern of hers. Later, in the bathroom, I attempt to re-create the motions of my mother's hands in the mirror. My magically locking hair and sweating palms work determinedly against me, and I begin to panic, because I know I must fix my hair before my mother sees it. I create a precarious series of knots that veer in one direction for a spell, then capriciously lurch in another.

My mother meets one sorry little girl after school that day. I wear a gradually unraveling semblance of a braid on one side of my head and an ecstatically liberated tangle on the other. The precise, knife-edge part is still maintained in between. As my mother approaches me and I explain, I see the tension in her neck and I feel my betrayal of her in my scalp, feel how I have betrayed her to a little white girl who wanted to put her hands in my hair and whose hands felt so good.

The next day, from three rows away, Reggie and I share looks behind the teacher's back. My mother had requested the move.

You say you want to know when and how I knew.

I realize that you might not understand that the first time I parted a woman's legs and bent my head down between them, I trusted the smell and knew I could follow it because it was familiar. At that point, I turned my mind off and could feel gears waking up inside me, moving against rust. Knowledge that I had never drawn on, or known existed, revealed itself to me. When I felt my lover's pelvis jittering against my palm for the first time, I felt the pressure building, the insistence of my fingers, and I came from watching her because watching her and touching her were enough.

I know you didn't ask me that, but I wanted to tell you.

And I want to tell you this, too.

Mama never told me girls could be this good.

———••——

Currently pursuing a master's degree in social work at Hunter College in New York City, Carla Richmond works with adult literacy students who are poets and writers. "Their discipline and commitment to writing put me to shame," she says. A poet and writer herself, Richmond was born in Jamaica. Raised in the Bahamas, she earned her B.A. from Columbia University in New York City and now lives in Brooklyn. Her story "How Did This Happen Anyway?" appeared in longer form in Ma-Ka: Diasporic Juks: Contemporary Writing by Queers of African Descent (1998).

THE
AUTOBIOGRAPHY
OF MY MOTHER

AN EXCERPT FROM THE NOVEL

Jamaica   Kincaid

His mouth was like an island in the sea that was his face; I am sure he had ears and nose and eyes and all the rest, but I could see only his mouth, which I knew could do all the things that a mouth usually does, such as eat food, purse in approval or disapproval, smile, twist in thought; inside were his teeth and behind them was his tongue. Why did I see him that way, how did I come to see him that way? It was a mystery to me that he had been alive all along and that I had not known of his existence and I was perfectly fine—I went to sleep at night and I could wake up in the morning and greet the day with indifference if it suited me, I could comb my hair and scratch myself and I was still perfectly fine—and he was alive, sometimes living in a house next to mine, sometimes living in a house far away, and his existence was ordinary and perfect and parallel to mine, but I did not know of it, even though sometimes he was close enough to me for me to notice that he smelled of cargo he had been unloading; he was a stevedore.

His mouth really did look like an island, lying in a twig-brown sea, stretching out from east to west, widest near the center, with tiny, sharp creases, its color a shade lighter than that of the twig-brown sea in which it lay, the place where the two lips met disappearing into the pinkest of pinks, and even

331

though I must have held his mouth in mine a thousand times, it was always new to me. He must have smiled at me, though I don't really know, but I don't like to think that I would love someone who hadn't first smiled at me. It had been raining, a heavy downpour, and I took shelter under the gallery of a dry-goods store along with some other people. The rain was an inconvenience, for it was not necessary; there had already been too much of it, and it was no longer only outside, overflowing in the gutters, but inside also, roofs were leaking and then falling in. I was standing under the gallery and had sunk deep within myself, enjoying completely the despair I felt at being myself. I was wearing a dress; I had combed my hair that morning; I had washed myself that morning. I was looking at nothing in particular when I saw his mouth. He was speaking to someone else, but he was looking at me. The someone else he was speaking to was a woman. His mouth then was not like an island at rest in a sea but like a small patch of ground viewed from high above and set in motion by a force not readily seen.

When he saw me looking at him, he opened his mouth wider, and that must have been the smile. I saw then that he had a large gap between his two front teeth, which probably meant that he could not be trusted, but I did not care. My dress was damp, my shoes were wet, my hair was wet, my skin was cold, all around me were people standing in small amounts of water and mud, shivering, but I started to perspire from an effort I wasn't aware I was making; I started to perspire because I felt hot, and I started to perspire because I felt happy. I wore my hair then in two plaits and the ends of them rested just below my collarbone; all the moisture in my hair collected and ran down my two plaits, as if they were two gutters, and the water seeped through my dress just below the collarbone and continued to run down my chest, only stopping at the place where the tips of my breasts met the fabric, revealing, plain as a new print, my nipples. He was looking at me and talking to someone else, and his mouth grew wide and narrow, small and large, and I wanted him to notice me, but there was so much noise: all the people standing in the gallery, sheltering themselves from the strong rain, had something they wanted to say, something not about the weather (that was by now beyond comment) but about their lives, their disappointments most likely, for joy is so short-lived there isn't enough time to dwell on its occurrence. The noise, which started as a hum, grew to a loud din, and the loud din had an unpleasant taste of metal and vinegar, but I knew his mouth could take it away if only I could get to it; so I called out my own name, and I knew he heard me immediately, but he wouldn't stop speaking to the woman he was talking to, so I had to call out my name again and again until he stopped, and by that time my name was like a chain around him, as the sight of his mouth was like a chain around me. And when our eyes met, we laughed, because we were happy, but it was frightening, for that gaze asked everything: who would betray whom, who would be captive, who would be captor, who would give and who would take, what would I do. And when our eyes met and we laughed at the same time, I said, "I love you, I love you," and he said, "I know." He did not say it out of vanity, he did not say it out of conceit, he only said it because it was true.

His name was Roland. He was not a hero, he did not even have a country; he was from an island, a small island that was between a sea and an ocean, and a small island is not a country. And he did not have a history; he was a small event in somebody else's history, but he was a man. I could see him better than he could see himself, and that was because he was who he was and I was myself, but also because I was taller than he was. He was unpolished, but he carried himself as if he were precious. His hands were large and thick, and for no reason that I could see he would spread them out in front of him and they looked as if they were the missing parts from a powerful piece of machinery; his legs were straight from hip to knee, and then from the knee they bent at an angle as if he had been at sea too long or had never learned to walk properly to begin with. The hair on his legs was tightly curled as if the hairs were pieces of thread rolled between the thumb and the forefinger in preparation for sewing, and so was the hair on his arms, the hair in his underarms, and the hair on his chest; the hair in those places was black and grew sparsely; the hair on his head and the hair between his legs was black and tightly curled also, but it grew in such abundance that it was impossible for me to move my hands through it. Sitting, standing, walking, or lying down, he carried himself as if he was something precious, but not out of vanity, for it was true, he was something precious; yet when he was lying on top of me he looked down at me as if I were the only woman in the world, the only woman he had ever looked at in that way—but that was not true, a man only does that when it is not true. When he first lay on top of me I was so ashamed of how much pleasure I felt that I bit my bottom lip hard—but I did not bleed, not from biting my lip, not then. His skin was smooth and warm in places I had not kissed him; in the places I had kissed him his skin was cold and coarse, and the pores were open and raised.

Did the world become a beautiful place? The rainy season eventually went away, the sunny season came, and it was too hot; the riverbed grew dry, the mouth of the river became shallow, the heat eventually became as wearying as the rain, and I would have wished it away if I had not become occupied with this other sensation, a sensation I had no single word for. I could feel myself full of happiness, but it was a kind of happiness I had never experienced before, and my happiness would spill out of me and run all the way down a long, long road and then the road would come to an end and I would feel empty and sad, for what could come after this? How would it end?

Not everything has an end, even though the beginning changes. The first time we were in a bed together we were lying on a thin board that was covered with old cloth, and this small detail, evidence of our poverty—people in our position, a stevedore and a doctor's servant, could not afford a proper mattress—was a major contribution to my satisfaction, for it allowed me to brace myself and match him breath for breath. But how can it be that a man who can carry large sacks filled with sugar or bales of cotton on his back from dawn to dusk exhausts himself within five minutes inside a woman? I did not then and I do not now know the answer to that. He kissed me. He fell asleep. I bathed my face then between his legs; he smelled of curry and onions, for those were the things he had been unloading all day; other times when I bathed my face between his legs—for I did it often, I liked doing it—he would smell of sugar, or flour, or the large, cheap bolts of cotton from which he would steal a few yards to give me to make a dress.

What is the everyday? What is the ordinary? One day, as I was walking toward the government dispensary to collect some supplies—one of my duties as a servant to a man who was in love with me beyond anything he could help and so had long since stopped trying, a man I ignored except when I wanted him to please me—I met Roland's wife, face-to-face, for the first time. She stood in front of me like a sentry—stern, dignified, guarding the noble idea, if not noble ideal, that was her husband. She did not block the sun, it was shining on my right; on my left was a large black cloud; it was raining way in the distance; there was no rainbow on the horizon. We stood on the narrow strip of concrete that was the sidewalk.

One section of a wooden fence that was supposed to shield a
yard from passersby on the street bulged out and was broken,
and a few tugs from any careless party would end its useful-
ness; in that yard a primrose bush bloomed unnaturally, its
leaves too large, its flowers showy, and weeds were everywhere, they had prospered in all the wet. We were not alone.
A man walked past us with a cutlass in his knapsack and a
mistreated dog two steps behind him; a woman walked by
with a large basket of food on her head; some children were
walking home from school, and they were not walking
together; a man was leaning out a window, spitting, he used
snuff. I was wearing a pair of modestly high heels, red, not a
color to wear to work in the middle of the day, but that was
just the way I had been feeling, red with a passion, like that
hibiscus that was growing under the window of the man who
kept spitting from the snuff. And Roland's wife called me a
whore, a slut, a pig, a snake, a viper, a rat, a lowlife, a para-
site, and an evil woman. I could see that her mouth formed a
familiar hug around these words—poor thing, she had been
used to saying them. I was not surprised. I could not have
loved Roland the way I did if he had not loved other women.
And I was not surprised; I had noticed immediately the space
between his teeth. I was not surprised that she knew about me;
a man cannot keep a secret, a man always wants all the
women he knows to know each other.

I believe I said this: "I love Roland; when he is with me I want
him to love me; when he is not with me I think of him loving me.
I do not love you. I love Roland." This is what I wanted to say,
and this is what I believe I said. She slapped me across the face;
her hand was wide and thick like an oar; she, too, was used to
doing hard work. Her hand met the side of my face: my jawbone,
the skin below my eye and under my chin, a small portion of my
nose, the lobe of my ear. I was then a young woman in my early

twenties, my skin was supple, smooth, the pores invisible to the naked eye. It was completely without bitterness that I thought as I looked at her face, a face I had so little interest in that it would tire me to describe it, Why is the state of marriage so desirable that all women are afraid to be caught outside it? And why does this woman, who has never seen me before, to whom I have never made any promise, to whom I owe nothing, hate me so much? She expected me to return her blow but, instead, I said, again completely without bitterness, "I consider it beneath me to fight over a man."

I was wearing a dress of light-blue Irish linen. I could not afford to buy such material, because it came from a real country, not a false country like mine; a shipment of this material in blue, in pink, in lime green, and in beige had come from Ireland, I suppose, and Roland had given me yards of each shade from the bolts. I was wearing my blue Irish-linen dress that day, and it was demure enough—a pleated skirt that ended quite beneath my knees, a belt at my waist, sleeves that buttoned at my wrists, a high neckline that covered my collarbone—but underneath my dress I wore absolutely nothing, no undergarments of any kind, only my stockings, given to me by Roland and taken from yet another shipment of dry goods, each one held up by two pieces of elastic that I had sewn together to make a garter. My declaration of what I considered beneath me must have enraged Roland's wife, for she grabbed my blue dress at the collar and gave it a huge tug, it rent in two from my neck to my waist. My breasts lay softly on my chest, like two small pieces of uprisen dough, unmoved by the anger of this woman; not so by the touch of her husband's mouth, for he would remove my dress, by first patiently undoing all the buttons and then pulling down the bodice, and then he would take one breast in his mouth, and it would grow to a size much bigger than his mouth could hold, and he would let it go and turn to the other one; the saliva evap-

orating from the skin on that breast was an altogether different
sensation from the sensation of my other breast in his mouth,
and I would divide myself in two, for I could not decide which
sensation I wanted to take dominance over the other. For an
hour he would kiss me in this way and then exhaust himself on
top of me in five minutes. I loved him so. In the dark I couldn't
see him clearly, only an outline, a solid shadow; when I saw him
in the daytime he was fully dressed. His wife, as she rent my
dress, a dress made of material she knew very well, for she had a
dress made of the same material, told me his history: it was not a
long one, it was not a sad one, no one had died in it, no land had
been laid waste, no birthright had been stolen; she had a list, and
it was full of names, but they were not the names of countries.

What was the color of her wedding day? When she first saw
him was she overwhelmed with desire? The impulse to possess is
alive in every heart, and some people choose vast plains, some
people choose high mountains, some people choose wide seas,
and some people choose husbands; I chose to possess myself. I
resembled a tree, a tall tree with long, strong branches; I looked
delicate, but any man I held in my arms knew that I was strong;
my hair was long and thick and deeply waved naturally, and I
wore it braided and pinned up, because when I wore it loose
around my shoulders it caused excitement in other people—
some of them men, some of them women, some of them it
pleased, some of them it did not. The way I walked depended on
who I thought would see me and what effect I wanted my walk
to have on them. My face was beautiful, I found it so.

And yet I was standing before a woman who found herself
unable to keep her life's booty in its protective sack, a woman
whose voice no longer came from her throat but from deep
within her stomach, a woman whose hatred was misplaced. I
looked down at our feet, hers and mine, and I expected to see my
short life flash before me; instead, I saw that her feet were with-

out shoes. She did have a pair of shoes, though, which I had seen; they were white, they were plain, a round toe and flat laces, they took shoe polish well, she wore them only on Sundays and to church. I had many pairs of shoes, in colors meant to attract attention and dazzle the eye; they were uncomfortable, I wore them every day, I never went to church at all.

My strong arms reached around to caress Roland, who was lying on my back naked; I was naked also. I knew his wife's name, but I did not say it; he knew his wife's name, too, but he did not say it. I did not know the long list of names that were not countries that his wife had committed to memory. He himself did not know the long list of names; he had not committed this list to memory. This was not from deceit, and it was not from carelessness. He was someone so used to a large fortune that he took it for granted; he did not have a bankbook, he did not have a ledger, he had a fortune—but still he had not lost interest in acquiring more. Feeling my womb contract, I crossed the room, still naked; small drops of blood spilled from inside me, evidence of my refusal to accept his silent offering. And Roland looked at me, his face expressing confusion. Why did I not bear his children? He could feel the times that I was fertile, and yet each month blood flowed away from me, and each month I expressed confidence at its imminent arrival and departure, and always I was overjoyed at the accuracy of my prediction. When I saw him like that, on his face a look that was a mixture—confusion, dumbfoundedness, defeat—I felt much sorrow for him, for his life was reduced to a list of names that were not countries, and to the number of times he brought the monthly flow of blood to a halt; his life was reduced to women, some of them beautiful, wearing dresses made from yards of cloth he had surreptitiously removed from the bowels of the ships where he worked as a stevedore.

At that time I loved him beyond words; I loved him when
he was standing in front of me and I loved him when he was
out of my sight. I was still a young woman. No small impressions, the size of a child's forefinger, had yet appeared on the
soft parts of my body; my legs were long and hard, as if they
had been made to take me a long distance; my arms were
long and strong, as if prepared for carrying heavy loads. I
was in love with Roland. He was a man. But who was he
really? He did not sail the seas, he did not cross the oceans,
he only worked in the bottom of vessels that had done so; no
mountains were named for him, no valleys, no nothing. But
still he was a man, and he wanted something beyond ordinary satisfaction—beyond one wife, one love, and one room
with walls made of mud and roof of cane leaves, beyond the
small plot of land where the same trees bear the same fruit
year following year—for it would all end only in death, for
though no history yet written had embraced him, though he
could not identify the small uprisings within himself, though
he would deny the small uprisings within himself, a strange
calm would sometimes come over him, a cold stillness, and
since he could find no words for it, he was momentarily
blinded with shame.

One night Roland and I were sitting on the steps of the jetty,
our backs facing the small world we were from, the world of
sharp, dangerous curves in the road, of steep mountains of
recent volcanic formations covered in a green so humble no one
had ever longed for them, of 365 small streams that would never
meet up to form a majestic roar, of clouds that were nothing but
large vessels holding endless days of water, of people who had
never been regarded as people at all; we looked into the night, its
blackness did not come as a surprise, a moon full of dead white
light traveled across the surface of a glittering black sky; I was

wearing a dress made from another piece of cloth he had given me, another piece of cloth taken from the bowels of a ship without permission, and there was a false pocket in the skirt, a pocket that did not have a bottom, and Roland placed his hand inside the pocket, reaching all the way down to touch inside me; I looked at his face, his mouth I could see and it stretched across his face like an island and like an island, too, it held secrets and was dangerous and could swallow things whole that were much larger than itself; I looked out toward the horizon, which I could not see but knew was there all the same, and this was also true of the end of my love for Roland.

<hr />

An exquisite stylist with a flawless ear, Jamaica Kincaid came of age in the Caribbean island of Antigua. In 1966, stifled by the routines of island life, she headed north to New York City. There, she began to write for such magazines as Ms. and The New Yorker, Rolling Stone, and the Paris Review. In 1976 she became a staff writer for The New Yorker. Her fractured relationship with her mother is a recurring theme in her work, weaving through her short-story collection, At the Bottom of the River (1983), and her novels, Annie John (1985), Lucy (1991), and The Autobiography of My Mother (1996). That strained mother-daughter bond is also a presence in her nonfiction works, A Small Place (1988), about political and commercial compromises in Kincaid's birthplace, and My Brother (1998), the story of her brother's losing battle with AIDS. Kincaid currently lives, gardens, and enjoys family life with her husband and their two children in Vermont.

WEDDING
SYMPHONY

Gale P. Jackson

Her first thought on waking to the sound of rain was to go back to sleep and forget the whole damn thing. Turning back her side of the covers, she imagined the rain perched, a vulture on the sky's dark shoulders, gleeful with bad omens and laughing as it was blowing the breath that rattled her venetian blinds. Her dreams called her back to the abandon of sleep, but her eye had already gotten caught in mildewed curtains, and the housekeeper in her was making a mental note to go to Woolworth's for the umpteenth time. She threw her legs over the edge of the bed and felt for her slippers. Silver bells of papier-mâché, arched on ribbons over the lamp at her bedside, greeted her. Steady rain beat down outside. But too many arrangements had been made. It would easier to go on through than to try to undo. *Okay*, she said to herself, *let's get to getting on with this day*. Then, to his back, she added, "I guess you might as well get five more minutes." He snored his response, but it sounded like one of gratitude. Making her way to the washroom she sang, "Love sweet love, it makes a woman, yes it makes a woman." And that's how she woke the baby, singing. "Come on, sugar," she called to him. "Rise and shine. It's Mommy's wedding day."

Five dollars an hour for a sitter on a Sunday was a high price to pay, but she would not turn back now. The storm winds compelled her. The cancellations made her more determined. The original sitter's basement had, over the night of torrential rains, been flooded. Her sister's plane, because of heavy clouds and no visibility, had been circling New York for over an hour. Her bridesmaid's car would pick this morning to stall out in Montclair. All these things pushed her on. She sat drinking lukewarm unsugared coffee, jotting notes or striking things from her list with a pencil she kept in hand while the phone stayed crooked between her ear and her shoulder. Each time she replaced the receiver the phone rang again, until she had heard from everyone who wasn't coming: friends from the office, family, neighbors, the woman downstairs who insisted that a rainy-day marriage was the most blessed kind. She thanked her neighbor for her wisdom. She remained a gracious telephone host to both family and friends, letting them all off the hook without giving anybody a hard time. Yes, this weather was too awful to drive through, to take a chance with, to come out in. Then she began to make calls of her own. Lightning streaked the sky. The rain was pouring down. The florist could be convinced easily. He had only put off the delivery because he thought, with such a storm, she would have postponed. The church, dear mercy, was open as usual and the pastor was there "all the time." She ran down her checklist and with one very formally polite but pointed threat to the photographer ("Mr. Green, you were contracted and paid in advance"), she was able to make it solid enough to warrant waking Jerome.

It was nine-thirty and, if anything, raining even harder than before. Feuan was mashing sugar, milk, raisins, and cornflakes into his favorite breakfast montage. She went back into the bedroom holding the cereal box in one hand (to keep him from getting any more) and a pair of ivory stockings in the other. Ivory stockings with small bells sewn into the ankles. The bells tinkled lightly against her arm. With the face of resolve, she sat on the bed's edge, softly calling his name—the same way she woke the boy. He pretended to sleep for a few minutes to listen. When she called his name like that, one thread in the fabric of ten years, he'd always wake or come, picturing her coralline, the dark lips surrounding, the blueberry or plum beyond. He had studied her for a long time but never ceased to wonder at the luxury of her spiraling southern drawl. Filled with her voice, he jumped up suddenly and announced, "Rain, snow, hail, winds—baby, I'm yours." She sighed real relief, then scolded, though havoc played with her voice. "This our wedding day and you oversleeping as usual. Come on. Come on." She wagged a finger, pointing first with the cereal box, then with the stockings, before realizing how silly it looked. She fell back on the bed. They hugged and giggled and laughed and laughed.

He tugged at his tie. She fastened the cummerbund from behind and snapped the suspenders at the back. He pulled them over his shoulders and then slid on the vest, leaving the jacket on the chair until it was time to leave. She, satisfied now that he would be ready when the cab arrived, disappeared back into the washroom. He fussed around, deciding what to put in his pockets and talking with his son in the other room. When she reappeared moments later (she had the commendable habits of a woman able to get ready beautifully, quickly), he wished, hoped, and sent up a silent prayer for the rain, which steadily grew more forceful, to end. She had insisted on white and seeing her now, he understood why. Against her almost purple skin, white was a joyous incantation. The dress, charged with her darkness, came alive as it never had in the department store. She stood in the sheer ivory stockings, wearing a pillbox hat rimmed by her hair, with a waist-long veil attached. "How I look?" she beamed, and he was in love one more time. "Beautiful," he said reverently, unhappy only that she did not look waterproof. He was smiling and staring. She waved off his appreciation but was secretly glad that he was enjoying this, too. She turned from him, stepped into her white satin pumps, and he could have sworn he heard bells ringing.

"With a start like this, baby, nothing can dampen our spirits." Jerome toasted her and lifted his glass to the photographer, who for ten extra dollars acted as a witness. The rain had stopped when they emerged from the storefront, but the wind was high and thrashing fallen leaves and branch and bough. Despite the ominous sky, she insisted on taking pictures in Prospect Park, so, much to his amusement, they tiptoed like burglars through the winds and the mud toward the white-columned enclosure on the park side. The angry photographer trudged behind. The white satin shoes sank immediately and deeply into the wet ground. The dress was muddy at the hem. On his rented suit, they rolled up the pant legs. "Okay," they said to each other when they reached the enclosure, which from the inside felt like the top of a wedding cake. Her veil whipped in the wind like the half-dressed treetops charged with the heady winds of the storm. He took her arm, they stood close, Jerome shouted, "Take it from the top," and the photographer shot the last of his plan number one wedding portfolio.

Poet, teacher, librarian, and storyteller, Gale P. Jackson received a National Endowment for the Humanities fellowship for her work in African American history. An assistant professor at Medgar Evers College of the City University of New York, she lives in Brooklyn. Her collections include We Stand Our Ground and two new volumes, A Khosian Tale of Beginnings and Ends and Bridge Suite: Narrative Poems Based on the Lives of African and African American Women in the Early History of These New Nations. Jackson is also the coauthor of an anthology of South African and North American art and writings called Art Against Apartheid: Works for Freedom. "Wedding Symphony" is excerpted from a longer work of fiction, which the author describes as "wedding portraits from a writer's album." Jackson recalls that the story "began with a couple I saw, her white train dancing in the storm's winds, while I was out jogging one rainy weekday afternoon. I was so moved by the image of them, alone with the photographer taking wedding pictures in Prospect Park. As I continued to jog toward home, the music began as I imagined how life and love had brought them out to face that storm."

ACKNOWLEDGMENTS